PRISONER
OF HOPE

David Wild

The Book Guild Ltd.
Sussex, England

The Book Guild Ltd.
25 High Street,
Lewes, Sussex.

First published 1992
Reprinted 1992
© David Wild 1992
Set in Baskerville
Typesetting by Southern Reproductions (Sussex)
East Grinstead, Sussex
Printed in Great Britain by
Antony Rowe Ltd.
Chippenham, Wiltshire.

A catalogue record for this book is
available from the British Library

ISBN 0 86332 711 7

CONTENTS

'Turn ye to the stronghold,
ye prisoners of hope'

Zechariah 9.12

For Mary

ACKNOWLEDGEMENTS

I would like to acknowledge the help and encouragement that I have received from many in the preparation of this book: from Richard Ollard, Sir Charles Troughton, Auberon Waugh, Neal Ascherson and General Sir John Hackett; from Mrs Mabel Granger, Anthony Parkinson, George Rimmer, and Vince Egan in Australia, who supplied me with photographs and Peter Birch who reproduced them superbly from very small snapshots; and most of all, from Paul and Emma Rogers, who saw the point of the story and bullied me into working on the manuscript and bringing it to a conclusion.

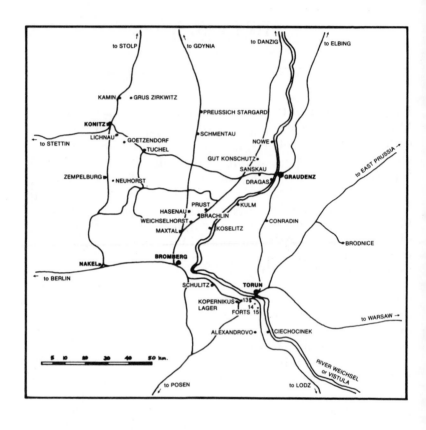

to STOLP to GDYNIA to DANZIG to ELBING

KAMIN • GRUS ZIRKWITZ

•PREUSSICH STARGARD

KONITZ• •SCHMENTAU
LICHNAU• •GOETZENDORF NOWE•
to STETTIN •TUCHEL

•GUT KONSCHUTZ
ZEMPELBURG• •NEUHORST SANSKAU•
DRAGAS• •GRAUDENZ to EAST PRUSSIA

PRUST• •KULM
HASENAU• •BRACHLIN
WEICHSELHORST• •CONRADIN
MAXTAL• •KOSELITZ •BRODNICE

NAKEL• BROMBERG• •SCHULTIZ
to BERLIN TORUN•

KOPERNIKUS• 13
LAGER 14
FORTS 15 to WARSAW →

ALEXANDROVO• •CIECHOCINEK

5 10 20 30 40 50 km. RIVER WEICHSEL or VISTULA

to POSEN to LODZ

10

PREFACE

I was a prisoner of the Germans from the time of Dunkirk, May 1940 to January 1945. After fifteen months in officers' camps (Oflags), I was allowed to exercise my ministry as a chaplain in camps for other ranks (Stalags) for the rest of my captivity.

During the months following my return to England in April 1945 I scribbled down into old notebooks all that I could remember about my five years as a prisoner. I had no thought of publication; the writing was a kind of unconscious therapy, getting it all out of my system. Counselling had not then become a commodity available to all.

More than forty years later, in 1988, I looked again at the notebooks and realized that what I had written gave a picture of POW life very different from that portrayed in many books of wartime reminiscences, most of which were about the experiences of officer POWs.

Encouraged by others, most of whom were not even born in 1945, I have tried in this book to give a picture of how thousands of British other rank POWs coped with captivity in Nazi Germany in a wide variety of conditions. Regular soldiers, volunteer members of the Territorial Army, or young conscripts, they came from a wide range of backgrounds. They were segregated on capture from their officers, and as prisoners they had no control over their work or their living conditions, or any choice of companions. Wherever they were they had to work out a way of living together, often in deplorable conditions, and of coping with their guards and their employers. For them there was no Miracle of Dunkirk.

An impression may be given in these pages that life was not all that hard in German captivity. It is true that we were fortunate to be prisoners of the German army. With that strange attachment to what is 'korrekt', they frequently protected us from being subjected to the brutality and ruthlessness of the Gestapo and the SS, and made a show of conforming most of the time to the requirements of the Geneva Convention. We knew little or nothing of what was going on a few miles away in Treblinka and other concentration camps. But captivity is captivity, and it was a severe test of character for young men parted from their homes and families, for five of the best years of their lives, 'tilling an alien soil', with no certainty about the duration or outcome of the war.

I have interspersed my story with extracts from the letters that I wrote to Mary, my wife. Alas, none of hers to me have survived; they fell irretrievably into Russian hands on 20 January 1945. Mary was, and still is, an incomparable letter writer. I can only hope that the extracts from my letters to her will give some impression of how much her letters meant to me, and often to others who shared the best of them.

1

Introduction

So this was Berlin, and here I was in 1941, occupying the enemy capital city all on my own. At 8 pm on a November evening it was wet, dark and cold. My guard and I had travelled all day from Westphalia, and he took me from the station to some large barracks where we were allotted a small room high up in the building. We were given some food in a large cafeteria where men were endlessly coming and going. The place was obviously a transit camp for men of all three services travelling to and from their units. In my British khaki battledress I must have been fairly conspicuous, but no one gave me more than a casual glance.

Back in our bedroom I was flattered to see my guard carefully placing his revolver under his pillow; but after a long journey I was too tired to think of taking on the whole Reich unarmed and singlehanded. It was the Fifth of November, and I rather hoped that the RAF might put on a firework display for me; but the night passed quietly.

Next morning my guard escorted me down two floors to a communal washplace where numerous sailors, soldiers and airmen were performing their ablutions. I arranged my shaving equipment on a shelf above one basin. Next to me I realized my guard was wrestling with his conscience. It had not occurred to him to bring his razor down with him. He might have asked one of the other troops to keep an eye on me, but he wasn't prepared to risk it. I had to pack up my gear, and we climbed the two floors back to our bedroom, where we collected his razor and came down again. Fifteen-love. Petty perhaps, but it was one of those minor successes that lent occasional cheer to POW life, my Battle of Berlin.

I could hardly have imagined such a scenario when, more than two years earlier, on 3 September 1939, Mary and I had switched on the radio in our High Street house at Eton and heard Neville Chamberlain announce that, as Hitler had not replied by 11 am to his ultimatum, we were at war with Nazi Germany.

Two years earlier I had been appointed to the staff at Eton as Assistant Master and Chaplain, and a year later Mary and I were married. We had had just one year together.

After we had heard the broadcast we got out our bicycles and rode out across Dorney Common to Boveney Lock on the Thames. It was a lovely early autumn afternoon, and we sat for a while in the tiny ancient chapel close to the lock, trying to realize what was real in a suddenly unreal world. We could not then anticipate a five year separation, but when that was how it turned out, our thoughts often returned to that quiet moment together at Boveney.

In March 1939, when Germany invaded the Sudetenland, I was so much convinced that I wanted to be involved in what had to be done that I applied for a commission in the Royal Army Chaplains Department, and thereby became one of the only two masters on the staff at Eton liable for immediate call-up on the outbreak of war.

Towards the end of August, Mary and I set off in our car for a short holiday in Scotland. But when we heard that Germany and Russia had signed a pact we turned the car round and returned to Eton to await the inevitable call-up. Before that occurred, we were asked to take in as lodgers four LCC women teachers who had been evacuated from London with their pupils. For the next few days they sat with their feet up in our drawing room, waiting for Mary to produce another meal.

On 4 September my call-up papers arrived and we abandoned the house to the teachers, Mary going to her family at Streatley, and I to join the battalion to which I had been posted at Oxford. This was the 4th Battalion, Oxford-shire and Buckinghamshire Light Infantry, a Territorial Army unit in which I had held a commission for five years during my student days at Oxford.

Within a few days the battalion was moved for training to the village of Woolton Hill in the Downs south of Newbury.

There I was billeted in a large house where Mary joined me at the invitation of the friendly middle-aged lady who owned it. Mary had found a job as a land-girl on a farm several miles away, and was learning to milk a herd of pedigree Jersey cows.

After four months training at Woolton Hill, 48th Division, of which my battalion was a part, was sent to France to join the British Expeditionary Force. It was an exceptionally cold winter, and until the spring arrived the 'phoney' war proved to be a period of extreme discomfort and unremitting boredom and frustration. The work for the troops was grim; mostly it involved the digging of a tank ditch and the construction of concrete pillboxes. There appeared to be no obvious plan to prosecute a war; our equipment was of derisory quality, and replacement with more convincing weapons was absurdly slow. Worst of all, it became increasingly clear that the French population had no stomach for the fight and positively resented our presence.

It was almost a relief when the Germans attacked on 10 May. We advanced into Belgium according to plan and defensively occupied the line of the River Dyle south of Brussels. The Field of Waterloo was allotted to my brigade. Meanwhile the Germans had broken through into France, and the BEF had to fall back.

Our retreat nearly became a rout. Each night my battalion dug in on a new defensive line; each day they marched back to a new position, until after seven days they were back in France, utterly exhausted, in the line of tank ditches and pillboxes they had prepared during the winter. Unfortunately, these were now facing in the wrong direction.

Plans from above were being issued and countermanded almost hourly, until eventually the brigade was despatched to face westward as part of the perimeter defending Dunkirk, through which, unknown to us, an escape for the army was being prepared.

My battalion and the 2nd Glosters concluded their active service, defending the town of Cassel on the perimeter for four vital days. This action was entirely creditable and was important in the context of the evacuation of the BEF. Very few of the defenders of Cassel made it back to England. When the brigade finally left Cassel and attempted to reach Dunkirk, many were killed and the rest were taken prisoner in the early hours of 29 May. Our total active service had lasted just over fifteen days.

The German triumph was complete, and as far as we knew the BEF had been annihilated. An invasion of Great Britain seemed imminent. Added to the misery of our condition after capture was the utterly depressing prospect of our families being faced with invasion and subjugation. As we trudged along the roads of the Pas de Calais, hungry and thirsty in the blazing June sunshine, we endured the taunts of the German soldiers as they drove past in tanks and armoured troop-carriers, equipment of a quality that had never been matched by the BEF or the French army. Endlessly they were singing, *'Wir fahren gegen England'.* Our humiliation was total.

For a few days our miserable journey into captivity was halted at some barracks in Mainz. There we were told that Italy had jumped on the bandwagon and declared war. When a German officer approached a group of us and asked what we thought of the news, one of our party said, 'We had them in the last war. It's your turn to have them in this.' A trivial incident, but for me this struck a new note and indicated a kind of spirit that I was to encounter among our troops many, many times in the next five years.

To this point I was still wondering how and where a chaplain was meant to fit into the army set-up. Those chaplains who had joined from civilian life had received no 'coaching', and the meetings at GHQ at Arras to which we had been summoned by the Deputy Chaplain-General each month since our arrival in France appeared to be concerned with trivial matters of marginal importance, care of our cars, regimental etiquette, was it less embarrassing to other officers if we discarded our clerical collars at mess dinners, and so on. The only useful advice I received came from an unexpected source.

Shortly before we left England in January 1939, the chaplains of 48th Division were summoned to Divisional HQ for a talk from the new Divisional Commander, General Andrew Thorne. In brisk military language he said that he did not expect chaplains to go rushing around officiously, being more trouble than they were worth. 'But there are jobs for you to do,' he said, 'all kinds of pastoral jobs. You have got to be on the look-out for these. And if you don't spot them and do them, God help you. If you fall down on those there will be no respect for you or your office.'

The longer the job lasted the more I came to appreciate what General Thorne had said. A few days after we had been captured we were sitting around in an old fort in Doullens, waiting for our next move, very tired, shell-shocked and utterly depressed. Brigadier Somerset asked me to lead some prayers. I told them about the lesson that had actually been the lesson appointed in the Anglican Lectionary for the morning that we had been captured. It came from St Peter's Epistle. 'Beloved, think it not strange concerning the fiery trial that is come to try you, as though some strange thing happened to you; but rejoice, inasmuch as you are partakers of Christ's sufferings . . . Wherefore let them that suffer according to the will of God commit the keeping of their souls to him in well-doing, as unto a faithful Creator.' The New Testament often juxtaposes these three ideas, suffering, joy and the faithfulness of God. This was something I had to hang on to, and with this I could help others. I now knew for certain that I had a job to do.

Almost immediately after capture, officers and other ranks were segregated. Most of the other ranks were sent off to East Germany and Poland. With most of the other officers captured at this time, I was despatched to Oflag VIIC at Laufen in Ober-Bayern near Salzburg where the numbers later grew to twelve hundred with the arrival in June of officers of the Fifty-First Highland division, captured at St Valery.

Three factors dominated our lives in the first six months: hunger, absence of any news from our families, and anxiety about the course of the war. It was two months before Mary received any news of my survival and five months before I received any letter from her, ten months before I received my first change of clothes.

The tidy-minded Germans allotted us to rooms according to rank. My room with six sets of three-decker beds contained eighteen chaplains of seven different denominations – ecumenism run riot.

I was fortunate in that quite soon after our arrival at Laufen, the Senior British Officer commissioned me and Padre Richard (Pooh) Heard to plan some organisation for study and lectures. Pooh was one of the outstanding characters in the camp; he had been Dean of Peterhouse, Cambridge, and had served as Chaplain of the Queen Victoria Rifles, captured at Calais. By degrees we enlisted numerous officers who were prepared to stand up and share their knowledge or skills. Eventually the courses offered covered languages (ancient and modern), history, theology, accountancy, law, mathematics and general subjects ranging from contract bridge to soft fruit growing and Highland dancing. There were problems: paper was in scarce supply and accommodation was very limited; classes were advertised as taking place in corners of barrack rooms, in various corridors or, when fine, in the courtyards or on the exercise *platz*. Pooh's own remarkable lectures on any subject from the Acts of the Apostles to the Economic Condition of the European Countries invariably attracted over a hundred officers and usually had to be given 'under the large tree on the exercise *platz*'. All this was the start of what later became in almost all camps thoroughly efficient group study facilities. But for that we had to wait for books and other equipment. It was a sad loss to us when the Germans decided that Pooh was a dangerous influence and sent him off to be a founder member of Colditz, together with other officers whom they found difficult to control.

Before long we began to acquire pianos and other musical instruments, and the standard of musical events was remarkably high. We had some very competent musicians, and for me the high spots were the Carol Service at Christmas, and in Holy Week a remarkable adaptation of Bach's *Matthew Passion* – with choir, soloists and orchestra.

Morale in the camp was at times depressingly low, especially among the more senior officers. Among the professionals, career prospects were dismal; their chances of reaching high rank had gone. There were also many majors who had left the army in the 1930s when they were not going any higher and had started a new career in civilian life; as reservists they had been recalled on mobilisation, and had now lost out in both worlds and were content to settle down in prison to a life of bridge and boredom.

Chaplains and doctors, of whom there were nearly a hundred, were classed as Protected Personnel. According to the Geneva Convention they were entitled to repatriation, and repatriation became a constant topic of discussion among them, fuelled by rumours in correspondence from optimists at home. At an early stage I and one or two others decided that on no account would we accept an offer of repatriation if it was made. We had a ministry among our fellow prisoners, and that was to be our work. As far as I was concerned, my decision had been made easier by Mary; she had written in her first letter to me that she had heard rumours about possible repatriation of Protected Personnel, but that she did not imagine that I would consider leaving the job. It was a decision that neither of us ever regretted.

The Germans did make one concession to Protected Personnel. Several times a month doctors, chaplains and medical orderlies were allowed to go for a two-hour walk in the surrounding countryside. We had to march in a column with armed guards on either side. One could hardly call it freedom, but it was good to be outside the barbed wire, and the sub-alpine scenery around Laufen was beautiful. In summer we went to a lake, where we bathed to our great enjoyment.

In August 1941 rumours began to circulate that Laufen was to be closed and we were to be transferred. I did not want a change. It had been a grim place in the early days, but conditions had much improved; at least half the officers had already been moved elsewhere and I had been sharing the chaplaincy work with the only remaining chaplains, Gordon Fraser of the Church of Scotland, and Kenneth Grant, one day to be appointed Roman Catholic Bishop of Argyll and the Isles, two wonderful room companions. Laufen was a prison, but it had its compensations. The River Salzsach flowed under its walls and there were always the mountains beyond Salzburg to which, winter and summer, we could lift our eyes.

After various false alarms the camp was finally closed at the end of September, and we were transferred to Oflag VIB at Dössel Warburg in Westphalia, a hutted camp in a sandy waste, accommodating three thousand officers. As far as I was concerned, apart from the fact that I found there numerous old friends and former colleagues, there was nothing to recommend it. There were already enough chaplains to cope with the work, and I found myself superfluous. I submitted an application to be transferred to a Stalag. I had learnt that there was work to be done in such camps, and that no officers were allowed there other than doctors and chaplains. To my surprise, an order came through within three weeks that I was to proceed to Stalag XXA at Torun in Poland. And that was how I found myself in Berlin on 5 November 1941 on my way to a very different kind of life in Stalag XXA.

2

Move to Poland

Darkness had fallen when I reached Torun with my guard on 6 November. I sat in a crowded waiting-room while my guard rang up Stalag HQ to obtain instructions. About an hour later the waiting-room door was flung open and a cheerful trio of young British NCOs burst in, accompanied by a meek-looking guard. They gave me a smart salute and a hearty welcome, and, loading my two bundles on a sledge, off we went into the dark and snow. Talk was incessant as they plied me with questions about conditions in an officers' camp and about any of their officers I might have come across. After about half a mile they decided to have a rest, and without any reference to our guards we halted and had a smoke before proceeding to our destination, Fort XV. I was being given a glimpse of a very different way of handling the Master Race from what I was used to in the Oflags.

It is hard to do justice to my first impressions of this extraordinary camp that was to be my home for the next two years. The Feldwebel – Scarface, as I came to know him – was waiting to welcome me as if I was an important guest arriving at a four-star hotel. He dismissed the guard who had brought me from Dössel and personally escorted me through the main gate and across a bridge over a moat to the main door of the camp. As the huge steel door was opened, from a long, dimly lit, brick-vaulted corridor there came the rapturous sound of a choir belting out 'And the Glory of the Lord' from Handel's *Messiah,* a stunning welcome. Meanwhile the Feldwebel escorted me to my room rushing around, shouting to all and sundry, organising my bed, my supper, and any other amenity he could think of.

21

Fort XV was one of a string of forts constructed around cities on the eastern frontier of Germany out of reparations received from France after the 1870 war. It occupied several acres and was surrounded by a dry moat. To right and left inside the main door there stretched long corridors, off which were barrack-rooms, eight in each direction, all looking out on to the moat. A second storey of identical corridors and barrack-rooms lay below this top layer. The rest of the fort was reached along endless corridors leading to store rooms, ammunition stores, hoists and casemates, the whole complex forming a figure of eight enclosing two open-air exercise *plätze.* Above it all was a thick layer of earth and vegetation, including many shrubby trees. From outside and from above, no building was visible except the barrack section facing the moat opposite the main entrance. A walk around the top of the fort amounted to about a third of a mile. All the barrack-rooms and corridors were brick-vaulted, like sections of underground railway, and the rooms, like Nissen huts. The exercise *plätze* were two deep bowls with steep grassy banks stretching up to the top of the fort.

At the time of my arrival the fort housed some 400 Warrant Officers and NCOs, mostly British, with perhaps fifty French. All had exercised their right under the terms of the Geneva Convention to refuse any form of work except of a supervisory nature. Between the time of their capture at Dunkirk and the summer of 1941 they had been denied this option by the Germans. But in Stalag XXA a small number of men, having become aware of their rights, had consistently refused to work. They had been subjected to the strongest pressure; all had served various periods of strafe and solitary confinement; some had been roughly handled; some had bullet wounds to show; a few had been shot dead. Their resolute, at times heroic, behaviour, backed intermittently by the support of the visiting Protecting Power (the USA at that stage), had gained by August 1941 a recognition by the Germans of the right of all ranks from Corporal upwards to be excused compulsory work. From that date onwards Fort XV had become the designated camp for all WOs and NCOs in Stalags XXA and XXB who availed themselves of this right. A considerable number did not do so and remained in working camps. Their motives, as I came to discover, were various. Some reasonably decided that they ought to continue to look after the men, many of them very young, in their camps, and many did excellent, responsible work in this way. Others simply continued to work because conditions in many working camps were more agreeable – better food, more 'perks', and in many farm parties contact with local women.

About once a year when the numbers of men refusing to work had risen to more than 700, a draft of anything from 100 to 600 was despatched to a larger camp in Germany. In two and a half years I saw over 2000 men pass in this way through Fort XV, but the *'nix-arbeiters'* who were there when I first arrived were a particularly spirited type of NCO, many quite young, from both Regular and Territorial Army. To live among them for nearly a year before they were sent elsewhere, after fifteen months' experience of the apathy and defeatism of some in an Oflag, did much to revive my spirits.

There was a permanent camp staff which remained largely unchanged throughout my stay. It consisted of a Camp Leader or *Vertrauensmann* ('Man of Confidence' or linkman with the Germans), cooks, a tailor and bootmaker, gardener and sanitary men, and so on. Since 1940 the *Vertrauensmann* had been a lively Irishman, CSM Macdonald, of the Leicestershire Regiment. Though subject to periods of gloom, he was a real fighter and stupendously energetic. All day he was besieged in his room: 'Mac, can I . . .?' 'Mac, have you got . . .?' 'Mac, will the Germans . . .?' and so on. He was accessible to all and would fight the Germans for anything, serving the camp unsparingly.

Until the spring of 1943, the German Commandant was always an officer. Most of those who held the job, especially the one who held it longest, Hauptmann Schubert, left the internal administration of the camp entirely to Mac, supervised by a Feldwebel. The Commandant only came into the camp to supervise morning *Appel* (roll call). The Feldwebel named Benz, known to thousands of POWs as Scarface, was a unique character. As a young soldier he had been a prisoner in Scotland from 1917 to 1919, and had come away from this experience with two things – a great sympathy for prisoners and an unerring understanding of their tricks and dodges. One would not have taken him for a soldier at first sight, but in the presence of one of his officers he became tremendously smart, and as a weapon training instructor for stupid men – and he had plenty of those under him – I never saw his equal. He was coarse and noisy in manner, he went around bellowing like a bull, but his own camp guards, young and elderly, were devoted to him because he was considerate and at his best when dealing with prisoners who were sick or in any kind of trouble. He had no children of his own, but all the Polish children in the vicinity of the camp loved him. When they approached prisoners outside the camp he would roar at them, but they took not the slightest notice. And in fact he made it a condition of taking any of us out for a walk or a bathe that we should bring chocolate or sweets from our parcels for the children.

Scarface virtually lived in the camp instead of in his quarters across the moat. Every morning when he came in he shaved and had breakfast in our quartermaster stores, and all day long was in and out of the barrack-rooms, fooling about and joking with the men. When a written order reached him from his superiors at Stalag HQ he brought it in to Mac to read it. They would then decide how to carry it out – or ignore it without being caught out. Scarface knew that a prison camp must be contented if it was to run well, and his simple method was to reduce restrictions to a minimum.

It might seem that the prisoners in Fort XV were culpably quiescent or even collaborators. That was far from being the case. But the way that things were worked out between Mac and Scarface meant that we were not having constantly to quarrel with the administration on the spot about silly regulations. Likewise I would hesitate to call Scarface a disloyal German, even though it was he who brought our first wireless into the camp – at a price. He was quite a greedy man and he did take bribes. But though strange things went on in the camp, we, and Scarface, were far less troubled by visits from higher authorities than were other camps where the Feldwebels went around looking for trouble and reporting it to their bosses.

For myself I had every reason to be grateful. Scarface treated all British officers with exaggerated respect, and for more than two years did everything possible to help me and the doctors in our work. Permits for officers to visit other camps were often hard to come by, but on the slightest pretext, and sometimes with no authority at all, he would supply me with a guard to escort me to the hospital or to another camp. Occasionally I was refused entrance at the other end, but at least Scarface had done his best, and his views on the obstructiveness or stupidly literal adherence to orders by others were colourful. If I had to be called at four o'clock in the morning to go on some journey he would never entrust the job to an underling. He would stay up to call me himself, creeping into our room with ludicrous stealth to avoid waking the other officer.

On the day I arrived at Fort XV and he showed me into my room, I found only one other officer in residence, another C of E chaplain, Charles King, like me a TA commission. As there were numerous other camps without a chaplain, this arrangement was pointless, and after a few weeks Charles was sent elsewhere and a doctor came in his place. I consequently shared the room with one or two doctors for the next two and a half years.

Our position in the camp was curious. In German eyes we were simply there as doctors and chaplains. The camp was administered by a Sergeant-Major. In practice we observed this arrangement, but the Sergeant-Major came to us for advice and on rare occasions asked the senior doctor to interview a recalcitrant man and administer reproof if necessary; but otherwise we did not take charge except in our own spheres. The men treated our rank with respect, but they also liked us to share in their activities and visit their barrack-rooms, though I never did this without their permission.

7.11.41

. . . It is all rather like a dream. For the first time I am in a quiet room of ample size, a batman, hot bath, single-decker bed and much besides. Today I walked with a hundred and fifty men to another camp in the Stalag for a real cinema show . . . Last night I attended an amusing, well-organised debate on 'Town v Country', full of good cracks and spirited debating . . . There are choirs, bands and much lively entertainment and music. Some seem keen about services and we are planning arrangements for Sunday. The country is unbelievably dull and will, no doubt, be equally bleak later . . . I gather the repatriees are still held up. They must be frightfully disappointed. I hope some solution can be found . . . I had to leave most of my books at VIB . . . The Germans may forward them. I am sorry to lose them otherwise, but there is a good library here, though not of the kind of books that I need most . . . Is it too soon to wish you Many Happy Returns? . . .

12.11.41

No letters yet . . . We had a meeting with the eight doctors from scattered sections of the Stalag; most I knew at VIIC before they came here. I shall probably have the hospital to visit as part of my job . . . about a quarter of an hour's walk. One novelty here is that I never see a paper and rarely get news of any kind. In many ways I prefer this to a daily dose of the local brew, but you will write and tell me when the war is over, won't you? . . . Did you get my letter telling you that Ingrid's husband Kai died suddenly of apoplexy at a dinner? Randi's father and mother spent summer and Jo's children their holiday on a farm and are all well. [These items of news referred to the family of Mary's sister-in-law in Denmark. Jo Dessau sent me wonderful parcels from occupied Denmark]. Please send Bromo by most rapid method. I hate newspapers or letters . . . I am well off here, better than since capture, except for letters. . .

16.11.41

. . . I am getting to know people . . . feature of this room is conversation between me, one of the Polish officers who talks German and a little French, and

26

one of the Frenchmen who also talks German. My contribution is School Cert. French, mixed with a few odd German words. Polish is beyond me; my mouth is the wrong shape . . . Charles King has a mandolin which is rather a menace . . . It will take a little time to settle in and work out possibilities of this job, but I am delighted to have been able to come . . .

21.11.41

. . . Life is supremely uneventful . . . I take my exercise daily on top of the fort without catching frostbite . . . Charles and I share a servant, Private Fry, who does everything except feed and dress us; he cooks for himself and for us, does our washing, 'in fact, my dear, he is a treasure,' in spite of having had seven tommy gun bullets in him. Last night I was first witness in a mock trial, brilliantly staged, lasting three hours; the opposition spent all their ammunition entirely destroying every shred of character I have ever had. We are all now set on rehearsing a carol service on the lines of last year's . . . The only real blight is continued lack of news of you, seven weeks now . . . I shall feel like October 1940 all over again when I hear at last . . . theatricals will weigh heavily against my ever taking over a parish. That is very unfair, as the shows are extraordinarily good . . . but it is the length and frequency and hard-arse seats that get me. Our [censored – presumably 'Polish'] friends leave tomorrow and Charles too may go elsewhere . . . I shall become a solitary or mystic or learn the trombone or something . . . Our Fry is a sexton or parish clerk at home; his mother writes, so he tells me, that his younger brother is acting for him and there have been a 'fine lot of funerals' . . . What a silly letter, but I do try to tell you what we do and think, when we are not eating and sleeping. . .

28.11.41

At last your October 8th, forwarded from VIB. What a thrill . . . What a miserable business it all was. [The collapse of the proposed repatriation when all the home-going party were sent back from France to Germany] . . . It sounds as if the announcing at home could not have been worse handled . . . We have two additions to our room, a doctor and a half-tamed squirrel. [It never became tame and we released it in the early spring]. Great thrill my first personal parcel here, and what a parcel, attaché case and contents all complete; I do not know how you can bear to part with the chocolate . . . Since 1940 I have had nine different sets of room-mates, so I cannot call life dull . . . Charles for ever worries about home matters, and seems to trust his wife to decide nothing. Perhaps I have not helped you enough, but, posts being what they are, I felt you could do better without interference . . .

On Sundays I held two services in my own camp, early Holy Communion, and at the hospital a mid-morning service. Owing to crowded conditions at Fort XV I never felt justified in asking for a room as a permanent chapel or quiet room, and the subterranean bunker that we used for services was not a cheerful place. The number of communicants was small, but those who came were regular and a particularly good lot of men, who performed many useful but unostentatious acts of service to the community. The evening congregation fluctuated greatly and quite unpredictably in numbers. We had a simple service to suit men of various denominations, and they sang enthusiastically any hymn that was familiar to them, which was a very small number. Few had had much experience of worship, and I always felt that most of those who came looked to the sermon to give them something to take away. One well-educated man, a bank employee, serving as a sergeant in a TA unit, said to me: 'I enjoy the sermon every week, because I like to hear a serious subject treated seriously. During the rest of the week I hear nothing in my barrack-room except trivial or bawdy conversation.' I know that many others felt the same; they enjoyed no privacy, no quiet for serious talk or reading, and the service met a real need. Certainly I have never prepared my sermons with greater care than in that camp.

A non-working NCOs' camp, like an officers' camp, had to work out its own amusements and diversions. Except in the four or five summer months, little was possible out of doors, as the ground was frozen or under snow. At other times football was played on a ground outside the camp to which players and spectators were conducted by a posse of elderly guards. Inside there was little room for anything except basketball. During the first winter that I was there we had a number of French NCOs, some of whom were superb players. After some months of intense practice and keen inter-room competitions, a British team eventually managed to score the odd victory over the French; but it was they who introduced our men to a game of great skill, and none of our referees ever really mastered the fine points.

18.12.41

. . . Have just given a talk on Christmas Carols. Four of us, two RC sergeants and a 'presby' church organist and I, illustrated the talk by singing unaccompanied all or parts of fourteen carols from the Oxford Carol Book. Fun, but slightly under-rehearsed. Now we face the larger Carol service on Sunday with some trepidation . . . We have been fitting together band and chorus. The band is five violins, two saxophones, one clarinet, two trumpets, a trombone and a double bass. I have to use tact explaining to the band that some carols are better with no accompaniment or strings only, especially as there are only fifteen singers . . . I shall keep your birthday on Saturday, but this year without liquor . . . Charles and I had a good walk by the big river [Vistula]: deadly dull country, but a river bank always fun. I have on my table some pussy willows that I picked, a German custom for Christmas our guard told us . . .

29.12.41

What a girl, my Mary! Three lovely letters on Christmas Eve . . . I knew just what you would think about my staying behind . . . I am sure that we were right and I have been inexpressibly happy inside since the decision was made. When I met Brigadier Somerset at Oflag VIB he said, 'I was sure that you would not go,' and he was pleased when I was sent up here. I have been terribly sorry about Cyril all this week. [My brother who, as I thought wrongly, was in Hong Kong. He was in Singapore]. Apart from that I had a lovely Christmas. I share my room now with a Major Boileau, very 60th, but nice, and two really delightful over-50s, a Captain Shannon (hereinafter called 'Skipper'), and Chief Engineer Annan (Chief), all from Greece or Crete . . . On Boxing Day all the officers were allowed to meet at one of the other camps; we attended a concert there, and the 'boys' gave us such a hand when we came in that I just wanted to burst into tears, as I did many times during those few days, as when the young Polish prisoners brought us presents . . .

31.12.41

More changes; we are expecting two more doctors . . . we shall be a slightly tighter fit . . . I have just delighted my companions (none of whom, being Cretan caught, get private parcels, nor even letters yet) with a cup of American Nescafé, the best tinned coffee in powdered form that I have ever tasted. I wish that Jo [in Denmark] and all the others who have sent us parcels could realize how many people have derived pleasure from them. Since September 1940 in every room I have been in I have asked everyone just to chuck everything into the common cupboard as larder. We then draw stores from that and cook communally for every meal, laying the table first and generally trying to live like civilized human beings, instead of the endless dividing up and private cooking and even eating out of tins, which some prisoners never grow out of . . . We get a snow-storm every day, sometimes very severe, and icy winds . . .

1.1.42

Well, we saw the New Year in vociferously after the manner of English, Scottish, Irish, Polish, French, Serbian, Arabian, Cypriot and others, with one thought at least in common to all, that every man may arrive safely and in peace to his own land and family. I hope that 1941 will have been the only complete year that I shall ever spend in jug. Another party arrived last night from Greece, almost all Australian medical personnel, including some doctors and a Presby chaplain. So we are very full now . . .

A major upheaval occurred in Fort XV on New Year's Eve with the arrival of nearly 150 Australians and New Zealanders. The party consisted of the staff and a few patients of the Fifth Australian General Hospital. The hospital had been left behind in Greece when the Allies abandoned the country in face of the German invasion in May. Casualties from the ill-fated campaign were assigned by the Germans to this hospital for treatment, as were also casualties from the subsequent and equally disastrous Crete debacle. Also left behind by the retreating British was a complete New Zealand dental unit. It was a tragedy that a highly skilled group of dentists and their trained technicians should have travelled thousands of miles just to land up in captivity almost before they had unpacked their drills. Their misfortune was, however, our good fortune, as they were to give excellent treatment to hundreds of fellow prisoners in the months to come. They were shocked by the condition of the teeth of most British prisoners, as no New Zealand soldier was sent overseas without a dental overhaul. The conditions under which the Australian hospital in

Greece had functioned throughout the summer and autumn of 1941 had steadily deteriorated, and when it was finally closed in December the men were in poor condition to endure a week-long cattle-truck journey in mid-winter from Greece to Poland. On their arrival, Fort XV turned on all the hospitality that it could offer and shared everything that had been saved up, to give the newcomers a tolerable New Year's Day and a chance to recover. Many of the Australians had never seen deep snow and were soon indulging in crazy snowballing like a lot of kids.

The average age of the Australian hospital staff was high by our standards. Quite a number of the men had served in Europe or the Middle East in the 1914/18 war and a few claimed that since then they had sat around the Sydney waterfront waiting for the next one. Forty was the maximum age for enlistment for service overseas; many of the men well past that age had walked into the recruiting office and passed themselves off as thirty-nine. I doubt if they had bargained for Poland in mid-winter.

The senior officer in charge was a Major Brooke Moore. A caricature of an extrovert Australian and a larger than life character, he was the right man to be in charge of a unit which contained a fair number of thoroughly disgruntled men. He was a good doctor and had coped well with a tremendous load of difficult work with inadequate resources in the aftermath of the Greek debacle. He was also something of an exhibitionist: a popular entertainment that he would put on was to remove tattoo marks by surgery in front of an admiring audience, with whom he carried on a ribald and highly entertaining conversation.

His ancestry was Ulster Protestant, and he introduced me to all the deplorable language and ideas of anti-Catholic bigotry. He removed from a book a picture that he had found of King Billy crossing the Boyne on his white horse, framed it, and, when the Irish Roman Catholic chaplain from Fort XIII was due to lunch with us on his monthly visit, hung it on the wall of our room.

Among a pile of oddly-assorted books brought to our camp by a representative of the International YMCA I found one, published in the 1870s, entitled *'The Papal Claim to Infallibility'*. Written by a protestant professor of Trinity College, Dublin, it was, as one would expect, a devastating refutation of the claim. I lent it to Brookie. For two days he was absorbed in it, lying on his bed and rolling about with uncontrolled merriment. Finally he returned it to me, saying: 'There is only one untrue statement in that book, Padre; in the Introduction it says, "Controversy is distasteful to me, and I enter upon it with reluctance." '

There was never a dull moment when Brookie was around, and when he visited me at Eton some years after the war, he had remembered a promise made in prison and presented me with a small purse made out of a kangaroo's scrotum.

Once they had recovered from their gruelling journey the Australians began to infuse new life into all fort activities, especially sport of any kind. They introduced rugger and ran some excellent athletics meetings with very thorough organisation and, of course, plenty of betting. Prison life offered scant opportunities to the Aussies to bet, but I could usually find a group in fine weather sitting for hours on the top of the Fort at a point overlooking the main railway that ran eastwards towards the Russian front and increasingly carried troops and materials frontwards and casualties westwards. They were betting on the direction from which the next train would come.

7.1.42

Nothing this week except your v. nice Oct 28. The address situation seems to have been acute in October, but you were well justified in writing anywhere and everywhere. As I told you the forwarding system in this country is excellent, and everything seems to reach me in time. I long to hear good news of Cyril, but I fear that when it does come it is unlikely to be good . . .

16.1.42

Five kilos of apples from Jo [Denmark], rather pulped, having arrived via Oflag VIB, but a super

33

present, excellent when cooked. [We scraped the pulp out of the cardboard box and baked the mush in the delousing cupboard] . . . I borrowed some music catalogues from Stalag HQ to order some piano stuff; you have no idea how much pleasure I get out of studying catalogues as a substitute for all the music I cannot hear here. I am reading Houghton's *'Life and Letters of Keats'* . . . he did write lovely letters, esp. 19 Feb. 1818 to Reynolds. It gives me an idea for the value of enforced idleness:

'He who saddens at the thought of idleness cannot be idle, and he is awake who thinks himself asleep.'

. . . The endless talk of some of my companions about repatriation or boredom is just irksome . . . These last three months have been almost the most contented in my life, 'patiently abiding' . . . a wonderful feeling of inward peace, compounded of faith and hope . . .

22.1.42

Jo [in a letter from Denmark] says, 'We too had an old-fashioned Christmas, and it sounds unbeliev- able that we are still able to do so. in wartime . . .' Here we had big changes today; our combatant officers left at 5 am for Oflag. We gave them a huge plate of porridge at 4 am to keep out the intense cold. I was very glad to climb back to bed. They have very much enjoyed the peace and civilized messing arrangements of this room after the rough and tumble of life for eight months in Crete, Greece, hospital etc. Both put on pounds in weight and I am quite proud of them . . . I wish you could see the meals we have been given lately by the young Polish prisoner who helps Fry. His pancakes from Red Cross powder are excellent. At the moment he is frying German sausage, Red Cross bacon, potato, to be followed by tinned strawberries with milk powder 'cream' . . . so sorry to make your mouth water . . .

28.1.42

. . . great news that you are now with FGH again. You
know how glad I am that you will not be battling
with the elements again for another winter [as a land
girl], and I hope that you will be happy at Bradmore
Road. [Mary had returned to Oxford to work as
secretary to an old friend, Dr F G Hobson, and was
living with my mother and sister-in-law, Celia.]
How I hope the spring will bring better times; we
seem to be going through a thin time at present . . .
[The Japanese had sunk the *Prince of Wales* and the
Repulse, and almost all war news was bad] . . . Here
we are fast in the grip of winter; one has to be really
careful when one goes out not to get any part frost-
bitten, but it is a wonderful clear atmosphere . . .

[The temperature one night reached –40C and on the East
Front –52C. It was this winter that really broke the German
morale in the east. They had made no proper preparation for
a winter campaign in Russia. It might have been different if
they had reached Moscow and Leningrad before winter set
in.]

2.2.42

. . . John's [my eldest brother, Fellow of University
College, Oxford] last letter encourages me to think
that Cyril was not in Hong Kong . . . I am ashamed
to say that I am still in bed, I have cured my cold, my
tino-sinovitis of left Achilles tendon and my violent
tummy ache, and now have only a vile sore throat.
My otherwise drab life is cheered by the Aussie
doctor, Major Brooke Moore, who would amuse
you greatly. A huge man, he sprawls over the end of
my bed and convulses me with one medical story or

vulgar joke after another. Under a rude exterior he is very able, has a heart of gold, is very well read indeed and much travelled . . . 'If you were in my hospital in Athens I would X-ray you night and day and blind you with flashes of pure science; you would not be any better, but you would think I was very clever . . .'

5.2.42

. . . What shall I tell you tonight? We have had a very good supper, tinned meat and veg, and fried potatoes, and stewed apple rings and powdered cream. The Skipper is in bed and a very nice Welsh Guards sergeant is chatting with him and Major Duffus. D is rather stiff, having been with other doctors to skate on the moat around the hospital. Fry having washed up is playing bridge. When I have finished this I shall make Ovaltine for all, and so to bed . . . I have a picture on my wall now. In it across three snow-covered fields I look down on an Alpine village grouped around a church, just like Galtür. The sun catches the red roofs of the comfortable warm *Gästhause* and their cream-washed walls. Away up the valley stand two great snow-mountains against a clear blue sky, 'We will go there next week.' Tonight you and I and Will [Mary's brother] will come back deliciously tired, our faces tingling with cold, down the lane that runs past my left hand, down through the last three fields, to a tea of cakes and *Glühwein,* all warmth and fun, while outside the ice crackles under the stars . . . delighted to find *All Trivia* in our library today . . .

12.2.42

. . . On Saturday our fortnightly meeting of Stalag doctors and chaplains, here for the first time, pleasant gathering of over twenty; we gave them a great spread for tea . . . [These meetings were later banned] I did my Sunday duty again to the hospital for two hours yesterday, icy cold twenty minutes walk . . . Read Chesterton's *'St Francis'* and Q's *'Art of Reading'.* I like Q, but he makes me feel ashamed to think that I ever dared to teach anyone English, though to do that well would be one of the most satisfactory tasks in the world. Another two and a half months of winter ahead of us . . . I just go right away in imagination to Oxford just beginning to show its spring loveliness . . .

19.2.42

. . . very boring week with cold and severe sore throat . . . I made the mistake of starting work again before I was fully fit and after a walk to the hospital and work there I went down with a bump that evening. The news has not been such at this end to fill one with good cheer; . . . I have been improving my time in bed with Boswell . . . the sort of thing one has to go to prison to do. I am glad you like Philippians; every word of it now has meaning for me . . .

Singapore had fallen. I had every reason to think that Cyril, my third brother, must have been involved. In the late summer of 1940 he and his wife Celia had returned to England from Japan, where for nine years he had been working for the Rising Sun Petroleum Co. He was commissioned and joined the Oxfordshire and Buckinghamshire Light Infantry in Northern Ireland. When Japan declared war he was sent out to Malaya and as a staff officer took part in the withdrawal down the peninsular to Singapore. There he became more and more involved in the events leading up to the surrender. Finally he accompanied General Percival to the actual surrender in the Ford factory, where he acted throughout as the general's interpreter.

Two photographs appeared in the German newspapers,

one of the General, accompanied by Cyril and two other British officers, carrying a white flag and a Union Jack towards the factory, and one of the scene of the surrender with the British and the Japanese facing each other across a table. In both Cyril was clearly visible, and I was able to write home to Celia with the news. Later on, when I knew that there was no effective postal service between Great Britain and British prisoners in Japanese hands, I wrote a number of letters vaguely addressed to a British POW camp in Singapore, via the Red Cross in Geneva. After the war I learnt to my surprise that at least four of these letters had reached my brother, almost the only letters he received in three and a half years.

22.2.42

Poor Celia, I suppose that she is quite without any news and likely to continue so. Was your pet aversion to blame for that show? I gather he [Duff Cooper] got himself out, as so many like him have done. Nice service this evening, I read Ecclus 2. Felt much better in voice than for many weeks past. So I hope to see another cherry-picking. I praught better than usual, on sin: I was against it. I have a small church choir now who lead the singing; we are even tackling Canticles, and I let them sing a less well-known hymn as an anthem . . . I am sitting close to our stove which is a marvellous object, 9 feet high by 3 by 3, covered with plain tiles with a very small grate. It must be an elaborate system within of brick flues as its entire surface gets very hot on quite a small, slow (when door shut) fire and heats this large room wonderfully, ideal for hall of a large house . . . A dull letter, but I have not been going places much lately and only just taking much interest again . . .

27.2.42

. . . Today I had one of my few back teeth out,

perhaps the cause of half my troubles. After Christmas I was very run down . . . got in a nervous state too, news etc upset me as never before, and it has been hard to get right . . . but I am far better now and slowly getting back to work . . . Today a man rushed in and said, 'Please sir, we have had an argument and will you settle it? Was Jesus conceived of Mary or of the Holy Ghost?' Typical; we are the last resort of all barrack-room arguments on any and every subject . . .

3.3.42

. . . So Winton is to be Ebor, grand but sad. A visit to Wolvesey was one of the treats I looked forward to. [The Bishop of Winchester had been made Archbishop of York. I had been his Chaplain in 1935, and he had married us in 1938. Throughout the war he wrote constantly to me and to Mary and sent wonderful parcels of books to me in prison] . . . I loved to hear about your visit to London, what abandon and what fun.

9.3.42

. . . book parcels galore. Who are donors of Sophocles 2 vol., Thucydides 4 vol., Wesley 4 vol., *I Bought a Mountain, Surfeit of Lampreys. Greek N T,* Raleigh's *Milton,* Quick's *Sacraments,* Kirk's *Vision of God,* Kilvert, *Choir Invisible,* and Marett's *Life?* And Celia's grand music parcel. Thank all so much. I have enough now for two wars at least . . . Blank three weeks for Red Cross parcels, great gloom in the Fort . . . The Skipper had a letter from his wife in South Africa, first letter for twelve months. He is the nicest possible room companion and a marvellous cook. I live in daily dread of his going to a new 'situation' . . . Nice Sunday yesterday, my evening service is always 'house full', great joy, and oh! such singing, about 120 men packed in a low brick-vaulted room. These early spring days give one such a longing for freedom; Kilvert has a heart-rending description of walking on such a day over the Marlborough Downs, sun, wind and larks singing everywhere . . .

13.3.42

. . . the Skipper, alas, has departed to Oflag, much to my sorrow . . . he was a lovely companion and we shared many stock jokes, like always 'marking the passage of time' by covering the table with a blanket between meals, even if we had only just got breakfast cleared before lunch arrived at 11.45. So are the civilities maintained and 'our hard won civilization hardly keeps at bay the age of acorns' . . . I think so much of poor Cyril and Celia . . . are things as bad as they sound to us? . . . What a variety of PGs you have at Bradmore Road; I like the pair of whom Mrs Waterhouse writes, 'can pay little and come on condition that they work hard and eat little, the kind of PG I should like to have.' Momentarily I have this room to myself and am free to answer all the astonishing questions that men delve in their spare time out of the more obscure Prayer Book rubrics; but soon I expect four doctors to move in. Last Sunday I got the choir to sing Harris' lovely tune to 'Lead, Kindly Light', with great success . . . all these little ploys, or great, help to speed the time, but never lessen one whit the ache of longing for home . . .

3

Spring 1942

Within a month of my arrival in Stalag XXA at Fort XV I
obtained permission from the German authorities to visit the
hospital at Fort XIV on Wednesday afternoons and on Sunday
mornings. It lay about three quarters of a mile away. I
continued these visits for two years, until I was transferred to
live in the hospital shortly before Fort XV was closed for good
and the NCOs transferred elsewhere. They were some of the
most rewarding that I enjoyed, quite apart from the pleasure
of taking a walk outside the camp, albeit accompanied by an
armed guard.

Fort XIV was much smaller than Fort XV, but the moat
surrounding it was a real moat, full of water, and the living
accommodation, the wards etc were not underground but in
wooden barracks on top of the mound, looking down on the
moat. The patients, French and British, were brought in from
working parties all over the Stalag area. By going round talking
to them I was able to get a good picture of what was going on
throughout the area, which covered a large part of the old so-
called Polish Corridor. The staff consisted of two British
doctors, one French doctor, and a team of medical orderlies,
mainly British.

I always had a particularly warm reception from the French
patients. Their morale on admission was invariably shockingly low and they were most appreciative of the care that they
received from the British hospital staff. It has to be
remembered that the French nation had capitulated and that
their homeland was under German occupation; but even so,
few British patients would have had such sentiments tattooed
on their torsos as *J'ai souffert beaucoup* or *trois années sans amour.*

41

The latter was an unconvincing statement, seeing that on the farms where they worked the French were far quicker off the mark with the Polish girls than their British counterparts.

The patients in the hospital were a mixed lot. On the surgical side were a few appendices, many haemorrhoids and hernias, and men with various fractures and small injuries. The operating theatre was not equipped to deal with more serious cases, which were usually sent off to a German military hospital in Torun.

On the medical side, gastric cases of various kinds predominated and did very well on the Red Cross diets supplied from home. Until the six-monthly system of repatriation of chronic sick was established in September 1943, there were apt to be some long-stay cases. There were always a few TB patients, sometimes waiting several months for transfer to a TB hospital in Germany. There was also an infectious ward, and a ward for skin cases. The ultimate decision about admission and discharge of patients lay with the German Stabsarzt, Weidermann, who could be extremely awkward; but most of the British doctors learnt how to handle him pretty effectively, aided by an invaluable interpreter, Sergeant Estival, who spoke fluent English, French and German, including all the most technical medical terms in all three languages.

In the summer of 1942 I obtained permission from the authorities to pay a fortnightly visit on Friday afternoons to the German Reserve *Lazarett* (Military Hospital) in Torun, where at the top of one block were three very small wards for prisoners of war whose ailments could not be handled in Fort XIV. My original permit was to visit a particular man who was dying of cancer. When he died I asked my Fort Commandant, Hauptmann Schubert, whether he would renew my permit.

'How often?' he asked.

'Once a fortnight,' I said, 'Or once a week when anyone is seriously ill.'

'You may go every day, if you think it necessary,' he said, and he instructed Scarface to see that I had a guard whenever I wanted.

So, every Friday, punctually at 2 o'clock Scarface fetched me from my room and escorted me to the *Wache*. There he handed me over to some elderly guard. If it was one that I had not had before, he said, 'Take the Herr Pastor to the Reserve *Lazarett*. He knows the way, and don't be a nuisance.'

It seemed like freedom, nearly three-quarters of an hour's good walking each way. For half a mile the road ran through a scrubby wood of stunted pines, little better than a track, in summer ankle-deep in soft sand, in winter rough frozen snow, and in spring a morass. At the railway sidings the road became rough cobbles for another half mile to the *Hauptbahnhof*. As we turned to pass under the railway we were confronted on the left by the most prominent feature of modern Torun, the five-hundred-foot-high wireless mast erected by the British before the war. We crossed the river by the railway bridge, a steel structure nearly half a mile long, the near half consisting of short spans curving towards the south bank of the Vistula, the further half consisting of three huge spans over the river. The footway was fortunately on the west side of the bridge, fortunately because the steel superstructure gave some protection from the blistering east wind and because we had a superb view of the old city of Torun with its lovely red brick churches, city walls and ancient gateways. It looked like a rather grim version of the 'View of Delft'. The magnificent Vistula swept away westwards towards where the Germans had replaced with a wooden structure the fine road bridge, *'gesprengt'* by the Poles in 1939. In winter the river was a solid, rugged mass of ice blocks, on which were sitting innumerable shivering wild duck. When the wind blew from the east, crossing the bridge was frighteningly cold, and I pitied the sentries who had to stand there on duty. More than once our British medical orderlies were sent down at night to bring in the corpse of a man who had died of exposure at his post.

At the north end of the bridge a civilian policeman was checking passes, but accompanied by a guard I passed without any question and arrived in the main streets of the city. There appeared to be barely any life at all; there were few people in the streets, a few soldiers loafing along perhaps and a few civilians hurrying past with joyless faces. A small squad of soldiers from the Hindenburg Kaserne would march listlessly by, singing unenthusiastically to order. The shops had only two kinds of window display: either packets of what looked like Vim or bird seed, or a bust of the Führer set off by shabby red and black draperies.

43

The Reserve *Lazarett* was a large general hospital. It occupied several large brick blocks standing in their own gardens, most of which were cluttered with temporary wooden huts, and it overflowed into two large schools across the road. From the winter of 1941/42, when thousands of frostbite cases began to arrive from the East Front, it was grossly overcrowded and the staff became quite unable to cope with the situation. There was only one really competent surgeon in the place, the *Chef Arzt,* Dr Hoffmann. He was a distinguished-looking man with the head of a lion and a mass of snow-white hair. He had been a professed anti-Nazi at one time, and, though he had been placed in charge of this huge hospital, he was granted no higher rank than that of Oberleutnant. I was told that he had appeared one day in the hospital with his white coat emblazoned with a large golden '25'. When asked why, he replied that it was the twenty-fifth anniversary of his promotion to Oberleutnant in the Wehrmacht. Shortly afterwards he was promoted to Hauptmann.

On arrival at the office we were directed through the garden to the surgical block, where we climbed to the top floor. Here was a veritable gathering of the League of Nations. Opening off a short landing there were three seven- to ten-bed wards, containing soldiers from the British Commonwealth, France, Belgium, Poland and Russia. Later these were joined by men from America and Italy. They were all patients who had serious or abstruse diseases or injuries that could not be treated in their own prison hospitals.

The nursing staff consisted of four British RAMC private soldiers, all very young. No one was officially in charge, but, until he was repatriated in October 1943, the lead was taken by a remarkable young Scotsman, Jimmy Finney. When I first visited the wards he himself was a patient, recovering from the second of two severe abdominal operations, and was still confined to his bed. In spite of this, I could see that he had complete authority in the wards. I heard him administer a sharp reproof to an elderly 'regular' RSM for being out of bed and remonstrate effectively with a recalcitrant Frenchman in another ward.

Of the other orderlies I was particularly impressed by George Rimmer, a young Liverpudlian, who later took over command from Jimmy. George found himself in a curious situation. Having acquired some knowledge of operating theatre procedure, he had drifted into the job of being Dr Hoffmann's chief instrument man. Hoffmann had come to regard him as indispensable. There was not a single Sister or German medical orderly who had not at some time been slung out of the theatre by an enraged Hoffmann, but never George, whom he treated with respect and courtesy. On one occasion, Stalag for some reason had recalled George to Fort XV. Hoffmann immediately went on leave and would not return and continue operating until George was sent back. On another occasion, in the middle of a difficult operation Hoffmann, in a temper, made some insulting remark about the British. When the operation was over, George walked out and only returned a fortnight later when Hoffmann implored him to do so. It was a difficult situation for George: clearly he was voluntarily assisting the enemy, but the resulting benefit to the seriously sick prisoners upstairs of his relations with Hoffmann was beyond question. At his request Hoffmann, who often operated from 8 am to the small hours of the next morning, would visit one of the prisoners at any time of day or night and would hold up a long operating list of German patients to perform an emergency operation on a prisoner. No patients in the hospital received better treatment.

Apart from visits from the hard-worked Hoffmann and other German doctors, the nursing given by our young orderlies was better than that of the German sisters or male orderlies, most of whom were clumsy and ill-trained. Patients of all the nationalities in the ward told me how well these young lads looked after them, often when they were desperately ill, with outstanding care and devotion. They rarely saw a doctor. they had no time off, as they had to sleep in the wards. For the most part, they were left on their own over a period of four years to do work that would have taxed to the full the best of our Nursing Sisters.

Invaluable help was given to the young British orderlies by a remarkable woman, Wanda Zakzewska. This intelligent, cultured wife of a Polish surgeon who had been killed during the German invasion had come to work in the Reserve *Lazarett*, and though she had no medical qualifications, she became responsible for the oversight of the POW patients on the top floor. She had complete freedom of movement throughout the hospital and her close contact with the German doctors and administrators, supported with occasional 'sweeteners' of Red Cross tea and other items supplied by our men, resulted in a surprising amount of skilled attention being given to the POW sick. She was also a source of valuable information, and even provided advanced warning when she learnt that the Germans planned a search of the POW wards. All who worked or were patients in the wards remember her as an ever-cheerful, caring and courageous woman.

Besides all this, the orderlies maintained a continuous atmosphere of good, at times even uproarious, humour in the wards. They were also the nerve centre of a large part of the POW black market in Torun. They had innumerable contacts with venal German and Polish civilians, and a steady stream of contraband goods passed to and fro through their hands and the hands of other POWs, coal-shovelling parties or out-patients and X-ray cases, who had to visit the Hospital. Each week an ambulance brought patients from our hospital at Fort XIV to be X-rayed. It returned in the evening loaded with contraband, thanks to George and his friends.

On my visits I reached the hospital at about three o'clock. My guard pushed-off into the town, leaving me for an hour and a half to talk with patients and staff. The British patients, even the very sick, were in good heart. Of the French and Belgians, new arrivals were invariably suffering from very low morale, but on subsequent visits I found them far more cheerful, and obviously deeply appreciative of the treatment they were receiving from the young British orderlies.

There was not much I could do or say to the young Russian soldier who mysteriously arrived in the ward except to enquire, '*Gut*, Joe?', to which he would reply with a beaming smile, '*Ja, gut heute*', which was about the limit of his German and mine. I never discovered how, out of all the tens of thousands of Russian prisoners dying without any medical treatment, he alone had the luck to be admitted to *Reserve Lazarett*. Our orderlies managed to keep him there many months. When eventually he was allowed up, he almost fought with a little Italian convalescent to wait on the British orderlies who had nursed them back to health. They prepared

46

their meals, washed their clothes and rushed to help them in any way they could.

I had a peculiar dread of falling seriously ill in prison; I think that most of our men felt the same. But the courage and cheerfulness of the British patients in that ward, many of them very sick indeed, was moving in the extreme. One man I shall never forget. It was to visit him in particular that I first received my fortnightly pass. Harry Lauder was, I imagine, in civilian life a casual labourer in Glasgow. Aged about forty-three, but mentally a lot less than that, he had led a hard, rough life. His marriage had broken down, but he had subsequently lived happily with another woman and her two children, of whom he spoke with affection. When I first saw him he was suffering from cancer of the oesophagus, which was making it increasingly difficult for him to talk or eat. After a time he had to feed himself through a tube into his stomach. He was always cheerful, and it never seemed to occur to him that he was dangerously ill. When I spoke to him he would rap with his fist on his chest and say: 'I'll be all right, sir, when I get rid of this lump.'

After seven months, when I had learnt something of his affairs from a relative at home, I felt I must ask him if he had arranged his affairs so that, if anything happened, the woman with whom he had lived and the children would get whatever might be due from him, and not his wife. When I broached the subject to him he replied somewhat peevishly, 'Aa fuxed that wi' ma Kerrnel at Aldershot in 1940.'

Then he sat up and, fixing me with a fierce stare, said: 'Aa'll no be dying. Aa'll be as reet as reet when aa get this shufted.'

He calmed down, and before I left that evening, I found him lying very quietly, quieter than I had ever seen him. I said the Lord's Prayer with him, and he repeated most of it with me, and I gave him my blessing. He died that night, and the orderlies told me that he barely woke after I left. We had all grown very fond of Harry, and I was glad that God took him so quietly in the end.

My visit always ended with a splendid tea, and my guard was also given something to keep him quiet. In winter it was dark when we left at five o'clock, and in summer it was still broad daylight. It was the spring and autumn evenings I liked best, when I could enjoy the sunsets, reflected in the river and warming to a rose-red the old churches and city walls. In that flat country one hardly seemed conscious of a horizon; the view seemed to pass imperceptibly into the infinity of the sunset, and on such evenings it needed only the smallest effort of the mind to carry me home. The 'barbed wire' was still there. but those hundreds of dividing miles shrunk almost to nothing. I felt then more poignantly than ever the spirit of fine men like George Rimmer and his fellows, who were creating in those three small wards an atmosphere of home for their unlucky fellow-prisoners.

29.3.42 – Palm Sunday

Such a lovely spring Berkshire Downs day . . . I got out the paints on Friday and lost myself in two hours painting, not very satisfactorily, the not very exciting view of the prison gates from my window . . . two nice birch trees which came well. How extra-ordinary about Cyril's last cable. His friends [Japan] seem terribly uppish still; I wish Dakin [USA] would do something. It is hateful with all God's world turning so lovely to have this eternal feeling of expecting great issues to be decided. At times 'my heart within me is even like melting wax', but then I try to see through it all in the spirit of Psalm 93, 'The Lord is King . . .'

6.4.42

. . . In spite of my cursory method of acknow-ledgement I do love getting all these letters, esp. yours. You give such a lovely picture of your life, just all I want to know . . . We have had a nice Easter weekend, all my services well attended – by army, not by parish standards, on Good Friday here and at hospital, and yesterday fifty-five communicants here and forty-five at hospital, and a very full evening service. The Fort Commandant kindly got me distemper and four small hydrangeas, so with the altar end of our tunnel-like chapel colour-washed and with flowers we had everything looking cheerful . . . Am reading Wesley's *Journal,* an uncomfortable man to have in a POW camp, but he might have converted the guards, who knows? . . .

The early months of 1942 brought me sad family news. My brother was indeed a prisoner of the Japanese, and in February my mother died. She had had a sad two years; my father and only sister had both died in 1940, and now two of her sons were prisoners of war. It had been characteristic of her to insist that she must attend the wedding in Belfast of an elder brother, Patrick, also an Army Chaplain. She obtained the necessary permits and made the return journey to Northern Ireland, a formidable journey for an elderly lady in wartime and in mid-winter. It was just the kind of challenge she enjoyed, and she was clearly delighted to have been present at the wedding. It was hard for my Mary to have to break the news to me of her death, as she had had to break the news in 1940 of the death of my father and sister.

8.4.42

. . . thank you for writing so wonderfully about dear Mother. Her going from us is a terrible blow for us all, and I know how terribly you must have felt it, not for yourself only, but also for me . . . it was such a lovely afternoon and I had been out in the sun sketching, before I came in to find your two sad letters. It seemed so impossible to read your lovely words about her, when I had been thinking so much of her, as I always do when I sketch. She taught me to paint. But I can only feel really glad for her with the Easter message so fresh in my mind . . . These last two years must have been agony for her, but she had that marvellous capacity for entering into life fully that seems to set grief in its proper place and proportion. Her friends were without number. But

49

you, what burdens you have borne for me, and for us all . . .

As in other prison camps, theatre offered an occupation for talented men of many different types. Originally our theatre was just one of the subterranean bunkers at the back of the Fort. Its shape was that of a tube tunnel or Nissen hut with brick vaulting, about sixty feet long. In time it was completely transformed. A neat stage and an attractively decorated proscenium arch were constructed. An orchestra pit was sunk through the concrete floor, and seats for nearly a hundred men rose in tiers towards the back. The electrical equipment was excellent, and it was impressive when for the first time the house lights slowly dimmed to the first notes of the overture. The material resources of Fort XV were inferior to those of Fort XIII where men going daily to work would by one means or another lay their hands on all kinds of material for staging, scenery or dresses, and our shows were consequently less spectacular, but the standard of acting was high.

As I said earlier, the first sound I ever heard in Fort XV was a choir of twenty men giving out a triumphant rendering of 'And the Glory of the Lord' from the *Messiah*. None of the singers could read music, and they had learnt every note of the parts by ear from their conductor, Corporal Brown of the Royal West Kent Regiment, who had been a chorister at Westminster Cathedral. The same choir had turned to, and in less than a month worked up for me a lively Carol Service at Christmas, at which a band of good army bandsmen accompanied carols and hymns. In the low brick-vaulted chapel the combined orchestra, choir and congregation produced some stirring sounds.*

Camp musicians, like musicians anywhere else, were a diverting crowd. On my arrival in the camp I was asked to serve as Band President. I did not know what I was in for. At that time there was an excellent band of experienced instrumentalists, including several first class players like CSM

---

*Bandsmen in the Army served in their units as Medical Orderlies and, like RAMC personnel, were 'protected' under the Geneva Convention, and so like Warrant Officers and NCOs were exempt from work and qualified to be in Fort XV, among those who had exercised their right not to work.

Henderson, first trumpeter of the Royal Scots, and PSM Sawyer of the Grenadier Guards, a double bass player and no mean musician, who could do all the necessary scoring. For ten months, before most of them were transferred elsewhere, in the intervals between fearful rows, they gave splendid concerts in Fort XV and at the hospital, particularly those they gave out of doors in the summer.

My role as President had its problems. From time to time the other three members of the Band committee would summon me to a Band meeting. This usually meant that Bandsman A and Bandsman B had refused to play in any band that contained Bandsman C or Bandsman D, or was conducted by Bandsman E. I felt somewhat out of my depth dealing with men, many of them older than myself, who had played in Regimental bands for anything up to twenty years; but the meetings had their entertaining moments. We discussed all kinds of unimportant questions in an atmosphere of deceptive calm, until eventually I put the question: 'Is there any other business?'

A combative voice then said: 'I think the conductor is putrid, sir.'

Then followed a hard-hitting discussion. Finally I closed the meeting by saying that they might be good instrumentalists, but that my feeling about real musicians was that they were prepared to sink such petty differences and give all the music they could to audiences that really wanted to hear them. Usually peace was restored, and when the Germans eventually moved them on to other camps they wrote me a touching letter, thanking me for my interest and encouragement, 'without which there might have been no Band at all.'

They were succeeded by a younger lot of instrumentalists, who were even more quarrelsome. Sawyer and I tried to hold them together, but they preferred to go their own way, and we never knew from week to week whether there was going to be any kind of band available.

15.4.42

. . . I have started a Literary Society; twenty of us

51

meet on Sunday afternoons. Last week, our first, an ex-King's man read a paper on Goldsmith, and I am to follow on Kilvert. Most of the men are very shy at tackling such a task, but I hope to show that it is worth giving us a simple appreciation with extracts from any author they may have been reading; they were very keen . . .

20.4.42

. . . you say you are in bed after visiting Eton . . . I can see that I shall have to stop this war and come home to look after you . . . I keep having to sort things out with men who have been keeping away from services because they have misunderstood my last sermon . . .

One regular Sunday evening attender was an austere-looking Sergeant-Major in the Corps of Military Police. When I noticed that he was missing on several successive Sundays I sought him out and asked him why. He said he had been upset by some remarks of mine – very guarded remarks they had been – about the Creation stories in Genesis. After some talk, I asked him to take the MS of my sermon and an excellent small book on the subject by C H Dodd, which stated the generally accepted view of all but extreme fundamentalists on the early Bible stories. Less than six hours later I found he had returned them to my room. Fearing the worst, I sought him out again. To my surprise, he said he had found them most interesting and totally convincing. His father had been the strictest of Plymouth Brethren, and at the age of forty this man had never encountered anything but the most extreme fundamentalist interpretation of the Bible.

26.4.42

. . . last night I saw an excellently acted play by the hospital staff, Cronin's 'Jupiter Laughs', suitable for

52

its subject . . . the standard is really staggeringly high, female parts and all . . .

3.5.42

. . . After three weeks alone in this room I now have two Aussie doctors, Moore and Meyer, a Yorkshire doctor, Knight, and a NZ dentist, Spencer. The faithful Fry still looks after us. I have been thinking a bit about after the war. . . I feel that I should like to teach, but not boys; there is a tremendous need for adult education . . . I do not know in what sphere I could do it . . . many are so keen to make up for what they have never learnt. . .

10.5.42

. . . I did see both photographs of Cyril [in the *Völkischer Beobachter*], one carrying out the flag with three others and the other at a conference table facing the foe, who were all looking towards him as if he was talking. But neither was clear and the latter was back view. It must have been a fine, though melancholy bit of work. I hope your menage with Celia will run well. I shall be thinking of our lovely Inkpen walk on Thursday [Ascension Day] . . .

25.5.42

. . . the loveliest and 'pangiest' week in the whole year; everything has burst right out, trees and such blossom as there is, and some grand flowering shrubs, and such sunshine. The Fort has gone completely berserk this weekend, Whit, an endless succession of mad frolics, unbecoming in grown men! – fancy dress basketball, a gruelling Treasure Hunt, fun-fair – all most amusing and Hampstead Heath. They somehow managed to sandwich in my evening service, which we held out of doors for the first time . . . Can you manage slippers sometime? Old ones have worn out, and most useful, esp. in long stone corridors at night on way to the 'Aunt'. How I envy you the Handel/Purcell ballet. I miss it more and more here, and had an entranced three minutes lately of *Brandenburg* on the wireless, wafted through a window as I waited outside the German guard-room. We do, however, have wonderful birdsong within the prison, including the nightingales . . .

29.5.42

. . . so glad to hear of your 'chaplaincy' at Wolvesey, [Mary had spent a weekend at Winchester and had driven the Bishop to a service at Basingstoke and supper at the Vyne, the Elizabethan home of the Chute family]. I never went to the Vyne, so you are one up there. What a cad Tony Chute Vicar of Basingstoke saying nothing about me. I knew him well there, and previously at Southampton. I have been thinking all day with thankfulness of the miracle that spared me when poor Joseph Thorne was killed beside me, [at Cassel in May 1940]. Dick saw it all and went off to report our deaths. When I walked into Brigade HQ an hour later he looked as if he had seen a ghost . . . It has been an extraordinary and rather wonderful year since then . . . Fancy St John's [ground landlords of much of North Oxford] allowing hens to be kept in North Oxford; there must be a war on somewhere. I hope they will flourish. Brooke Moore says; 'Be a sport and keep a rooster too.'

1.6.42

. . . nice open air band service at 6 pm as the sun went down. Am reading Vol 1 of Bryant's *Pepys* . . .

what a dog he was and how unlike our present celibacy. Amusing debate on Thursday on 'Should Divorce be Easier?' at which neither side knew the present law; but what matter? Some of the birds in the Fort are wonderful. This morning I woke for their Matins, an astonishing chorus led by the nightingales, golden orioles and others unknown to me. A swallow is nesting in a passage a few yards from this room. So you can see things have improved on the desolation of Oct/May. I hope you get time to stand and stare occasionally in your busy life as bread-winner . . .

7.6.42

Such a week of June the Fourth weather, the old unforgettable days of lilac, laburnum and love . . . Good about the hen's first day. Do you have to 'set' hens like marrows? . . . I am preparing a blitz on the many square miles of English poetry I have never read, having acquired some new ideas on the whole subject of the 'purpose of poetry', 'the meaning of meaning' and other hitherto incomprehensibles. Hoping to read it 'around' with some interested folk . . . The picture of Singapore has appeared again in the papers, very clear indeed, Cyril stepping out with the General and three others to the last meeting, looking really grand and very fit . . .

14.6.42

. . . in spite of all my temporal blessings I have been having a dry time spiritually, a bad spell of accidie. I seem to be getting nowhere in this place . . . due to letting myself get very lazy in reading etc. To keep mentally active and healthy one needs here to be constantly working at something fairly tough. I now get cracking on Tawney, *Religion and the Rise of Capitalism,* so I hope for better things . . . Don't

55

imagine I shall return bursting to do things . . . You will be lucky if you can drag me into the garden to do an hour's weeding with the promise of an egg for tea . . .

4

Half Way 1942

How did we spend our days as we passed the two-year mark in our captivity? About 7 am our batman, Colin Fry, arrived with cookhouse tea in mugs. We rose, washed and shaved. I insisted that three times a day the table in the middle of the room should be cleared, a cloth and the table set, however frugal the coming meal might be. We shared all our supplies, German or Red Cross, rather than each man hogging his own. Some newcomers to our mess were surprised at this and were hesitant to conform, but I am sure that it helped us all to maintain some degree of civilized behaviour. For breakfast there might be porridge of Red Cross oats with two slices of bread, and tea. The doctor went off to his sick parade and ward rounds, and while Fry cleaned the room, I went to collect Red Cross tins from the Red Cross store where we had our Mess locker under German lock and key. Some of the troops who scoffed their Red Cross parcels as soon as they arrived used to mock my more frugal methods of house-keeping and maintained that the officers' tins grew moss on them.

For the rest of the morning I played the piano or walked round the top of the Fort, or in the summer found a place to spread a blanket and sunbathe. I did not carry much surplus flesh at this time, and there were those who compared my jutting ribs with those of the Polish horse that brought the sludge truck into the camp.

A pleasant diversion was to walk two miles to Stalag HQ with the post party, starting just before nine o'clock and returning when business was done, in time for lunch. Sometimes I had business to do there with CQMS Granger, the Stalag Man of Confidence; but I began to realize that the Germans were suspicious of British officers who hung about Stalag HQ, where there were always men from many working parties collecting mail, clothing and other stores. It seemed wise to avoid going there more than necessary, though I missed the walk.

At lunch we ate our only German meal, soup and potatoes from the cookhouse. Two or three times a week I went out in the afternoon visiting one or other of the hospitals from two till five, or later, and was given a cup of tea there.

When the doctor had finished his afternoon round I usually spent some time chatting with patients in the *Revier* (sick-bay) until it was time to see to supper. This, except for some potato saved from lunch, was a wholly Red Cross meal, and for three years, even when parcels had failed to arrive for some weeks, thanks to my 'mossing up', I always managed to find something from our store for our Mess supper. John Irwin, an immense Irish rugger International doctor, was a problem when he was a member of our Mess. After the only course he would push his plate forward, saying, 'a good beginning to a meal'. We all suffered pangs at times, but he more than most.

After supper there was perhaps a theatre show, a concert or a lecture, or I visited a barrack room for a game of bridge, or just to talk, ending as a rule in the QM stores where our patriarchs, CQMS 'Pop' Townsend and RSM Eames, would be finishing their nightly game of crib. The formula was always the same. 'Well, who won tonight?'

'Just about level, wasn't it, Pop?' Eames said.

'Yes, just about level, although you may just have had it,' said Pop.

'Well,' said Eames, 'I'm off to my virtuous couch.'

Veterans of 1914/18, they were a rocklike pair in what was often a rather volatile and explosive society.

At about eight o'clock the news bulletin reached the barrack rooms, the high spot of the day. Our clandestine listeners recorded the World Service bulletin in shorthand from the radio night after night, and we hardly missed a single day's news between the summer of 1942, when we acquired our set, and January 1945. The fewer people around the set the better for security, but I did occasionally attend the session and hear the news for myself. Receiving authentic news, even bad news, in this way was the greatest factor of all in maintaining morale, even greater than receiving mail or parcels.

No account of POW life can omit reference to the parcel service conducted by the Red Cross and the Order of St John. Once the system got going it functioned with great efficiency. Theoretically every prisoner received a weekly food parcel, though there were periods when the system broke down for several weeks or even a month or two, such gaps being usually followed by a 'spate'. In addition, families could send a quarterly clothing parcel up to eleven pounds weight, which could include chocolate, the only food allowed. In course of time I did not need more clothes, and for several years I was sent parcels consisting of nothing but chocolate saved from their rations by Mary and various kind friends and relations. The German censors practically swooned at the sight on opening such parcels. There was in addition no limit on cigarettes and tobacco parcels sent to individual prisoners, and, best of all, no limit on book parcels. The only limiting factor really was transport, and in wartime one could not be surprised when the system creaked, or even, after the Allied landings in 1944, more or less collapsed. To the credit of the Germans, there was little or no pilfering, at least in our area. We were very, very lucky to be looked after so generously by those at home. Parcels from other sources were an agreeable bonus. An Eton colleague passed news of my capture to two Old Boys, Prince Alexander of Jugoslavia and Blaikie Purvis, son of the splendid Head of the British Purchasing Commission in USA for a time. Both sent me generous and most welcome parcels. But even more I appreciated the extraordinary kindness of a Danish sister-in-law of my wife, who continued throughout the war to send me a succession of parcels from German-occupied Denmark. (See excerpts from letters in previous chapter.) The last parcel from this source reached me on Christmas Eve 1944, at a time when we had long ceased to receive Red Cross parcels. What I did not know at the time was that some months earlier Jo Dessau had escaped with her three children to Sweden, but before leaving had made arrangements, perhaps with the Danish Red Cross, for a continued supply of parcels to be despatched to me.

28.6.42

. . . today I got a paper on Johnson off my chest; went well; not so my sermon, which was good, but the service concluded prematurely after the collect for the day, owing to circumstances over which I had no control. [We were unexpectedly ordered out on parade.] So I am a sermon in hand, a *bisque, n'est-ce pas?* . . . I have a new UK companion now, very nice Capt. Irwin, Irish rugby International, who has swapped jobs with Quag Meyer. I am pleased, a huge man and very quiet . . .

28.6.42

. . . How ghastly the family junk must be. [Mary and my brother John were sorting my deceased parents' effects]. I always thought it would be . . . Do what you like with my stuff; in theory there are some things I would like to keep, but in practice I am not likely to care a damn if I get home and start all over again . . .

5.7.42

. . . Summer has come; real grilling weather . . . Sad things happen here; a New Zealand sergeant had his first letter since capture in Crete in May 1941 and learnt that his wife died that month . . . John says the hens flourish, but your vegetables don't. I do enjoy the way you make it possible to enjoy the family jokes . . . I wish I could give you an equivalent picture of life here . . .

12.7.42

. . . with the importance of which day I have just been acquainted by Irwin. 'To the glorious, pious and immortal memory of that most illustrious Prince of Orange, etc.' I gather that I ought to have staged a much more stirring service with petitions for preservation 'from the power of the Bishop of Rome and all his detestable enormities' . . . I preached on Ezekiel 11.16. ['Although I have cast them far off among the heathen . . . yet will I be to them a little sanctuary in the countries where they shall come']. I think a 'little sanctuary' is to be able to walk out of an argument in one's barrack room up on to the *platz,* and stand and look at the sky and trees and birds, and then, after five minutes, say 'thank you' and go in again. At Laufen there were always the mountains and I had a special corner where I learnt to do it as never before, and I think it means more to me than any attempt at coherent prayer. It is the cure for all 'Martharing'! What some people don't realize is that you don't in this way abandon interest in the problems that have been vexing you, but you come back to them a different man . . . Tell Celia that I would do any job under the sun, if I could come home and be husband to you both. I do hope she will hear from Cyril soon; I have such a good photo of him . . .

19.7.42

Another *Sonntag,* and a very nice one too – Communion here, service at hospital and crowded evening service with grand singing. A paper by an Aussie in the afternoon . . . This should reach you on holiday, and I hope that you will have a lovely time, undisturbed by all the too usual bad news . . . CSM Shillingford of whom I told you gave an excellent lecture on big game shooting. Some of these fellows can give talks about any part of the world. I am going to give a Brains Trust a go this week, but I doubt if we have men with sufficient general knowledge . . . I have tried writing again to Cyril through Geneva; one never knows if it might not

61

work better than from home . . . This has been rather a good week . . . It is curious that every now and then the real needs of some of these folk break through the normal rather heart-breaking crust of apparent indifference and reserve, and a chance talk here and there shows how worthwhile one's presence and work has been all these months . . . It is very little, but it works like a tonic on me . . .

26.7.42

. . . Such a lovely clothing parcel arrived complete yesterday, shirts, blanket, what a beauty! . . . I won't exactly say that the heap of chocolate turned bitter in my mouth, but it does seem awful that you should restrain yourself, having collected such a marvellous lot . . . I am the most popular man in the room . . . Tip-and-run with a tennis ball in our limited area is now the rage; fifteen a side and all must bowl one over . . . Two sad cases this week, one man dying of cancer, and yet another man's wife has produced a baby . . . I hope your hens continue to lay . . .

3.8.42

. . . Bank Holiday today, but so are all the other 364 days in the year in this camp for all. So no difference, except that I got the band to play on the *platz* this afternoon. Your suggestion of a Brains Trust was a brilliant success. I took the chair and four men for an hour and a half rocked a crowded house of two hundred and fifty men with excellent talking and sparkling repartee. I included such topical questions as 'Is the afternoon siesta a bad habit?' and 'Is an accordion a musical instrument?', over which feelings ran high. The best thing in some ways that we have done yet, and no one more surprised than the Trust themselves, who had

62

anticipated a ghastly flop. Anyway, thank you very much . . . The officers have been made hon. members of one of the smaller barrack-rooms and we play in an inter-room competition, which lasts a week, between teams from each room – bridge, draughts, teni-quoit, crib, darts, basketball, tip-and-run, etc. and a general knowledge quiz, from which the officers are disqualified. Great fun and gives us pleasant contacts with men we do not know . . . Ploughing through *Tom Jones*, a splendidly virile novel compared with so much nineteenth century stuff . . .

23.8.42

. . . Incredible hot weather this last fortnight; I sunbathe and play teni-quoit and very strenuous basketball and am as brown as a berry all over. Getting as fit as possible before the interminable winter of these parts. Some of the men are like niggers and I am envious, as most of mine comes off in the weekly bath. Major Moore has moved to Oflag, so the moral tone of my letters may improve. I miss him; he was good company in his wild 'aborigine' way. [His own epithet, only he put emphasis on the second and last syllables] . . . Cigarette parcel from Alice Coleman in USA; you ought to see an Aussie's mouth water when I offer a Lucky Strike . . .

One major feature of camp life in the summer was the remarkable form of cricket devised by the Australians. In the very restricted area of our exercise *platz* they laid out an almost perfect clay and matting wicket with a bowler's run up from one end only. Apart from ordinary short runs to balls played within the area, runs were counted according to where the ball struck the banks sloping up from the *platz*. There were some good cricketers in the camp, English and Australian, and the quality of the play can be judged from the fact that when five

'Test Matches' of 1942 were played, the barrack rooms were almost deserted. Day after day, seven or eight hundred men occupied the steep grassy banks of the 'bowl', looking down on the playing area. Every ball was followed with a wealth of comment that combined the liveliest and most vociferous features of the Surrey Oval and the Sydney Hill. I spent many happy hours watching every ball as closely as I had ever done in the Parks at Oxford or at Lords.

30.8.42

. . . eventful day yesterday; in the afternoon a Fun Fair in which I correctly guessed 3000 dried peas in a box; after tea Highland Dancing in kilts by four very good performers, band intermissions, and eleven three-round boxing bouts, mostly well fought . . . Today we had the last of the five 'Test Matches', which the Australians won, 3-2. Don't imagine the cricket is like anything you ever saw . . . but even so skill counts, and the barracking and betting is tremendous. Excitement is intense . . .

6.9.42

. . . Have been particularly busy. By the time I have finished here there will be hardly any pastoral problem which I have not had to deal with, some of them very tragic and disillusioning. One of the best things I learnt from Garbett was that the first hearing of a problem is seldom the right one . . . Irwin is a good bridge player, so I have resumed after six months' rest from the game. It passes the evening pleasantly, and our opponents always appreciate a quiet evening in our room. Our band gave an excellent concert last night out of doors, now an all military band and twenty good players. The *Unfinished Symphony* makes particularly good summer evening music and I had a lovely home-sick evening lying on the grass. I hope you hear

good music sometimes; I just have to imagine and
remember it, as almost the only sane thing in this
mad world . . .

Besides entertainment, more serious activities were running all the time. Thanks to the Red Cross organisation, men
were able to sit for many forms of examination, invigilated by
officers. In spite of many shortages, chiefly of text books and
paper, classes went on all the time of a practical type,
shorthand and book-keeping, advertising etc, but quite a
number of men studied languages with other prisoners who
were proficient in them.

I was lucky to be well supplied with books sent to me by
Mary and other friends and relations. My reading in 1942
included Boswell's *Johnson,* Wesley's *Journal,* Bryant's Pepys
volumes, Kilvert's diaries, *Bevis, Tom Jones,* McNeile Dixon's
Human Situation, and various books sent at my request on adult
education, and much Theology. All this in spite of the fact that
the library I had begun to build up at Laufen and Dössel had
been left behind when I moved to Poland. I doubted if I
would ever see these books again, but after about eight
months they all turned up, a great tribute to the German
authorities who permitted this service.

There was quite a good camp library at Fort XV which was
well patronised; but few men did any serious reading,
conditions of quiet and privacy being what they were. Our
Librarian, Alan Dickinson, of the Quaker Ambulance Unit
captured in Greece, kept a record of books borrowed.
Roughly it indicated that of every hundred books borrowed,
eighty-five were Westerns, ten were thrillers, three were light
novels, and two were biography, history or classics. This
record was kept in 1943. I think that serious reading might
have come out more favourably in 1941/42 when the original
crowd of NCOs were in the camp.

A tribute should be paid to our two Quakers who arrived in
Fort XV from Greece in December 1942 with the Australians.
My memory tells me that their unit had been sent originally to
Finland and, when that campaign fizzled out, they found
themselves by some circuitous route in Greece. In spite of
their non-combatant status they were treated by the Germans

as prisoners, and it was curious for them to find themselves in a camp of army personnel. But their high ideals of service were respected by all. Alan, a quiet, tortured soul, ran our library most efficiently, but in 1942 he suffered a mental breakdown. For weeks volunteers watched over him in pairs day and night, but eventually he broke away from his guardians, threw himself from a window into the dry moat and suffered terrible injuries. There was no way in which he could continue to be kept in the Fort, and he was taken by the Germans to an asylum, where he died not long after.

The other Quaker. Michael Mounsey, a graduate of King's College, Cambridge, was a tougher character altogether. When the Germans relieved Macdonald of his job as Camp Leader, and replaced him with CSM Rogers of the RA, the men claimed their right to choose their own Man of Confidence. Seven hundred combatant Warrant Officers and NCOs and a hundred and fifty Australians proceeded to elect as their representative a conscientious objector. Michael was a fluent German speaker and, being shrewd and scrupulously fair to all, he carried out the job with distinction for over a year. I cannot imagine soldiers of any other army making such a choice.

In the camp there were men of such varied professions and interests that it was possible to run weekly lectures on a wide variety of topics. Some of the most interesting lectures were given by unexpected men. Isaak Walton could not have spoken with more affection for his sport and a greater wealth of detail than a Lincolnshire corporal who spoke with simple eloquence about fishing in the Fens. I seemed to go with him beneath the wide dome of the fenland sky as he rode ten or fifteen miles on his bicycle the night before his fishing day to lay his ground bait, and shared his shocked surprise when his wife scolded him for breeding and colouring his maggots all over the house. It was also touching to hear a Manxman, who twelve months before had been shot through both lungs in Greece, tell us of his island home in a husky, uncertain voice.

13.9.42

. . . Have been invigilating exams here for a few men

the last four days; it is a pity more do not take them [professional exams of various kinds], but text books and facilities for study are the problem. CSM Shillingford tells me that the Parks at Oxford are shut now . . . you must miss them terribly. [This was luckily not the case.]

20.9.42

Mail ban again in force . . . actually I don't seem to get your letters, ban or no ban . . . We are now a small community of about 230 men, more than half Australian Medical Corps men. The other 720 odd left for good on Wednesday. I was very sorry to see them go, but that is prison life, always saying goodbye to good friends. All very quiet now, but one wonders what will happen to one next. In this room our chief recreation is hunting fleas. Pause while I reflect on Dick Spencer and all his ancestors. He was searching in his shirt over my head and suddenly exclaimed, 'Hell, I missed him.' The hunt is up; Spencer, Irwin and Fry all at it at this table, driving them towards me, and I cannot concentrate at all. I know what the Psalmist meant by 'the patient abiding of the meek'. Well, they are waiting for my trousers now, so I must say 'Good Night' . . .

27.9.42

. . . have restarted my English classes, and fortified with Whale on Christian doctrine am giving a fairly stiff course on Sunday evenings . . . If you ever feel like a glass of beer in the High, drop into the Bear and tell Mrs Ellis that her son, Cpl Lay, was in good form when he left here last week, a 4th Bn man, who worked in Corpus normally. I miss the great crowd who have gone, my 'parish' for ten months, and am feeling all the reactions of knowing how many men did not get the time they wanted and I could have given them, and how very few I really got to know and did anything for. Most would never come to a parson again . . . Thank you for your glorious letters . . .

4.10.42

. . . another pious letter from the Chaplain's Dept . . . funny to think of you alone in a canoe. I cannot imagine being alone now and picture myself going on the Cherwell with a guard at the back of the canoe . . . I have been having an orgy of art in this fine autumn weather, now that there are so few onlookers . . . I have had notices of books sent off from home . . . doubt if it is much use sending more . . . really our library is very good now . . . Irwin is a keen and good bridge player, but I am constitutionally incapable of remembering what Mr Culbertson said in answer to two no trumps in 1928 . . .

11.10.42

Letter ban still in force . . . very autumnal here . . . We have a French officer with us temporarily [en route to Oflag after serving a sentence in the *Strafe Gefängnis*], good for my French, because Irwin pretends that he knows none and Dick is very lacking. He is nice and easy to fit in with; I hope he stays awhile. I arrived at the hospital today in time to have a few words with a young New Zealand private, who died soon after – sad, but he has long been ill. A young lad from Bicester in the 4th Bn. has made a great recovery since coming in very sick a few weeks ago . . . Faithful Fry retired to bed with 'flu and we all waited on him, taking him his meals. He lives in a little annexe to our room and has his share of all our meals, pooling his Red Cross with the rest. I have just re-read *Beside the Bonny Briar Bush,* a favourite of

Mother's, sentimental in parts, but it is easier to understand her wonderful character in reading it. Her deep faith combined with astonishing tolerance is an occasional product at its best of that narrow but very sincere Bible Christianity common among our older Scottish Presbyterian cousins. I am glad to have found it again . . . I have had such bad hands this week that I even think I shall have to give up bridge if you will have me back. I mean that, so do hurry up and get cracking . . .

18.10.42

. . . loved your account of the wedding. John, impossible man, would say no more than, 'Mary looked very well in blue'. I suppose he has not got words like 'celestial', 'smashing', or 'ravishing' in his academic vocabulary. If you still think in terms of parcels will you remember toothpaste (block) and razor blades, if available, even if you have to give up shaving for a week or two . . . I am launching a Choral Society tomorrow, a hard thing to keep up enthusiasm over, and suitable music hard to come by . . . We are just on the threshold of our third six month's hard in this camp, in some ways, however, better fortified than previously, clothing fine and larder fuller, thanks to the Red Cross . . . Your father once wrote to me of your 'great task of happiness' . . .

25.10.42

I have left your letter to last, having spent the whole evening writing difficult letters about those endless matrimonial tangles. Garbett says they are uncommon but he is not right. They are: and only a proportion as it is have come to a head. Two lovely letters from you – the envy of our room. Lovely to hear of you having outings, esp. to anywhere as nice as Birdham, memories of that last sad summer . . . St Crispin's Day, and I re-read and re-loved Henry V's speech. And it was not of France 1940 that I thought, but of the splendid spirit of these men here in the last two years . . . Our local Colonel, Dr Mackay, has now come to live with us . . . Today was glorious, more like spring than autumn, and I enjoyed my walk to the hospital . . . Have found a man at last who has a nice voice and enjoys something better than jazz; am enjoying teaching him some Schubert and learning the accompaniments . . . We are in a state of flux, men coming and going, and it is hard to settle down to any useful organisation for winter programmes . . .

During my twelve months in Fort XV there had been frequent changes of the occupants of my room. In addition to the variety of doctors, British and Commonwealth, who seemed to come and go, we even had the occasional French visitor, such as the officer who had been discharged from the *Strafe Gefängnis* at Graudenz, waiting to go back to an Oflag. This coming and going, however, came to an end with the arrival of Colonel Mackay, and a Polish officer, Lieutenant C Radzynski, of whom more will be told hereafter.

1.11.42 – All Saints Day

. . . I am glad that Garbett supports me over a shady piece of RC work. [A priest in England was retrospectively bullying the wife of a man in my camp because as an Anglican he had not at the time of their wedding signed away control of his prospective children to the RCs. He had not been asked to do so by the priest who married them. The new priest had sent the man a form to sign and told him that if he did not comply the marriage would be regarded as void and the children born out of wedlock. Both the man and his wife were deeply

70

distressed, and at my request Garbett took the matter up with the Catholic hierarchy]. We are still enjoying the loveliest St Luke's summer that I ever remember. I have entered for the fifty yards Open in the sports; after two days' practice I am so stiff that I cannot even walk. But the bookies are cautious and my price has dropped from ten to four to one . . . I was so glad to hear of your short holiday at Birdham; I know how much such outings must help to break the monotony . . . All your happiness is mine.

8.11.42

Well, I have done a year here and it has been very possible; to celebrate the occasion we moved into the room next door while my little companions were gassed. I start my year with a clean blanket, if not a clean sheet. Our Frenchmen departed and likewise to my great regret the two Padres from Fort XIII were sent to Oflag. Whether they will be replaced I do not know, but they will be greatly missed. I said goodbye to them at a splendid concert in their camp . . . a first-rate variety show, lovely 'girls', riotous knock-about, good singing and acting, and the whole backed by the best band by far that I have heard here. Too early to think of Christmas and your birthday; how I hoped that I would be there this time . . . Col Mackay praises my house-keeping, so I shall devote myself to that while you go out bread-winning; you seem to be so much better than I at it . . .

15.11.42

. . . I am at present visiting two carcinoma cases, one of whom, poor fellow, is not likely to last many days . . . Two new chaplains have arrived in the Stalag – C of E and RC, both of whom I knew in 1940. From

71

them I had news of many old friends . . . Dick Spencer has designs on all my teeth, but they have been X-rayed and he can prove his case against only one, thank God; so I may yet return respectable . . .

29.11.42

. . . Our menagerie has another French officer, Capitaine Pavillet. Last night he cooked us a too, too French meal, all garlic . . . Winter has arrived with a bump and I plod through wind and horizontal snow to my various duties. We buried James Sproat of Ayr on Wednesday, and I wrote to Charlie Fergusson [my cousin, General Sir C F], commending his family to some discreet and kindly folk. I wish you could see the wonderful work done by two very young medical orderlies in the British ward of the German hospital where we send bad operations. Under the German surgeon they run the show entirely by themselves, and I have never seen more conscientious and kindly nursing any where. I find it most moving here and there to find prisoners like these who in their marvellous work for the rest of us seem to have completely forgotten their own misfortune. So glad you enjoyed Livingstone's book *Education for a World Adrift,* on adult education. He is a man I should love to meet – and work for, if only he, or someone like him, would get cracking after the war. The idea of his books has become part of me . . .

6.12.42

Nearly Christmas and I have not done my shopping yet. Very hard to get anything going; a gross darkness seems to cover the people and I cannot arouse any enthusiasm to learn carols etc. Dacre [Balsdon] is far more lyrical on your charms than my prosaic brother. I am sending photographs [of the officers] . . . I am not allowed to mark myself with a cross, but I hope you will find me. Folk come and go here these days, which is always interesting, but unsettling. Latest addition is about twenty-five marines and naval personnel, very good men. One of the 4th Bn. was here for two days, a nice local yokel from Tetsworth. I always like meeting the real Oxfordshire lads, very solid and sensible. Last week I heard a brand new record of Isobel Baillie singing, 'I know that my Redeemer liveth', quite perfect; such beauty and refinement is in overwhelming contrast with this extraordinary life here. It seems to come from another world, an echo of that 'other country' from which at the moment we are strangers, but whither I shall come some day, to find my Mary and everything else that I love . . .

13.12.42

. . . blank week for letters, so nowt to say. You need not try to floor me with medical terms; I have a dictionary here with 10,000 of them . . . What you won't know about famous Oxford 'interiors' after this war will not be worth knowing. We might settle down at Garsington or somewhere nearby and live on the immoral earnings of your knowledge . . . I had a lovely walk to the hospital today wearing the excellent new shoes. Duckers seem to have hit off my oddly shaped feet. The shoes are better than the boots they made for me when I was at home, yes, three years ago. Two and a half years gone now behind bars. I hope that all my reports have been good, or doesn't the Head send one until it is all over? I have been trying to save all the chocolate from your last parcel till Christmas, but I have had to bury it in the bottom of my suitcase to avoid having nibbling raids on it. We have saved a Red Cross parcel each, intact, for the day, which is lucky, as we have gone on half rations for parcels lately.

Great comings and goings here lately . . . mostly younger men than before. I am almost the oldest inhabitant of this camp now . . .

20.12.42

. . . how have you spent your birthday? I had a special treat, a good recording of the *Ninth Symphony* . . . Post's all to pieces . . . Am working hard to produce some carols for Christmas with a small, unskilled choir, but some have nice voices and are gradually learning, note by note. But two good Welsh soloists, who in addition to some solo carols are singing Vaughan Williams's 'Wither's Rocking Song' and Cornelius's 'Three Kings' . . . *Times* calendar arrived from Mrs B; I hope not to have to tear off every page, but fear that that is too optimistic now . . . I am going to start a new course in English, based on books we have here in the library, a kind of reader's guide, anything from thrillers to Gibbon. We have a good library, but most of the men are very vague about what to read, and shy off the better stuff. It may help them, and good practice for me . . .

27.12.42

Well, another Christmas has passed . . . Everybody was in tremendously good form here. The Christmas show ended on Wednesday night and I had my Service of Lessons and Carols on Christmas Eve, well attended. Choir and soloists repaid all my work a thousandfold by singing better than ever before. Nice services here on Christmas Day, and at the hospital, and came back in time for our evening meal, which flattened me in traditional style. All credit to the Red Cross who got the Christmas parcels here, plus plum puddings and all. Various 'itinerant' concert parties in the Fort, one of which, complete with piano and band, arrived en bloc in our room and played to us even when we had gone to bed. The Polish officer, whom we call Felix, dreamt that he was sitting in front of an enormous pudding, while I, dressed in the uniform of the local police, was standing over him and insisting with dire threats that he finish it. It was the best Christmas so far in prison, and I think everyone had a good time. At the hospital some of the decorations and room 'spreads' were a great sight. On Boxing Day we had our annual officers' gathering at another camp, saw the Stalag Art and Crafts Exhibition, at soccer England drew with Scotland, and more over-eating. In spite of our preoccupations I know that everybody was thinking of home and many men were saying to me that they hoped that their wives and children were having as good a Christmas and wished that you all knew what a great time everyone here was having. The family spirit was wonderful . . .

And so we came to the end of another year, and our third Christmas in captivity. At the beginning of the year all had been gloom. The Japanese were advancing on all fronts in the Pacific, and Singapore fell in February. Even India was threatened. Rommel was threatening a final breakthrough in North Africa, and though the Germans had not actually broken Russian resistance, they were threatening Moscow and Leningrad and were heading for the oil fields in the Caucasus. By the end of the year the situation was more encouraging in some sectors. El Alamein in October had heralded a change of fortune in North Africa, and the Germans, having run out of steam in Russia, were facing imminent disaster at Stalingrad. But in prison it was hard to appreciate that the tide had really begun to turn, and there was little to suggest that we would be on our way home in the foreseeable future.

5

Felix

It was in August 1942 that Felix first came into our lives. We became aware that a stranger had been housed in the punishment 'bunker' on the other side of the moat close to the main entrance to the Fort. When we discovered that it was a Polish officer, we persuaded Scarface to let us send him Red Cross food and cigarettes with his rations that were drawn from our cookhouse. Some days later he was allowed to come into our room in the evenings and have supper with us. He was a lively person, short and very dark. His uniform was worn, but he was always neatly turned out.

At first he was reticent about himself and his affairs, but by degrees his story emerged. He was not a regular soldier, but had held a reserve commission in the most famous regiment in the Polish army, a regiment whose officers at some time had included some of Poland's most famous names. He was of good Polish family, and before the war had been Managing Director of PPG, the largest rubber factory in Poland, at Graudenz.

He had been taken prisoner when Poland capitulated and, after various vicissitudes, he had become Adjutant of an Oflag at Lübeck for 7000 Polish officers. Without warning he had suddenly been transferred from Lübeck to Torun. This transfer had been requested by the German political services, alias the Gestapo. As there was no POW camp for Poles in Torun he was placed by the Stalag XXA authorities in Fort XV, the camp for non-working British NCOs. He was something of an embarrassment to the XXA authorities who had no reason to keep him in solitary confinement, and within ten days of his arrival the very 'korrekt' Oberst Dulnig visited him

76

and gave orders that he was to be treated as an ordinary POW and not subjected to any form of close arrest. As usual the army took some pleasure in thwarting the political services.

We might at that stage have asked for Felix to be transferred to our room, but I found out that from his bunker on the other side of the moat he was able to communicate with various clandestine organisations. On the very first night that Felix arrived in this bunker, the elderly sentry on duty had spoken to him through his small slit window. Felix had recognized him as a former sergeant in his own Polish cavalry regiment. That very night the sentry conveyed a message to the Polish 'underground' organisation in Torun, informing them where Felix was. Subsequently Felix made less use of this man, who was, after all, now serving in the German army. Instead, agents from Torun brought and fetched messages by means of a small wicket gate in the prison wall just outside Felix's cell. He was able to leave messages under a stone while at exercise, just outside the sentry's line of vision, and they could be reached from outside.

A week or two after his arrival, Felix was taken by a German officer from Stalag XXA to the Gestapo HQ in Torun. There he was interrogated for three hours by the local Gestapo chief, who had in front of him an alarming dossier. Before the war Felix, acting in collaboration with the Polish Secret Service, had sent engineers and travellers from his firm into Germany; these were in fact secret agents. In the dossier were papers from the Polish Secret Service HQ in Warsaw that confirmed these activities. Many incriminating files had not been destroyed by Poles who had fled abroad in 1939, and several members of the service had assisted the Germans in their investigations, on being captured. I think that under the terms of the Geneva Convention a POW should not be charged with activities as a spy before the commencement of hostilities; but it was doubtful whether the Germans would abide by the Convention in such a case.

There were two hopeful features about this initial interview. First, the Germans seemed to want to be more certain of their ground before proceeding further. They knew that the Wehrmacht would not hand Felix over unless there was a cast-iron case. Secondly, the Stalag officer accompanying Felix appeared to be on his side. He took Felix with him when they went to lunch, and would not allow the interview to continue in his absence. On more than one occasion he agreed that Felix need not answer a question.

Felix had been brought to Torun to be interrogated on matters that were likely to lead to a capital charge, but he seemed to have kept a steady nerve throughout the first interview, and reckoned that he had won the first round. When asked for references on this and on subsequent occasions, he gave the names of Poles whom he knew to be dead, or to be alive but by that time in England or Russia. His chief reaction was to double his efforts to conduct clandestine correspondence. He squared Scarface, and on Sunday afternoons when few Germans were about, Scarface allowed him to see his wife, who arrived from Graudenz with a suitable bribe.

Her story was fairly remarkable. She was his second wife. His first wife, a Catholic of an aristocratic Polish family, had died giving birth to their first child, a son, who was safely in America. Felix had then defied the wishes of his family and married a young girl of the minority Protestant faith. When Poland fell in September 1939, she, being pregnant, had escaped to Switzerland where she had somehow acquired Swiss papers.

In the first winter of the war, when Felix was already a prisoner, she had returned with her baby to Poland on her Swiss passport and was living in two or three rooms with her parents and Felix's mother. Protestants in Poland had always been suspect as good patriots; they were too closely identified with the large German Protestant minority. But Mrs Felix was a true Pole; besides caring for these three old people, her own child and the two children of the Polish Protestant minister at Graudenz, who had been arrested and sent to Dachau, she had, unknown to Felix, thrown herself into various underground activities. She had also become secretary to the new German manager of her husband's own factory.

Her contacts were fantastic. Among them was a man called B. Before the war he had been chief engineer of the factory. In 1938 he had caused a sensation by marrying a Nazi German girl in Danzig. On the German invasion he had shown his hand and assisted the invaders. By 1942 he was Deputy Chief of the Gestapo in Western Poland, with his HQ at Bromberg. But by 1942 he was already sitting on the fence. He was in communication with Mrs Felix, and within twenty-four hours of each of Felix's interrogations at Torun he supplied her with the latest report of the official Gestapo views on the case. That the case became so long drawn out was also apparently due to the fact that B had a way of moving Felix's case to the bottom of the pile.

A hitch in Felix's arrangements occurred in late September, when for no apparent reason he was transferred to Fort XIII where he was put to live in the room of the British doctors and chaplains. He continued his correspondence with the underground world, largely through British soldiers who went from the Fort each day to work at jobs in Torun, but it was not so easy. In November, when an additional British dentist arrived, Felix told the Germans that he was an encumbrance to the British officers and asked to be transferred back to Fort XV where the officers had more room. His request was granted and for the next fourteen months he shared a room with Colonel Mackay, the doctor, and myself.

He was a wonderful room companion. Language might have been a difficulty; he could speak no English and very little German, and he had no language sense. My German was equally bad, but we worked out a hybrid language of our own, unintelligible to others but adequate to achieve a good understanding between ourselves. He must have been terribly bored much of the time; he had practically no Polish books and, though by nature an active and vigorous man, he had no obvious outlet for his energy. But he was capable of the most rigorous self-discipline. Each day he spent much time over his personal toilet, making his bed, shaving, washing and so on. He made himself into the perfect valet, mending and ironing his own clothes, and often ours too. He took regular exercise in all weathers round the top of the Fort and spent much of the day visiting our barrack-rooms, chatting with men who had been out working in country districts and playing chess with them. He was liked and admired by all. In the evening he went into consultation with our batman, Colin Fry, and out of what Red Cross stores were available in our cupboard he concocted delicious and exotic meals, cooking them on our illegal electric stove.

It was over cooking that he nearly came to blows with a French visitor. This officer having completed a sentence and been released from the *Strafe Gefängnis* at Graudenz, was sent to live with us for two or three weeks pending his transfer to an Oflag. He was quite a pleasant fellow, but Felix, like most Poles, regarded with contempt a member of a nation that had signed an Armistice with the Germans. It was not an easy fortnight. One evening Felix announced that he was going to make a jam omelette for supper. A heated argument started up, the Frenchman saying that there was no such thing, that the word omelette was French, and that therefore only a Frenchman could make what was rightly known as a crêpe. Felix retorted that one name might be a crêpe, but that he had travelled all over the world and whenever he had ordered a jam omelette that was what he had got. John Irwin offered the suggestion that if he asked for one in England he would get it, but that it would be called a pancake. Feeling was running high, and the question whether the Frenchman should be allowed to make it was still undecided when he returned from a short visit to the medical Inspection Room, where he had gone to be weighed, with a badly cut lip. The spring balance from which he had been hanging had pulled out of the ceiling and hit him in the face. Felix felt that he had won by default and served up for supper excellent jam omelettes, crêpes or pancakes.

In the summer Felix persuaded Scarface to let him cultivate a strip of ground inside the main gate on the other side of the moat; it was close to his old cell and gave access to the wicket gate where he left and collected his notes. He grew there a prodigious quantity of lettuces and tomatoes which were a welcome addition to our diet in the late summer and autumn. He tended them assiduously, carrying up at least twenty buckets of water a day from a spring in the dry moat. I was ashamed not to have helped him, but I refrained, partly because I was lazy and partly because he had chosen this public place, ostensibly under a sentry's eye, to forward tricky clandestine activities that were his private concern. In the autumn of 1943 he learnt through B that, in answer to a Gestapo enquiry from Bromberg, Hauptmann Goedecke, Abwehr Chief of Stalag XXA, had reported that he was a quiet, law-abiding prisoner who spent his time gardening.

He took a close interest in the course of the war and on few nights failed to join the listening-in party on our hidden radio. News of any action involving Polish forces thrilled him, and he nearly burst with pride one night when the BBC played the march of his old cavalry regiment. On Polish national days he wore his best uniform with medal ribbons, and when Marshal Sikorski was killed in an air crash he refrained from all Fort activities and concerts during the month of official mourning.

We never questioned him about his underground activities, but much went on under our noses and he told us as much as he wished us to know. I think that he did not wish to involve us in any disaster that might befall him. He would question me closely about details of my travels and my visits to working parties and other camps, and he could have made use of me, but he never asked me to meddle in his affairs.

By contrast he appeared to have compromised most of the German officials to some degree. His wife supplied the money, even in gold, and the Hauptmann, Scarface and various lesser fry were all recipients of his bounty. In January 1943 a Stalag letter censor, Äsche by name, who was always on the make, called on Felix and said he could arrange to bring Felix's wife to see him for a consideration. When Felix refused the offer, Äsche went to Graudenz and made the same proposition to Mrs F. She also refused, for the good but undisclosed reason that she was already seeing him, and she wrote through the normal post informing Felix of Äshe's proposal. Felix was in a quandary, but finally took the bold course.

He asked for an interview with Oberst Dulnig at Stalag. There he was interviewed by Dulnig, Major Loeffler, the elderly Adjutant, and Hauptmann Goedecke of Abwehr. Felix asked them by what authority a member of the Censor staff visited the wife of a Polish officer who was in prison and made such a proposition. They expressed astonishment. Äsche was put under arrest, and we saw no more of him; no doubt he ended up on the East Front. They also asked Felix if he would like to see his wife, and he replied that he would rather they continued free of the pain of such a meeting, as they had already been for three and a half years. They thanked him for his information, as also did the Hauptmann of our Fort, who in fact countenanced, if he did not actually arrange, the visits of Mrs F. Hauptmann Schubert was a close friend of Loeffler, and I have no doubt he also knew the facts. They were all reasonably humane men, and no friends of the Nazi overlords.

Various civilians used to visit the Fort on business, electricians, chimneysweeps and the like. In theory they should always have been accompanied by a guard while in the camp, but they rarely were. By degrees I learnt that most of them were Poles, and some were engaged with the underground movements. Invariably they spent some part of their time in the Fort closeted with Felix in our room or in some other corner of the Fort. On such occasions Felix was a man transformed; the night before they arrived he wrote endlessly in minute handwriting on cigarette papers, and next morning he was no longer his cheerful, irresponsible self, but nervous and tense. He talked with his visitors with excited gestures, and when they had gone he remained tense and preoccupied.

Among these occasional visitors the most remarkable was one of the chimneysweeps. He worked always with a harmless-looking little *Volksdeutsch* man, who may have been unaware of his companion's activities. In the traditional top hats of their trade they had access to every room of every building in Torun, including the close guarded camp for the top French generals at Fort XVI and the Gestapo HQ. The larger sweep had the manner of a simple half-wit with his sooty face, but in conversation with Felix he was a changed man; he looked what in fact he had been, a smart young petty officer in the Polish navy. After the fall of Poland he had shed his identity and severed all connection with his family near Warsaw and set up as a simple chimneysweep in Torun. He had not, however, signed papers and become *'eingedeutscht'* (Germanised), and he was deeply involved in espionage for the underground movement.

For many months he was an active agent between the movement and Felix, but in August 1943, following the suspicious activities in the Torun area of a strange supposed British soldier, over a hundred Poles were rounded up by the Gestapo. They were mostly *eingedeutscht* folk who were belatedly running an underground movement of their own. Few of the real underground were among those arrested, but unluckily our chimneysweep was among them. After being held for a while in Torun, they were transferred in heavily guarded cattle trucks by night to Bromberg. En route the train was halted by a signal in the forest through which the train ran. Members of the underground who had arranged the halt broke open the right truck and extracted the chimneysweep and others. Two days later Felix received a note from him which ended with 'kind regards to the British doctor and chaplain'. We did not hear of him again, and he may well have died with many other of the finest Polish patriots in the Warsaw rising a year later.

Among other visitors seen by Felix in Scarface's room outside the camp was his uncle, a distinguished surgeon from Warsaw. Felix was no lover of the Jews, who were not generally popular in Poland before the war, but he was in tears when he told me of his uncle's account of the extermination of the Jews by the SS in the Warsaw ghetto. After the discovery of thousands of Polish corpses at Katyn, the Germans asked this eminent surgeon to go there with a commission to place the blame for the massacre on the Russians. He said that that was not his business, and was thereupon sent to Dachau concentration camp. There, at the age of seventy, this man, who had devoted his life and his skill to healing, was last heard of shovelling sand into trucks. We heard no more.

Felix was taken for interrogation to Torun several times during 1943, but no progress appeared to be being made in his case. At last in December, at the end of a typical interview, the Gestapo chief produced a copy of a letter believed to have been written by Felix to the underground movement. It was genuine all right, but Felix challenged them to produce the original. Apparently the recipients of this letter had copied this extract and forwarded it to the *eingedeutscht* crowd as concerning them. In the round-up in August this copy had been found, unsigned, but from the information it contained it clearly had its origin in our camp.

For the first time Felix was rattled. He told me privately that he would have to get out. The problem was Mrs F and the child. She came to see him on Christmas Day, bringing in a suitcase, for the second year running, a present to us of a cooked goose, wine, cakes and other delicacies. She promised Felix that she had now made all arrangements to go on her Swiss passport to Switzerland with the child. He told her he would not carry out his escape plans if she turned back again, as she had done once before, on the pretence that her papers were found not to be in order.

Meanwhile Felix had 'booked' a place on an escape route via Sweden to England. At that time it was taking two British prisoners each month. A British Warrant Officer, RSM Hawtin of the Oxfordshire and Buckinghamshire Light Infantry, was to go with him. The route was supposed to be foolproof once the pair had got out of the camp and contacted a car at a nearby cross-road.

The chosen day was 5 January. On 3 January Felix heard that his wife had left Graudenz and was to cross the Swiss frontier on the night of the 4th. I have little doubt that for a consideration, Scarface or one of the guards would have ushered Felix and companion out of the camp. But the risk of being double-crossed was too great, and a different plan was concocted.

Felix's old cell on the other side of the moat was now the bread store, and our Quartermaster had the key. Between the store and the main gate there was a new wooden barrack. This was by now our library, and we could cross the moat by day to visit it. After dark gates were shut and locked at both ends of the bridge. During the day the Quartermaster took civilian clothes over to the bread store and hid them there. Felix and Hawtin crossed over to the library during the late afternoon and, while someone engaged the sentry in conversation, they slipped round to the bread store and with a false key locked themselves in and were able to change.

Meanwhile I had gone to the hospital three quarters of a mile away on my weekly visit, escorted as usual by a British corporal and a guard. I told the corporal that we must leave the hospital punctually at 5 o'clock and reach Fort XV between 5.15 and 5.20. The plan was that our guard having reported our return at the Wache, would escort us on to the main gate and hand us over to the sentry inside. The sentry, having closed the main gate with a simple bar, would walk with us, unlock the first moat gate, cross the moat and finally let us into the Fort through the second gate. During that time, if they had not already escaped from the Fort, Felix and Hawtin would leave their hiding place and let themselves out of the main gate. It would be up to us to make slow progress across the moat and if possible engage the sentry in lengthy conversation.

As it grew dark at Fort XIV, I noticed with some concern that a brilliant moon was shining. We were at the guardroom in good time to allow our guard last words with his mates as he signed us out. A hard windswept crust of snow gleamed in the moonlight, and visibility was at least half a mile as we walked across the open fields. In the distance I saw two figures emerge from the dark mass of trees that surrounded Fort XV, and I bore off to the left to give them a wider berth as they struck out across the open fields. It seemed that our pair had made an early break. Months later I discovered that they had not done so and that we were right to carry out the rest of our part in the plan.

On arrival at the Fort, our guard signed us in but carelessly left us to make our own way to the main gate. As the huge iron gate swung to behind us, the corporal started an elaborate discussion with the guard about trade in chickens. The guard let us in through the first moat gate, and halfway across the bridge I stopped for a moment or two to tie a boot lace. From within the Fort was coming a cacophony of singing and banging of mess tins, designed to blot out any sound from the opening of the main gate. Inside the Fort I found the chief accomplice, a Warrant Officer, with a face as white as a sheet. 'They are away now,' I said, 'we saw them in the fields.'

Five weeks later I received a letter from my wife in England which said, 'Scatty [Hawtin] came to see me.' After all his troubles, Felix had reached safety. But he had no news of his wife and child. Poland, I suspect, meant even more to her and she had never left the country after all. She only wanted to make certain that he would go.

6

Spring 1943

As far as I was concerned, the early months of 1943 were uneventful and I can leave it to the letters that I wrote to give an impression of our life at that time.

3.1.43

Into another year which I never thought to spend in prison. Finishing wars is not as easy as I thought, and I am afraid that I do not think now that we have begun this one, not at least that great and terrible part of it that we shall all remember, when our little Dunkirks, Greece, Crete and North Africa will have passed into the limbo of forgotten skirmishes . . . I have just got into a reading mood again, which is fortunate, as I shall have to do a lot of reading for my two new courses in English which begin this week. Have just finished *Books and You*, Somerset Maugham, three good newspaper articles on the most enjoyable books to read, a book of Clarence Day, and Harold Nicholson's very good *Byron, the Last Journey*. Am now on Moran, *Viewless Winds*, an interesting and searching commentary on Australians and the Aussie outlook . . . I have suddenly been inundated with a great load of books forwarded from Oflag VIB, after thirteen months, very welcome too . . . If possible I should like drawing blocks and paints for the summer. My portrait by an Aussie appeared in the Stalag Christmas Art

Exhibition, where there was some very good work shown, esp. some of the handicrafts . . . Bit more wintry now. . .

17.1.43

. . . Celia must be pleased to hear officially that Cyril is a prisoner in Singapore, something, but very little . . . Very cold snowy funeral yesterday. The poor trumpeter, in spite of blowing on his mouth-piece all the way to the cemetery, found it was nearly seized up when it was his turn to blow . . .

24.1.43

Looking at your latest letters I am glad what you say about Dakin [USA]. Mary [Russia] looks likely to be the death of Walter [Germany] with her continual nagging; I always thought so when he took her on; but people do these stupid things in wartime. We have had a change round here; Irwin has gone to the hospital and Meyer is back here with me, the Colonel and Felix . . . I have had an orgy of reading Stevenson, skimming through fourteen books for a lecture. What an excellent book *Weir of Hermiston* is, if unfinished. The first chapter is one of the most striking things I have read . . . The new RC chaplain Gallagher borrows all my theological books when he comes here each week, but I haven't converted him yet. He is a Jesuit, so I reckon he is impervious or stagnant or something. I told my congregation how lucky St Paul was not to be confined to twenty-nine line letter forms in his prison. If I wasn't I would really try to tell you how much I love you . . .

31.1.43

. . . had a very rude letter from the relations of a man

here whom I was trying to help. At the moment I am trying to escape from a long bout of accidie, awareness of my failure to get anywhere or make much impression here . . . If I can stop people bumping their heads into a brick wall of misunderstandings I do so. I think I have helped a number of men here, but it has not been through services or sermons, but only because after my living with them for months and months some of them do come to think that I might be able in some way to help them. Somehow I seem to scare many of them away and I still suffer from an idiotic shyness. I do not think that many here would believe when I say that the first ten minutes of a visit to a barrack-room of private soldiers is agony to me, and I feel like dashing out. I shall never influence many people at a time, but if I go slowly and win confidence I may be able to help some . . .

7.2.43

. . . Another change here; Meyer has been replaced by Knight, an English doctor who comes from Leeds and was here earlier from Greece . . . Very nice letter from Garbett, who says that he remembers you and me daily at some hour that I cannot read; don't tell him that [the Archbishop's handwriting must have been a sore trial to the censors in England as well as in Germany]. One of the nicest things about him is that, though he is a confirmed bachelor, he gets a tremendous vicarious pleasure in having married us and made us the happiest people in the whole world . . .

14.2.43

. . . a nice letter from Jo Dessau [in Denmark], saying that they are leading a normal sort of life. Tonight I took part in my first concert; I accompanied a Welsh

tenor in five songs; all went well and a good
audience . . . wintry again and I ploughed through
an icy blizzard of wind and snow to the hospital this
morning for my service . . . So glad to hear about
Henry Coombe-Tennant, a most deserving case, I
reckon [He had been awarded an MC, having
escaped with others from Oflag VIB]. Bridge is
rather slack for me these days, you will be glad to
hear. Irwin is away and none of my colleagues play,
so I have to find some strange Sergeant-Major or
someone to partner me.

21.2.43

Just one very old letter from you this week, 17 Nov,
but none the less welcome for your having said
something naughty which I had to guess . . . I again
accompanied a piano and song recital, including
'Where e'er you walk' for which I had to work out
the accompaniment. These concerts are popular,
quiet and appreciative audience, good Sunday night
fare, after the orgy of jazz that goes on all the week. I
am attaching small photograph of self, taken in late
autumn by Mr Berg, the nice Swedish YMCA visitor
who, or one of his colleagues, comes here quarterly,
men I shall always remember for their obedience to
Our Lord's injunction. 'I was in prison . . .'. They
have more than earned their reward . . .

28.2.43

I am writing this in mid-week, as I go on a journey
for a week tomorrow. I now have the opportunity to
visit three of the larger out-lying working parties. It
will be interesting and a great change after eighteen
months in the same place. I find that I am very stale
. . . and am sure that, apart from the interest of the
trip, I shall come back fresher . . . I have launched
forth at last on an advanced English class with a

89

syllabus that will last at least sixteen months. I found that there were at least half a dozen men keen to tackle something of the kind and likely to remain here as permanently as any men are likely to remain. It should keep us all well occupied, but we will not be disappointed if we are not able to finish the course. At the moment I regret to say that I think we will . . .

Obtaining permits for chaplains to visit other camps was a constant problem. The local German authorities could only act within the rules laid down by the High Command (OKW) in Berlin and were nervous about interpreting such rules in our favour, even when they were inclined to do so. On our side it was important to give them no excuse to suspect that the visits for which we sought permission were for any other purpose than what they termed *'seelsorgerische Tätigkeit'* (soul-caring activity).

Apart from doctors and chaplains, no other officers could visit or reside in other ranks' camps. In the course of our visits it was natural that the men would ask questions or raise problems that in the strict sense were not our business as chaplains to deal with. In such circumstances we would give such advice as we could and, where it seemed necessary, take up matters they raised with the Germans. There was a danger that, if we constantly passed on complaints to the German authorities, they would assume that we were meddling with matters that were not our concern, or even encouraging trouble or discontent in camps that they allowed us to visit. In practice we dealt with a wide range of problems in the course of our visits, but common sense and discretion had to be shown.

During the late summer and autumn of 1942 the attitude of the Germans towards the chaplains had stiffened appreciably. Permission that had been granted to two chaplains at Fort XIII, one Anglican and one RC, to visit some of the larger working camps, was at first restricted and ultimately withdrawn altogether.

This embargo lasted over six months, but early in 1943 I sought to have it lifted. By the spring of 1943 there were few large parties; most of them had been closed and the men sent to work on farms. I asked for permission to visit some of the hundred and eighty odd small parties that had never had a visit. By all reports, many of them had come to feel an acute sense of isolation. As the authorities made no response I raised the matter with the representative of the Protecting Power, now the Swiss, on the occasion of his next two quarterly visits, in December and March. On each occasion he went into a huddle with the elderly Stalag Commandant, Oberst Dulnig, and the equally elderly but more genial Head of Abwehr, Hauptmann Goedecke. Each time I heard them raise objections, making some reference to something the *Katholische Pfarrer* had said or done.

However, at the end of the March visit Herr Achentaler, the Swiss, drew me into a corner and said that the C of E chaplains would receive permission. But he insisted that we should strictly confine our activities to our work as chaplains. The point was made at last, and though on our tours we were constantly involved in all kinds of questions about discipline, billets, working practices, the behaviour of guards and so on, it paid us to give the authorities the impression that *seelsorgerische Tätigkeit* was the real purpose of our visits. They certainly became more helpful and responsive in return.

In due course I was issued with my first permit. I was not very happy with the idea of going round the countryside for a week with an armed guard. 'Accidents' were known to occur, and the subsequent report simply said, 'shot while attempting to escape'. I thought that I could do with a witness. When I explained to Herr Goedecke that it was not customary for a British officer to carry his own bag and that I would like one of our men to accompany me for that purpose, he heartily approved, and from that moment it became standard practice on all our journeys to select a 'bag-carrier' from the men in our camps, who incidentally greatly enjoyed the outing.

It was glorious spring weather when in March I set out on my first working party tour, taking with me as my 'bag-carrier' Colin Fry, who for many months had been our Officers' Mess batman. We visited five camps in a week, staying two nights at Klein Bartelsee (about 450 men), where the resident doctor was the Australian Captain (Quag) Meyer, two nights at Brahnau (about 600 men in two camps), and three nights at

Schülitz Camp 48, from which I also visited Camps 34 and 129. Klein Bartelsee and Brahnau had been very popular camps at one time, working hard on sand-shifting by day, but full of well-organised life, music, sport and entertainment of various kinds out of working hours. But by March 1943 they had grown stale, and a strained atmosphere was apparent in both. No one much regretted their dispersal a month later. The three Schülitz camps by contrast were fine, lively camps. Camp 34 closed not long after my visit, but the other two, until the final evacuation in January 1945, continued to maintain the highest standards under two outstanding Camp Leaders, Corporal Waller of the Royal Norfolks and CQMS Robson of the Northumberland Fusiliers.

The organisation at both camps was impressive, and they had the Germans well under control. Camp 129 existed to supply labour to a yard on the banks of the Vistula constructing enormous barges. Every kind of tool and all kinds of equipment, including welding equipment, were available to our men, who used it all extensively for their own purposes, and their products found their way into many other camps in the Stalag.

The owner of the yard, Herr X, brought to Schülitz all manner of immense cranes and other machinery that he had dismantled in shipyards of countries occupied by the Germans in 1940. In theory all this material was meant to be reconditioned in the Schülitz yard. At least our men painted up these machines and they looked very smart, but it was not apparent that any of them worked or that they were put to any use. I was shown the barges being constructed in a huge shed. They were covered with ribald chalk graffiti in English, and one proudly carried the name of Lord Nelson. One of them, I was told, on descending the slipway reached the water and gently sunk to the bottom. Someone had apparently left the cork out.

Herr X held officer rank in the Wehrmacht and, being of age for active service, was in constant danger of being called up. But he had plenty of friends in high places, and whenever call-up threatened he declared that his yard was doing work of national importance and required another twenty prisoners to cope with it. His very elegant wife lived close to the yard and regularly traded through the wire, exchanging with the

92

prisoners chickens, ducks and other foodstuffs for chocolate and real coffee which she needed for entertaining her rich friends. When it was known in the camp that one of her visits to friends in Hamburg was impending, the price of coffee would rise steeply.

All such happy arrangements at Schülitz were what neither side wished to be disturbed, and they continued until the great evacuation when the Russians arrived in January 1945.

7.3.43

. . . Had a most interesting and enjoyable trip by train and on foot. In a week I stayed in three camps and visited four others, the smallest being over fifty men. In all I saw over a thousand men. Their hospitality was stupendous. I staggered out with Red Cross food for a week on my back, and brought it ALL back; they forbade me to contribute anything. The wonderful spring weather held throughout and I cannot tell you how much I enjoyed new scenes and new faces after all this time, in spite of the ubiquitous wire. . . . Sorry you thought me thin in the photos; it is in contrast with the monstrous Irwin. Assure you my weight is normal pre-war . . .

14.3.43

Three welcome letters from you . . . If you think your letters dull, what on earth do you think of mine, you dear chump! I try to lead a respectable life . . . warm enough to sit out most days. I have even done two sketches . . . I am trying to take my Advanced English course slap through *Paradise Lost,* but I think Book One shook them . . . I am glad you are getting so much practice 'finishing' people; I shall need it, especially my language, which sur- prises me at times . . .

93

21.3.43

... We now have a New Zealand doctor major here temporarily; he has been 'inside' for six months and looks like it. [He had been serving a sentence in the *Strafe Gefängnis*.] In fact I have decided to go straight ... My class is getting on with *Paradise Lost*. It sure is the right stuff, but it must be read aloud ... This amazing spring weather seems to be trying to rub in our incarceration, but we are lucky to have such a good *platz* whereon to enjoy it, the best in any prison I have seen, though I miss the VIIC view and would rather be in Oxford ...

By the beginning of 1943 we had lost most of our professional musicians and were short of competent entertainers. We did, however, have a valuable pianist, a young private soldier from Hull, with an immense repertoire which he learnt and played entirely by ear.

28.3.43

Tonight we had the fifth of our Sunday night concerts, given by Eric Williams, a young professional dance band pianist. He gives a varied selection of light stuff on the theatre stage, and I generally produce a singer or something twice in the programme to give him a break. Tonight I accompanied a good clarinettist in three pieces, one a lively piece with what he calls 'bags of clarinet stuff' ... I am afraid that mothballs will have to stay put for another year ...

Several times during the spring and summer of 1943 I was sent out to conduct the funerals of men who had died on small working parties. Such losses were deeply felt in these tiny groups of men who had been living and working together for perhaps two years.

To the first of these funerals I took with me CQMS Granger, the Stalag Man of Confidence. After the usual early start and a two hour train journey, we arrived at Conradin station where we were met by a corporal in the Royal West Kents from Krüschin camp. He startled the crowd on the station platform by giving me a very smart salute and then drove us four miles to Krüschin in a most uncomfortable farm cart.

We learnt that the victim was a young Lance-Corporal in the 2nd Glosters who had been killed instantaneously by lightning while working in a huge open field, together with three Polish civilians and three large cart-horses. After lunch we placed his coffin on a large farm cart, draped with a Union Jack we had brought with us, and with the remaining nine members of his party set off to follow the wagon seven kilometres to the nearest village cemetery. It was a heavenly spring evening as we laid this young soldier to rest, with the sun setting over miles and miles of wheat and barley fields stretching as far as the eye could see. I was much impressed with the morale of this isolated little party, saddened though they were by the tragic loss of one of their number. Most of the men had been formerly at one of the Schülitz camps, and seemed to have brought with them the fine spirit of that camp.

We had a quick supper on our return to the camp and started, rather late, to catch our train at another small station half a mile away. In the dark we could see the lights of the train already standing in the station, and all twelve of us with our two guards ran screaming up the line towards it. It started and then stopped again, and while all the passengers craned out of the windows to see what all the fuss was about, Granger and I and our guard scrambled in. I put my bag on the rack and turned back to the window to say goodbye. There on the platform were the nine men of Krüschin formed up in two ranks with the corporal at the salute. I was deeply moved by this sudden spontaneous demonstration by these young soldiers, prisoners of war for the last three years, and I am sure that it impressed the many German passengers on the train who saw it.

4.4.43

. . . I had an exceptionally nice letter from cousin
[General Sir] Charles Fergusson about the widow of a
man I buried here and about whom I had written to
him. He had been to see her himself. We are four
again here, the Colonel, Major Thompson, Felix
and myself. I am afraid I do not like being the
youngest by ten years or more . . .

11.4.43

. . . another regrettable landmark almost reached
[thirty-third birthday on 12th]. I find it hard to
realize that I was not thirty when I last saw you. I
wonder how Cyril kept his birthday [10th]. It seems
that things are better there . . . Here we jog along . . .
My class has reached the end of Book Four of
Paradise Lost; it has a great finish. I find reading
Milton in bulk gives me a distaste for lesser
literature, as being too trivial after such gigantic
scenes and problems, but no doubt the pendulum
will soon swing back to P G Wodehouse . . . I hope
your farmyard are beginning to do their stuff again . . .

18.4.43

My birthday marked by two lovely letters from you,
such lovely Oxford letters too. I am glad that one of
the indirect results of my captivity has been the
renewal of ties with Oxford. It is more home to me,
and I think to you, than anywhere . . . another
musical evening, in which my share was to accompany a Welshman whom I have slaved to teach
Schumann's 'Du Meine Seele' and 'Ich Grolle
Nicht' and other pieces. Last night we gave our
show twice at the hospital, in a ward and in the
theatre, with my clarinettist . . . Am reading a nice
Australian historical novel by Ernestine Hill, *My*

Love must Wait, about Matthew Flinders, very tragic but fine . . .

26.4.43

. . . Lovely spring evening after lousy day; most of the trees are nearly out and the cherry tree outside my window in full bloom with memories of Norham Road . . . enjoying all the pleasant rain smells and the birds singing evensong . . . all rapturous after a miserable day with what our hosts so graphically describe as a *'durchfall'* which started last night. Lucky it did not start till all my Good Friday and Easter services were done – very happy services throughout. The camp indulged in an orgy of sport all the weekend, very well organised . . . Felix said how amazed he was with the extra-ordinary good temper of all the sport here. In spite of that I have been whelmed in an orgy of peace-making here; the curious thing about my life here is that I am outside most of the activities that go on, with the result that most of the rows that I get called in to settle seem incredibly small, because I have no prejudice either way, and I think the partisans think me very frigid. One thing I find heavy to bear sometimes is the fact that I meet these men mostly in their troubles, local or home, while naturally in the happier side of their barrack-room life and comradeship I have little share. It is a great privilege and a good field of work, but living with three men much older than myself makes my longing to be with you and share the things we both enjoy more acute than ever . . .

2.5.43

. . . Almost all our trees are now out except the many fine acacias, which still look stone dead, giant skeletons amid all this beauty; but in a fortnight they will be a mass of white blossom . . . I saw a copy of the December 'Countryman' today, reviewing so many books I shall love to read when I get home and mentioning so many old folk I did not know had died . . . I don't like Cressy's behaviour [RAF thousand bomber raids], though it is something Walter [Germany] understands . . .

9.5.43

. . . So glad Mrs Kitchen's garden [French North Africa had been finally cleared] has been such a success. You are telling me that it takes a long time to get a place like that clear of weeds, but when it is done it is worth while. I may go on another tour this week to visit some working parties, some that have never had a visit. It will be a great change; things here have rather got on top of me; the Colonel and Major beat Dr R [a classic bore of our acquaintance] into a cocked hat . . . Today on my way to the hospital I saw in flower lilac, may, chestnut and laburnum . . . but no flowers in gardens; they don't grow in all this sand . . .

16.5.43

. . . our chief domestic event is that Colin Fry was passed fit for work and left for a working party after eighteen months of splendid work as our batman. I miss him more than I can say, a sterling chap who was prepared to put up with all our tiresomeness. On Thursday I went with an RSM to a small party of ten men to bury a young man of twenty-four, dead of heart failure, about sixty kilometres from here. Glorious day and lovely country, agriculture, forests and lakes . . .

I had taken to this funeral of a young soldier in the Royal West Kents his RSM, Sievers by name. The camp lay just outside the town of Gut Konschütz, close to an autobahn, and consisted of a tiny cottage and compound. The men lived in three small rooms, and the whole atmosphere seemed friendly and homely. When we arrived the men were putting the finishing touches to some wreaths. A meal was soon prepared for us and, with old-world courtesy, Mac, the elderly Highland sergeant in charge, asked me to say grace. I think I was found wanting, and he closed the meal himself with a much longer grace. After supper we had a short service at his request, and the men listened intently when Sievers and I followed this with an account of all that we had heard on our camp radio of Monty's campaign from El Alamein to Tunis and Bizerta, which had recently fallen. Sievers took the vacant bed and I was given Mac's – he slept on the floor – and talk went on until the decent elderly guard came in at midnight to shut us up. He even passed round a bottle of schnapps. It was two o'clock before we were asleep.

Next morning the men were excused from work. Before we fell in to march to the cemetery, Polish girls from the farm brought some lovely wreaths and handed them through the barbed wire of the compound. When Sievers fell the party in, every man was carrying one or more wreaths. It was a mile to the cemetery on the brow of a hill outside the village, and there we found a hundred Poles, mostly women. I conducted a short service in the cemetery chapel, and then we carried the lad to a quiet corner where his grave looked out over the wide farmlands where he had worked, and southwards down the great valley of the Vistula. Two well-dressed civilians, representing the German major who was Director of the State Farm, attended the service and laid a wreath.

After the service, RSM Sievers explained to the young soldiers that the army tradition was for the band to play a lively, cheerful piece on the way back from a funeral. Accordingly he led us back through the village singing 'Roll out the Barrel' and other popular songs. It certainly cheered the troops, but the Poles were rather shocked, as I heard later.

After lunch I went with Mac to thank the elderly Major, an old retired Prussian, for giving the men the day off and for making satisfactory arrangements for the funeral. He was obviously touched by our words, and rather stiffly replied that it was his *'Soldatenpflicht'* to do all that for a dead soldier. He was the type who treated our lads quite well, because they were soldiers of an unbeaten foe, and beat hell out of the Polish women and children who worked for him. Mac asked him if he could take Sievers and me for a walk round the estate unescorted. Our guard protested strongly, but he was overruled by the Major, who ridiculed his anxiety. The three of us consequently had a five or six mile walk round what was a magnificent estate of farmland and forest before setting off for our train home.

7

Goetzendorf 1943

In May the chaplains pressed the Germans to implement the agreement they had made with the Protecting Power to allow us to visit smaller working parties. Padre Lathaen, now resident in Fort XIII, and I both received permits to do so for a week. I chose an area around Könitz on the West Prussian border where many small parties were situated. I was accompanied by an elderly rustic guard and an Australian medical corporal, Bill Morison.

Leaving Torun in the afternoon, we had a slow rail journey with changes at Graudenz and Laskewitz. It was already growing dark as we approached our destination. The tiny country stations had no lighting, and we only knew that we had arrived at the right one when we heard the faint voice of the guard calling out the name of our station. A solitary porter put us on our road and said the *lager* at Goetzendorf was six kilometres away.

We hitched up our packs and set off on a strange walk across desolate country in pitch darkness. The guard was miserable and had no ideas about knocking up any of the cottages that we passed and asking the way, hardly surprising perhaps; a solitary German calling at an isolated Polish cottage on a dark night might well have wondered what kind of reception he would get. At one point we dimly saw a couple embracing in a ditch. Encouraged by us, the guard timidly advanced and, leaning over the pair, prefaced his enquiry by extending his right arm in a Nazi salute to them where they lay and said, '*Heil* Hitler'. After another mile we found a farm schnapps factory looming up darkly beside the road. I thought that this might be the *lager* and made him call out, but his feeble shouts gave back nothing but a hollow and desolate echo. 'Is anybody there?' said the traveller. . . There was nobody. At last by a small turning we found a wooden sign-board, pointing up a rough farm track and bearing the welcome inscription, 'Kgf. Lager 143'.

A large farm a hundred yards up the track appeared to be our destination, but at 10.30 pm there was no light visible anywhere. With a torch we found a door in the main farmhouse marked *'Wache'*, and after several knocks we roused a guard, a smart-looking Silesian Obergefreiter. He said that he had had no warning of our visit, but he accepted my pass without demur.

'Kommen', he said and led us across the farmyard to where a flight of stone steps led up the side of one of the farm buildings to a well-bolted loft door. I was beside him as he unbolted it and threw it open, and so had my first view of a typical farm *lager*.

By the light of two candles at the far end I could make out a fair-sized loft. All down the right-hand side were two-decker wooden beds. More of these occupied the middle of the left-hand wall, but at each end there was a more open space with a table and forms. The men were all asleep in bed except for a group of three who were sitting round the candles at the farther end. They were clearly surprised to see the guard and two strangers, and they peered at us enquiringly in the dim light. I explained who we were, and at once they greeted us warmly. The guard also hastened to make us at home. He allowed two men to go down to the cookhouse in the yard and asked the men if they had everything they needed for us. The British NCO in charge, Sergeant Gallagher of the 2nd Glosters, was organising things. Within a quarter of an hour he had me and Morison seated in front of a huge meal of bacon and forbidden eggs and great mugs of tea.

Some of the sleepers woke and joined the circle, plying us with endless questions. As always on these visits they were full of enquiries about their own officers, whom they had not seen for three years, but with whom I had spent the first fifteen months of my captivity. 'How is General Fortune getting on?' 'Did you meet my Company Commander, Captain X . . .?' 'How do the Germans treat them?' They laughed with genuine sympathy when I told them that I had last seen

Colonel X and Major Y discussing the respective merits of cherry leaves and German herbal tea leaves as a pipe tobacco substitute.

It was long after midnight when they showed us two beds, one being already unoccupied, and the sergeant and another man doubling up to provide another.

Early the next morning the guard unbolted the door and walked in, shouting *'Aufstehen'*. Nobody moved, and he went out again. Twice more he came in with the same peremptory command, but still nobody moved. At last Sgt Gallagher sat up in bed and said quietly, but firmly, 'Up, lads,' and at once the floor space was a scene of activity, dressing, washing, bed-making and hasty snacks. Within a quarter of an hour all the men had gone off to work on the farms except one youngster whom the guard, at Gallagher's request, had allowed to stay in to look after us. He brought us water for washing and shaving and cooked us an excellent meal.

When the men had gone to work, it was easier to inspect their living quarters. With great ingenuity this rude loft had been converted into a passable dwelling for thirty men. The walls were freshly colour-washed, the floor and tables were well scrubbed. Kit, eating utensils and the ubiquitous Red Cross parcels were neatly stowed away, and within each bed-space personal treasures and photographs were cunningly arranged. Everywhere was evident cleanliness, tidiness and good order that could only have been achieved by a group of men who had shaken down well together.

After breakfast the guard told me that for the next three days Morison and I were to have our meals on two adjacent farms. He pointed them out to us a quarter of a mile away and said we might go there unescorted.

In the spring sunshine the scene outside the *lager* was like a dream after the dreariness of Torun. The *lager* itself stood close to the bank of a fine lake which must have been the best part of a mile long and half surrounded by trees. Away to the north-east stretched gently undulating farmland, dotted here and there with very small farm buildings and rising gradually to a wooded ridge some miles away. There was no real village of Goetzendorf; what there was consisted of about fifteen farms distributed at intervals along two roads that were little better than tracks. Along one of these roads were larger and superior farms, at this time in German hands, while along the other at intervals of no more than four hundred yards were inferior farm buildings occupied and still worked by Poles. The largest farm, in the buildings of which was the *lager*, was the seat of the Ortsbauführer, the village head-man, who supervised for the State all the farming and who owned all the machines, tractors, etc.

After a lazy morning, Morison and I made our way to our respective farms for lunch. It was a strange experience to walk unescorted through the countryside for the first time in three years, and we sat for a while on a grassy bank to relish the sensation. At my farm I was given a great welcome by the Polish farmer, his wife, seventeen-year-old daughter and fourteen-year-old son. Their home was tiny. The front door opened straight into the kitchen, which was perhaps twelve feet by eight, and there were two small bedrooms behind. That was all. In the kitchen was a small range, a table, four chairs and two wall cupboards. While we ate, the room filled with livestock. Under the table was a box full of baby chickens; in another box were baby ducks, while walking around the floor were two dogs, two cats, some geese and innumerable ducks and hens.

A wonderfully friendly family, they fed me generously and talked without ceasing – the conversation was in very inadequate German on both sides, but I could make enough sense of it. They were embarrassingly pro-British, and told me many things about the English prisoners who had worked for them. The most impressive thing to them was an Englishman's way with animals. 'They call them all by name,' they said, 'and even feed the ducks by hand.' They talked about the German invasion of 1939 and conditions since then, and the wife became so outspoken that the farmer kept looking out of the door to see if anyone had crept up to listen. Entertaining a British officer was clearly an event of some moment to them, and I felt that anything I might say unguardedly would go round the village in a flash.

After lunch I called in at the next-door farm for Bill Morison. He was equally at home with another charming Polish family and their prisoner, Micky Dering, a young lad from Leeds. He was treated there like a son, and among his varied occupations he said he usually put the children to bed.

Morison and I spent the rest of the day visiting some of the other farms where our men worked, and after supper with our respective families we returned to the *lager* about 8.30 pm. While I chatted with some of the men at one end of the loft, Morison worked busily at the other end. He was among other things a skilled chiropodist, and having brought his weapons with him he did useful work on the men's feet that night and throughout the whole week of our tour.

The next day I explained to the guard that I wanted to visit some neighbouring working parties. He at once went off in search of bicycles, and returned with three that he had borrowed from local Poles, and on these we set off after lunch in lovely sunny weather. About a mile away were two very small camps, Stirnau and Lottin, grouped under one German guard and an English sergeant-major. The men were all out at work, so I arranged with the sergeant-major that they should visit us the next day, a Sunday, at Goetzendorf. I also chatted with an English lad in one of the camps who appeared to be heading for a nervous breakdown. The German guard agreed to take him into hospital on his next visit to Torun.

I was not much impressed with the sergeant-major, and formed the impression that it was not just caring for the men that kept him out working on a farm when he might be claiming his non-working rights in Fort XV.

Riding on from Stirnau for a mile and a half we came to the pleasant village green of Neukirch where our guard stood us each a beer outside the 'local'. Close by we found a British *lager* in what appeared to be a typical small village school. The corporal in charge, a smart young Corporal Breen of the Cameronians, was working on a farm just opposite. He came over at once, bringing some eggs for our tea, and he squared his guard to send a man on a bicycle around all the farms to bring his fifteen men back to the *lager*.

After a quick tea I left Morison, and rode on half a mile into the forest to another small camp at Koenigs Neukirch. Here the camp was but one room of an old country-house type of farm. We found the guard's room also in the house and the guard lying on his bed. He did not get up when we came in, and, still lying down, he refused my guard's request for his men to be brought in for half an hour. We showed him my authority, but he continued to refuse in an offensive way, and we could do nothing but retire. We returned to Neukirch, pushing our bicycles across fields, where on our way we found the Koenigs Neukirch men. Many of them I had known previously as Stalag workers at Fort XIII and this was their first experience of farm work. They had struck a bad farm and were not at all happy. At that moment they were just beginning to plant with potatoes the largest field I had ever seen, and I felt very sorry for them.

On my return to Torun at the end of our tour I reported to the Stalag Adjutant, Major Loeffler, the churlish behaviour of the Koenigs Neukirch guard. He replied, 'Captain Wild, in every army in the world there are men who do not obey orders. You have them in your army, the Americans have them in theirs, and I regret to say we have them in ours. I will deal with him.' The guard, as I heard, got a week's 'bunker arrest', and I learnt that things improved on the party.

At Neukirch we had little time for me to hold a service, celebrate Holy Communion, and talk to one or two men who had special problems. But Morison, who had a good pastoral sense, had already broken the ice and paved the way for me. It made a tremendous difference having with me a man who was at once well liked by the troops, a practising Christian and one who could see what I could do for the men on these very short visits. I liked the Neukirch men, I admired their young NCO and I could see that it was a well-disciplined, happy party.

We arrived back at Goetzendorf on our bicycles at about 9.30 pm for another evening of talk and pedicure. I spent some time with a corporal whose case was most distressing; his wife had recently been murdered by a Canadian soldier in England.

During our stay I learnt that the men had a secret exit from the *lager* by which they went out regularly at night. Apart from visiting their Polish friends, they made all night forays under Sgt Gallagher, going further afield. A farmer some miles away might wake up one morning to find one of his heavy carts perched on top of a shed. The expeditions were mainly pointless, just good 'dares', but I am sure that their morale value was enormous. Sunday morning was to me another revelation of farm-party life. After breakfast in the *lager*, all the men got busy. They scrubbed, cleaned and tidied the loft, they polished their boots, and washed and cleaned their clothes. Everyone was busy, and by the time they were due to go to their farms for lunch, the place was spotless and all the men dressed in their best. This was, as I discovered, normal Sunday routine on most of the farm parties. These men had been prisoners for three years, and such self-discipline greatly impressed both the German guards and the local inhabitants. It certainly impressed me.

I had lunch again with my Polish family, and returned to camp just as the Stirnau and Lottin parties marched smartly into the yard. All three parties, about forty-five men in all, then gathered by the lake for a service. It was a marvellous setting in a small glade, the trees giving some shade from the hot sun. Every man was there, including Sgt Gallagher and another Roman Catholic. I told them that in the last three days they had taught me more than I could ever tell them about the art of living together in real Christian fellowship. After the service a number of them shared Communion with me in this beautiful spot beside the lake.

The whole party then adjourned to a nearby field where the men of Goetzendorf did battle at football with the men of Stirnau and Lottin. Few of them had shorts or football boots, but it was a good, skilful encounter, played in the best spirit. Armed guards from each camp stood behind the goals and ill-concealed their partisan feelings. When the game was over the visitors, who had very properly won, were given a good tea before returning home. There had been a splendid feeling of neighbourliness pervading the whole day's gathering.

It was hard to leave Goetzendorf the next day. As it was the first, so it was the happiest working party that I ever visited.

On Monday morning Gallagher produced a carriage and pair from his farm and drove us across country to our next destination at Lichnau. He, Morison and I sat on the front seat and our guard with his newly-wedded wife sat behind, a strange sight.

The camp at Lichnau proved to be a very different set-up. Lichnau was a straggling village of many farms. The British *lager* lay on the outskirts, on the main road to Könitz, facing one end of an attractive lake. The building was a black, derelict-looking hut, divided into two large rooms. We found in the first room only five beds, squeezed into one corner. The other thirty beds were all crowded into the further room, and all the tables. The roof apparently leaked all over, but particularly in the first room. On first sight the *lager* looked indescribably dirty; I could see that there was dirt under all the beds, and every corner and shelf was coated with grime.

Soon after our arrival, in the early evening, the Obergefreiter in charge escorted us to a farm at the other end of the village where Sergeant L, the camp leader, worked. I had not met him before, and at first sight I was not impressed. A young TA sergeant, he had formerly been in charge of the big sawmill party at Zempelburg; but he had chucked the job up and returned to Fort XIII. There, rather than be sent to Fort XV as a *'non-arbeiter'*, he had signed his willingness to work and been sent to Lichnau.

We arranged with him that that evening we would eat what we had brought with us at the *lager,* but that next day his farm would give us lunch. We spent the evening talking with the men when they came in from work. They were not an impressive lot, and included some well-known Stalag 'bad-hats'. The camp had obviously never shaken down as a community, and most of the men were replacements, drawn from the 'bunker', for other men who had got bored and pushed off. One could not dignify such men as 'escapers'. There was no difficulty for a man who so wished to walk away from his place of work, where he was not under guard, and few such men had any idea of getting anywhere except back to Stalag via the 'punishment bunker', and so on to another party elsewhere. Later on the Germans countered this ploy by sending these 'escapers' back to whatever camp they had left.

It became apparent that evening that Sgt L had no control of the situation. Any instructions he issued were contradicted or altered by Corporal H, a tough-looking regular soldier, who had been in charge before Sgt L arrived.

Next morning after the men had gone to work, we wasted most of the morning arguing with the Obergefreiter about how we were going to visit other camps in the area. He was a lazy man, and refused to find bicycles or a carriage. When I said we would have to walk, he was obviously torn between getting out of a walk and rendering himself liable to a bad report from me at Stalag, where I assured him that my word carried a great weight.

Lunch at the farm was good entertainment. We were received in the grandest style, with the best room and the best crockery. The old Polish farmer sat at the head of the table and his wife, a portly matron, at the other end. Two lively young daughters, very good-looking, of about twenty-two to twenty-five years old, Sgt L, Cpl H, the Obergefreiter, Morison and myself made up the party. The old lady appeared to be in great discomfort. Apparently she had wished to eat in the kitchen, but the daughters had told her that she must attend in her best dress. They had called on Corporal H to put his knee in her back and pull her corsets tight enough to get her into the dress. It was a rich farm lunch, really too much for Morison and me, who were unaccustomed to such fare.

After lunch I dragged the reluctant Obergefreiter on to the road and we set off to walk six kilometres to Osterwick. This was a large state farm, lying a little off the main road, where ten of our men were employed. They had no warning of our visit, but as we turned off the main road we encountered a young English lad at work in a field. He was excited when we told him that we were paying his camp a visit, and escorted us to the farm where we found the camp leader, Sgt Hay of the 4th Bn. Cameron Highlanders, working in the blacksmith's shop. He went at once to the boss, a turncoat Pole of the Junker class, to obtain permission for the rest of the men to be brought in. The *lager* was at one end of a row of cleanly whitewashed cottages. It was really pleasant inside, four small low-ceilinged rooms – a living room, a kitchen, a sleeping room – rather a tight fit with two-decker bunks – and a store room, where the men hung all their clothes and great coats, and kept their boots and shoes in neat racks, all very well organised.

There was a dim-witted guard with whom I had an argument about how long the men might stay off work. We compromised with one hour and a half. But he made a condition that he should write in his log-book that I had given the order, and that I should sign the entry. I agreed, having little doubt that when the Kontrol Offizier next inspected his log he would be awarded a substantial spell in the 'bunker' for taking orders from a POW.

We had tea and a short service in the bedroom, where one of the party was sick in bed. I liked Osterwick; a fine group of young men, morale high, camp clean, and Sgt Hay from Skye the best type of TA non-commissioned officer. Men like these had been taken prisoner at around the age of twenty and were losing in effect five of the best years of their life, but what a good job they were making of their captivity!

The sick man had a roaring tonsillitis. That morning he had been marched by the guard twelve kilometres each way to the doctor in Könitz, who had ordered him to have cold compresses and come back in four days' time. He told me he had previously had the same complaint, and on that occasion the doctor had kept him in hospital. On admission he had a cold compress, which remained on for sixteen days unchanged, because he did not know what it was for. He was then seen again by the doctor and discharged as cured. Morison fixed him up with some more effective treatment and, on our return to Torun later in the week, I arranged for him to be brought into our Stalag hospital for proper examination and treatment.

After our service Sgt Hay produced a carriage, very handsome and complete with Polish coachman, who drove us on three kilometres to Schlagenthin. There we found the sergeant in charge working in a field close to the *lager*. He was a less impressive type, a regular soldier in the Buffs, without much push, imagination or initiative. He told me that it would be quite impossible to bring the men in before seven o'clock at the earliest. This was a slack time of year too. He did, however, take us a mile up the road to another *lager* of twelve men also in his jurisdiction, at the other end of the village. As we entered the farmyard we were met by a young Yorkshire lad, pitchfork in hand. He saw that I was something out of the ordinary and gave me the Polish salute, with only two fingers extended. Then with hand still at his cap, he came to and slowly extended the other two fingers. For several minutes he talked to me in POW German as we walked along. Then he recollected himself and apologized profusely. It was intriguing to see how young men like this had unconsciously settled into the life of the farm on which they worked, in many cases as the only man at work on the farm, all the local men,

110

German or Polish, having been called up.

The *lager* was the smallest that I ever saw, even for twelve men, two tiny rooms, probably harness rooms, attached to the stables. Only three of the men could be summoned in the time available, but we managed a short chat and a few prayers, which clearly moved them almost to tears. I was profoundly struck by the isolation of this little handful of youngsters and by the cleanliness and tidiness of their tiny hovel, which was considerably better than the sergeant's own camp. I asked them to tell their mates how sorry I was not to see them all, and to congratulate them on the state of their camp and their morale.

Back then to the sergeant's camp, where we found a message to say that the German Bürgermeister had heard that I was there and was asking at what time I would require his carriage. I ordered it for seven forty-five. Few of the men were in at seven, but at seven fifteen I was able to start a short talk and informal prayers. It was not a good visit, too short to be of much use, and the ice was never broken. I felt that the men wanted to open up in a friendlier way, but that the sergeant, who did not seem faintly interested, was a wet blanket.

At seven forty-five we set off in the Bürgermeister's carriage, complete with young Polish coachman in a dark blue frock coat with silver buttons and a silver-braided cheese-cutter hat, all several sizes too large. Darkness was falling when two miles from Lichnau there was a metallic bang and groaning from the off rear wheel, and we found that we had shed the metal rim. For half an hour we struggled to put it on again, efforts which, to my surprise, were eventually successful. It was nine o'clock when we arrived at Lichnau to find one of our men waiting to tell us that we had been expected to supper at the Ortsbauführer's house. He was a kind of District State Landlord, usually the largest farmer, who among other things was responsible for allotting POW labour to the local farms and for maintaining the condition of the *lagers* with contributions drawn from those farmers who employed prisoner labour. We were told that the Ortsbauführer himself had been scouring the neighbourhood on his motor-cycle for an hour trying to locate us. Accordingly we set off for his house outside the village where we arrived, full of apologies, at nine fifteen.

Herr Gabriel was a caricature of a German, stiff as a ramrod and awkward in his manner. We learnt that under the Nazis he had gone up in the world, having as a farm-inspector (manager) married the daughter of the former owner of the farm. She was a kindly-mannered woman, and her old father was a real character. I do not think that he liked his son-in-law, or any other Nazi, and repeatedly grumbled to me about his lack of tobacco, which he said all went 'quite unreasonably' to the Army and party members. The Obergefreiter, Morison and I were ushered into the best dining room where an excellent meal was served, Gabriel and his wife sitting at either end of the table, and the sixth member of the party being an elegant young lady who had been specially brought four miles from Könitz because she could speak English. Even with her assistance, conversation was sticky. I could not, for instance, offer much sympathy when Herr Gabriel told me that the crops were suffering from drought. We were relieved when it was time for us to return to the *lager*. It had been a long day.

Next morning we returned to Gabriel's farm for breakfast. Frau Gabriel had asked Pte Mackenzie of the Seaforth's who worked on the farm what a British officer had for breakfast. He very properly said 'two eggs and bacon', and two eggs and bacon we duly received. After breakfast back at the *lager*, where all the men were out at work, I was reading a book when the Obergefreiter walked in with the local Control Officer, doing his weekly round. They ignored me until I asked to be allowed to speak to the Oberleutnant, to complain about the state of the barrack and its leaking roof. I knew that he could insist on Herr Gabriel improving things on threat of withdrawing POW labour for the district. He hedged about this question and countered by saying that the men were unclean and lazy.

'*Niemann kann sagen dass dieser Lager sauber ist,*' he said. I had to agree, and then said that I intended to speak to the men about this. But I added that there must be a reason why they were worse than the other camps.

'You must have noticed,' I said, 'the high standard of cleanliness in other British camps in your area. The low standard here is due to the morale of the men being undermined by having to live in such a deplorable leaking building. If you would give them better quarters I am sure that their standards would be raised.'

He more or less agreed, but he had his reply and used it against everything that I said.

'Aber, niemann kann sagen dass dieser Lager sauber ist.' ('No one can say that this is a clean *lager*.')

Later in the morning we returned to Gabriel's farm for lunch, and I remarked to Morison that the meal was something of a sign of the times. There we were sitting at the table with the Orstbauführer and his wife, his father-in-law, his two daughters, our guard and the visiting Oberleutnant, and from the manner of all present, it was apparent that I was the chief guest. A year earlier we would have been lucky to be served a meal in the kitchen. Conversation was not easy, and on the German side it was exclusively about food, the most palatable way of cooking potatoes and so on.

After lunch Sgt L arrived with a carriage from his farm and drove us about six kilometres to the town of Könitz, where I wished to visit the British ward in the hospital, a large German military base hospital. It turned out to be one small room on the top floor with six beds, available for French or British patients from the many small parties in the neighbourhood. Any man sick enough to need attention from a doctor would be brought by his camp guard, usually some miles on foot. The doctor, an elderly Oberstabsarzt (Major), was a moody fellow. Usually he was pretty hard on our men, but if they spoke some German they usually got somewhere with him. One man at Lichnau, Frank Vagg, told me he had gone with his guard to get treatment for diarrhoea. The doctor did not examine him but questioned the guard all about it. As not much progress seemed to be being made, Vagg, who spoke fluent POW German, butted in and said, 'It's I who keeps running to the latrine, not the guard.' The doctor was so pleased that he signed him off work for seven days.

On our return to Lichnau we were taken to supper at another farm with a German farmer and his wife. They were hospitable people, and the friendliness of their manner was very different from the stiffness of Herr Gabriel. The farmer had been a prisoner in England in the 1914/18 war, and spoke well of his experience there doing farm work. He had always lived in the Könitz area and had therefore been part of the so-called 'oppressed minority' between 1920 and 1939. It was interesting therefore to hear them speak so well of conditions under the Poles during that period. Like many Germans I met who had lived in the same area, they would preface many remarks with the phrase *'in polnischer Zeit'* (in Polish times), as if it had been a kind of Golden Age. Considering that my guard was sitting at the table with us, I was astounded to hear some of the remarks they made. Speaking of the current drought, she said it was 'a judgment on Adolf Hitler and all his wickedness.' The farmer's old father, a jolly fellow of about eighty-five, had his meal in the kitchen with the Irish POW who worked for them. Perhaps he would have been even more outspoken.

On our return to the *lager* we found one of the younger men sick with violent stomach pains. Morison, an experienced hospital nurse, was convinced that it was appendicitis. The guard would do nothing that night, but next morning we insisted that he must be taken by carriage to Könitz. I went too, because I wanted to see the doctor at work on one of our men. He gave the man a cursory examination and said that he was 'fit for work'. Appendicitis or not, the man was still in considerable pain. The guard said he must go out to work and that he could not go against the doctor's orders. However, we frightened him by saying that the man might die at any moment and that he would be responsible. Eventually he allowed him to stay in for several days.

On our return from Könitz we lunched on the same hospitable farm and, the afternoon being hot and sultry, Morison and I both felt desperately sick from overeating. In fact we were both violently sick, and, feeling better, we set off to walk three kilometres to Granau. We had sent word that we would visit the party at four o'clock, and when we arrived the last men were just coming in from work to meet us. They were under a very dynamic Sgt Heasman of the Manchester Regiment, who on getting my message had been round to every farm and obtained permission for all his fifteen men to get off work for the remainder of the day. We had a pleasant two hours, with a simple service followed by Holy Communion. Heasman had previously been in charge of one of the big camps at Brahnau; he was a strong, conscientious Warrant Officer who was not afraid of carrying his rank and demanding high standards, and he did not expect to be popular. At Brahnau I understood that he had not been too popular, as he had a way with the Germans and had married a German woman during the occupation of the Rhineland. But from what I saw of him at Brahnau and Granau I formed a high opinion of him. Already at Granau he had vastly improved the conditions since his arrival, having acquired an extra room, and it appeared that there was a happier atmosphere in the camp since he had taken a strong line about the youngsters going out at night to local women. I enjoyed our visit to the camp, and so, I think, did the men, who were mostly very young.

The last night at Lichnau was bound to be difficult. I called the men together and told them, at the risk of abusing their hospitality, I had to take them to task. Their standards were lower than any other camp I had seen. No doubt the deplorable building in which they were housed had something to do with it, but that was no excuse for accumulated filth. Whatever interests they might have in the way of girls on their farms, the *lager* and community life in the *lager* must be their concern. I told them that I had tried to put in a word for them to the Control Officer, but that he had countered with justifiable criticism of the filth. Some of them had told me that eighteen men had escaped from the camp, but such 'escapes' were no credit to the camp; they only showed that any man who came there found such a mess and so little decent spirit that he could only want to get away. Privately I told Sgt L and Cpl H that they must cease the business of dual control, which really amounted to no control; it was incorrect and could only lead to misunderstandings among the men and with the Germans. The sergeant who wore three stripes must take charge and the corporal must back him up. Otherwise the sergeant should go back to Fort XV as a *'non-arbeiter'*.

A few of the men tried to say that the camp was beyond improvement, but the majority seemed to accept my criticism and advice. I never had the chance to pay another visit to Lichnau, but I often met men from the camp elsewhere and twice Lichnau provided a funeral party for me at Könitz. They always greeted me in a friendly way and, without being asked, some of them hastened to tell me of the latest improvement in their camp.

Lichnau was an unlucky camp. Later it was to lose three members in tragic circumstances. Two were inseparable friends, very young Welsh Guardsmen, Jones and Williams, who had been together at school in Anglesey. Some months after my visit, Jones died while swimming in the lake and Williams came into hospital at Torun in the terminal stages of pulmonary TB. Another older man, Gillan, was shot in cold blood after an altercation with a guard.

Morison and I returned to Torun after a week of great interest, having visited ten working parties. By this tour and by Padre Lathaen's a week earlier, we had opened up a new field and shown the small working parties that they were not forgotten. Word of our tours reached other camps, and many requests arrived for a visit from smaller camps throughout the Stalag area.

During our absence, twenty of our best non-employed medical orderlies, British and Australian, had responded to a call from the TB hospital in Germany for more staff. Morison would undoubtedly have volunteered and been selected if he had not been on tour with me. Instead he took over our Fort sick-bay, and by not going away was included in the autumn of 1943 repatriation scheme, which did not include those who had gone to Germany.

30.5.43

. . . you have no idea what memories cow parsley brought back on my tour; there is none around here. At the moment the local glory is the acacias which surround this place, in full bloom and look like a cherry orchard. The birds too are innumerable and sing day and night, nightingales, golden orioles, redstarts, goldfinches, other finches galore and many others. I am getting quite addicted to the place, but have every intention of going home as soon as possible . . . Major Thompson left us for Oflag, their misfortune. Now I have only the Colonel and Felix, the best companion I have had in prison. A small band played for my service tonight, three saxophones, a clarinet and double bass, most effective for hymns . . . No wonder Mrs Q's girl keeps 'giving way to guardsmen', but I bet that they have nothing on our lads on working parties on a Sunday . . .

13.6.43

. . . How nice of your bank manager. I suppose you got carried away in Wings for Victory Week and bought a few more Halifaxes out of my hard-earned savings. Most unseasonably I have had flu this week, very mild, but all aches, pains and shivers . . . Much better now, but this morning got caught in a downpour on my way back from the hospital and arrived like a drowned rat. Felix has a small garden here where he grows lettuces, radishes etc for our table. On Friday the first England/Australian Test is to be played. Would you kindly through Blackwells thank whoever sent two parcels of Shakespeares, air mail at half a guinea a time. Anyway tell Basil B. Such a thrill to see the old Blackwell's label in this arid waste; took me right back to the Broad and Oxford . . .

8

June 1943

In June I travelled to yet a third funeral, of an older soldier in the Royal Welch Fusiliers, who had been shot 'while attempting to escape' at Deutsch Cekzin near Könitz. I went to Könitz in the afternoon by train with Corporal Knox of the RWF. In the train there were three compartments full of British lads who had travelled into Stalag from working parties around Zempelburg and Könitz on various excuses, to collect Red Cross parcels, to have dental treatment and so on. At Nakel, where we changed trains, there were at least forty British prisoners milling about on the station, using all the available barrows to transfer their baggage and generally taking complete charge of the place. They were all at their liveliest; it was like a jolly Bank Holiday party, and the Master Race appeared unamused. I was not surprised when travel for such parties was much curtailed a month later. One party in our train, as they approached their station, threw packets of cigarettes out of the window to one of their friends who had brought his herd of cows to pasture near the railway line.

Knox and I were quartered for the night in the Hindenburg Kaserne at Könitz, and next morning after breakfast we made our way to the mortuary where we found the man's coffin and a guard of honour composed of twenty men from Lichnau. There was no representative from Deutsch Cekzin (the victim's own party), about which I later lodged a complaint, nor could I discover anything about the circumstances of the man's death. The coffin was placed on a flat dray, hideously draped with black, and drawn by two seedy-looking horses also under black draperies. We covered the coffin with a Union Jack and followed it through streets crowded with sympathetic onlookers to the Protestant cemetery outside the town. After the service, while the men filled in the grave, I searched for another grave where, I had been told, one of our men from Osterwick camp had been buried. He had lost his life going to the help of two Poles who had been overcome by gases in a well. I found that our standard POW cross marked the spot, but that the grave was utterly neglected. The sexton also showed me an unmarked grave which he said was the grave of an English POW buried in 1941. Later on, Granger was able to discover the name of this man and mark his grave with a cross.

I lunched with the Lichnau men at a neighbouring barracks before they returned to their camp, and afterwards questioned the Germans about maintenance of the British graves, pointing out that they had buried the man from Osterwick with full military honours as a hero, and now his grave was as neglected as a pauper's. I suggested that, where British prisoners were allowed access to the graves of their comrades, they kept them in good order. The Germans agreed that a working party from Lichnau should from time to time be allowed to tend the graves in Könitz cemetery.

After lunch I asked my guard to take me to the British ward in the hospital. On the way down the main street we were stopped by a policeman who told us it was *'verboten'* for prisoners to walk on the pavement. My guard strongly objected, but when he appeared to be getting nowhere in the argument I told the policeman that I always walked on the pavement in Torun.

'This is not Torun, it is Könitz,' I was told. When we said that I was not a POW but a *'festgehaltene Feldgeistlicher'* (an interned Army chaplain) he looked puzzled and asked what I was doing in Könitz. My guard told him I had come to take a funeral.

'When do you go back?' he asked.

'Today,' I said.

'To *England?*' he asked.

He then staggered me by apologising for having interfered, and explained that he had been misled into thinking that I was a POW by my uniform. He saluted smartly and waved us on with a grand gesture, as if to say, 'The whole Borough of Könitz is yours.'

Our guard on this trip was a good young soldier, keen to do his job well, helpful and respectful. Wherever we went he walked boldly up to the authorities and announced loudly, 'The British chaplain from Stalag XXA,' as if I were some important diplomat to be given special facilities. More often than not, his methods were successful.

Also in June, I paid the first of my three visits to the Wehrmacht *Strafe Gefängnis* at Graudenz. This was the punishment prison to which British, French and Belgian POWs in all parts of Germany were sent to serve sentences passed on them by German Courts Martial for offences committed in prison. Most of the British had offended by casting aspersions on the Führer or the regime, or had had a dust-up with guards or employers. Most of the French had committed offences against the 'racial purity acts' for which on farms with most German menfolk absent on active service there was ample scope. Before 1942 such offenders had been sent to Torgau, south of Berlin, where they were in the same camp as German servicemen under sentence, but in the summer of 1943 they were transferred to the 'glass-house' at Graudenz exclusively for POWs. Though living conditions and hours of work had been hard at Torgau, the food was better than at Graudenz, and the POWs had the satisfaction of seeing that they were treated with considerably less brutality than the Germans dealt out to their own malefactors. At Graudenz the work and the regime were less hard but the food was deplorable. Sick men occasionally brought from there to our hospital at Torun were seriously underweight, and Frenchmen came to us from Graudenz and its various satellite working parties suffering from self-inflicted wounds. Conditions had to be bad when a man was prepared to put his hand on a railway line in order to find his way into hospital. Short rations tended to be the favourite form of German punishment.

For the first few months after the move to Graudenz, the Wehrmacht *Gefängnis,* though it was in the Stalag XXA area, came administratively under Stalag XXB at Marienburg. When it was transferred to XXA, CQMS Granger set about seeing what he could do to improve conditions there. Instead of the one letter a month the prisoners were allowed being delayed by the Marienburg censors department, Granger soon had this dealt with in the censor department at Torun, and I never heard any more complaints about mail. He also arranged that both the Protecting Power and YMCA representatives should visit the *Strafe* prison that summer. This had not happened before, and it meant that conditions might be expected to improve. In fact, as a result of these visits, permission was also granted for Granger to supply the prison with a certain amount of food in bulk from our Red Cross supply. This could be used in the daily soups by all three nationalities. Permission was also given for a chaplain to visit the prison periodically to hold a service.

My colleague, Padre Lathaen, agreed to go first, and from his account it was an interesting and useful visit – as satisfactory as could be expected in a place under such a stringent regime. Although the *Gefängnis* was dependent on Stalag XXA for mail, parcels and much else, it was otherwise administered by its own staff who were responsible to the Oberkommando des Wehrmacht (OKW) in Berlin. We were therefore strangers to them on our visits and regarded with some suspicion, so we had to watch our step.

Two months later I went myself, taking with me CQMS Granger as my 'bag carrier'. It seemed a good chance to let him have actual contact with the place. We caught a train from Torun at 5.30 am and were at Graudenz by 7.30. As it was Sunday morning there was not much life in the large working party, Graudenz Internat, which was our first port of call. This camp was contained in a large, three-storey brick building standing in a dirty compound large enough to contain a dusty football pitch. It housed some four hundred and fifty prisoners who went to work each day in a variety of factories in the town. It was a depressing and overcrowded place with room after room full of three-decker beds. The camp had had a succession of bad Commandants since it opened in 1940, and the current Feldwebel – who lasted till December 1944, when he was arrested for embezzling rations – was a notorious obstructionist.

On the British side the main weakness appeared to be the man at the top, CSM R, an elderly Warrant Officer in a Scottish regiment. He had neither the push to challenge and harass the Germans effectively, nor the personality to gain the confidence of so many men. There were unfortunate divisions in the camp, due to the fact that the men working in factories were subject to varying treatment at work. Some worked short hours and enjoyed good 'rackets', while others were far less fortunate. A good camp leader who gave the men at least an impression of energy and firmness could probably have welded them into a happier body, and this, for all his conscientiousness, R could not do.

The camp always had one British or Commonwealth Medical Officer. At the time of my visit this was Lionel Sapsford, an Australian, with whom I had breakfast. It was agreed that I should celebrate Holy Communion for those who wished it in the morning, and that I would conduct a larger service in the evening on my return from the *Gefängnis*.

I talked with some younger men who had previously tried to hold a service each week in the camp, but who had become discouraged and allowed it to lapse. They were nice, serious types, but they clearly felt their efforts had not been worthwhile. I asked them to keep the services going if possible. I told them that a majority of the men in the camps, even though they did not come to services, seemed to value what was going on and appreciated that services were being held week by week. Men who rarely came to services that I took in Fort XV, and had not done so elsewhere, had often told me with genuine respect that in other camps where they had been, Private A or Corporal B had always held a service on Sundays. I know that these young soldiers did a good job at Graudenz, and witnessed well to their faith.

After lunch Granger and I set out on the long walk to the other side of the town to the *Strafe Gefängnis*. We rang the bell at the great iron doors, and after being closely scrutinised through a grill were admitted into the porch. While our guard checked us in at the office, various unpleasant-looking Unteroffiziers passed by, hungrily looking us over as new victims. We were then escorted through a tunnel under one block, the French block, and across a huge parade ground to the British block, a typical prison building with small heavily barred windows. Upstairs, through two more locked doors, we came to an office on the first floor where an Unteroffizier interpreter took us in charge. Later we learnt that he was nicknamed 'the Cockney' because he spoke perfect English

122

with a strong Cockney accent.

He took us first to the cell of the only British officer then in the prison, Flying Officer Dickinson, an impressive young man. With his Flight Sergeant, immediately after capture, he had attempted to overcome their guards while they were being transported to Oflag, and was now paying the price. We were joined in the cell by the Man of Confidence, Sgt Russell of the Cameron Highlanders, a quiet, conscientious and likeable man. For half an hour we were allowed to talk without supervision, though at regular intervals the door into the corridor was opened and a sub-human type of guard gazed silently into the room. Granger discussed with Russell ways and means of increasing deliveries of Red Cross food, and other possibilities of helping prisoners from the Torun end, while I talked with Dickinson. He was evidently taking his solitary life very philosophically, and I know that all the other ranks in the prison had a great respect for him. Eventually the Cockney returned to say that all the British prisoners were on parade ready to march over to the Chapel. As we walked past the men I could see they were all very thin and poorly clothed, and discipline was clearly severe enough to discourage them from taking more than a furtive glance in our direction.

The chapel was a surprisingly fine Gothic building in the style of the Sainte Chapelle in Paris – in its time the prison had been some kind of monastery – but it was dirty and uncared-for inside. The men, about 150 of them, filed into their places and the guards stood at the back. While Granger gave out hymn sheets I had a few words with some of them. We had a simple service and a short address, and in the end they warmed up with some unaccompanied hymns, which they sang well. After the service about twenty men were allowed by the Germans to stay and receive Communion, while the rest were counted and taken back to their cells.

I next asked the Cockney if I might visit some of the cells, and after hesitating he eventually agreed. While Granger managed some more private talk with Russell and others, I was taken to the various landings, on each of which I chose two cells. On either side of each was a double-decker bed with a very narrow space between, and at the end nearest the door just space for a small table and four stools. The men were not allowed to smoke or lie on their beds during the day, but on

Sundays most of them were allowed the 'privilege' of reading a book. They were under continuous scrutiny from guards on each landing, and one of the worst features of the life was the constant bawling of guards and the slamming of doors. It was bad enough while I was there, but considerably modified, I understood, for my benefit.

I had about five minutes each in six cells, the Cockney invariably moving out of earshot. The men talked freely and cheerfully, and in no way tried to impress me with the rigours of their plight. They all praised the improvement in the quality of the daily soup since the Red Cross supplies from Torun had been admitted, though still so far in small quantities, into the camp. As a result of this visit, Granger was able by degrees to increase substantially the amount of food, cigarettes and clothing delivered to the *Gefängnis* from Torun. There is no doubt that the Cockney and other Germans took a share of what was sent, but the condition of our men was much improved. This was obvious to me on my later visits, and we stopped getting emaciated men at our hospital from the *Gefängnis*. The handling of the Graudenz question was a great triumph of diplomacy – or was it intrigue? – on the part of Granger and successive Men of Confidence at Graudenz. One false step, and the whole traffic of supplies would have been disallowed.

Before leaving I persuaded the Cockney to take me to the Medical ward. I had been told it was a devil of a job to get admitted there as a patient, but once there things were not too bad. I talked with several British, French and Belgians, and they joined in a few short prayers. I asked the German medical orderly why vitamin tablets sent from Torun had not been issued to the men. He had quite a sensible answer – they were waiting till there were enough for each man to have a box. Next day they would be issued, and there would be inspections to see that they were not all scoffed in one go to stave off the pangs of hunger – an interesting admission.

There were many stories about the Cockney, both to his credit and his discredit. My own opinion was that, in a camp full of Nazi thugs, he alone realized that the standards of living and treatment in the *Gefängnis* were far below what any British troops would lightly tolerate. He had been in England long enough not to approve. In various ways he helped prisoners individually and collectively, but like most of the guards he was scared of his superiors, and he was crooked by nature. He would do good turns for a fat enough bribe, but would 'shop' anyone to save his skin.

When our visit was over, he said that he would like to see a British prison, and he accompanied us back to the Internat, this time by tram. We were too late to fit in a service, but when I explained that we had been allowed to stay longer than we expected at the *Gefängnis,* the Internat men heartily agreed it was right the *Gefängnis* should have priority. We nearly missed our train back to Torun because our guard, the Cockney and the guard on the Internat main gate had a 'shopping' match in front of the Commandant lasting nearly half an hour – each trying to prove that it was another's fault that the Cockney had got into the camp without a permit.

It had been a privilege to be able to pay a pastoral visit to men living under such conditions and a happy way to celebrate the anniversary of my ordination on another Trinity Sunday, 1935.

9

July 1943

For my July visits I submitted to the authorities a list of camps in the area south of Könitz near to Zempelburg. As escort I took with me a 1914/18 veteran, Sergeant Lovelace from Worthing; since his arrival in Fort XV earlier in the year, he had been a pillar of my congregation and withal a cheery companion. For the first time under a new Stalag arrangement, we had as guard an English-speaking censor, Unteroffizier Oldorp, a boring braggart. According to his story he had served on the Intelligence branch of Rommel's Afrika Corps. His story that the English cigarettes, of which he appeared to have an unlimited supply in his bag, were spoils from Tobruk taxed the credulity of the working parties we visited, especially when it was discovered that they had 'British Red Cross and Order of St John' printed on them.

We arrived at Zempelburg, a very small town, at lunchtime, and found the British *lager* close to the station. After an excellent lunch, the rather dim sergeant and a very forceful young German-speaking private soldier, Ted Lyne of the QVRs, showed me round the factory where a hundred of our men were at work. It was an interesting set-up, sectional huts being produced on mass production methods. Each saw was set at a particular angle to do a particular job, to cut one special shaped plank, so most of the labour required was unskilled. All sawdust and shavings in each workshop was swept into a corner where it was sucked up and drawn through vast pipes as fuel for the boilers.

After the factory we had a look at the camp. It appeared that at intervals the prisoners would approach the management of the firm and suggest that better quarters should be provided.

Already the wooden barracks were an advance on what they occupied previously, and would have been regarded as sumptuous by most prisoners. But not by the men of Zempelburg; already behind the existing camp a number of men were employed in putting the finishing touches to an even more luxurious barrack, supplied by the firm and erected in the firm's time. On the wall facing the main road was a board executed to the highest standards of sign-painting, bearing the information 'Jones & Wilcox, Painters and Decorators. Tel Zempelburg 1212'. Lovelace and I were entertained separately by a different room at each meal, a pleasant way of helping us to meet as many men as possible during a short visit. There was a good turnout to the service I took in one of the new barrack rooms, and many stayed on for Communion.

Zempelburg at that time was fortunate in having a really good Medical Orderly officially attached to them, a middle-aged man in the Leicestershire Regiment. In addition to dealing with all the ailments of the men in the camp, he was first-aid man to the factory, in which accidents were not uncommon, as the saws were inadequately protected. The overworked German doctor in Zempelburg also sent him most of his British patients from the many neighbouring farm working parties, to receive the treatment he prescribed. Through one of these 'out-patients' we arranged for a carriage to fetch us next morning to convey us to Neuhorst, five or six kilometres away.

I had put Neuhorst on my list, having been asked on a previous railway journey by a young private soldier to pay his party a visit if I was ever in their neighbourhood. In the morning we approached the camp in our carriage by a narrow sandy track leading further and further away from the main road. The camp itself turned out to be a very small brick building, one of some very poor farm-labourers' cottages. We found the guard in a neighbouring cottage and he let us into the camp, unlocking the gate of the tiny wire compound and unbarring the cottage door. All these precautions had been taken to ensure that my friend of the train, Don Cotton by name, who had stayed in from work indisposed, should not enjoy the fresh summer weather out of doors in the compound.

We were warmly welcomed by Don, who had no advance warning of our arrival, and there was a long discussion between the guard and Oldorp as to where Lovelace and I should sleep. The guard suggested a farm, but when I asked Cotton if they could fit us into their cramped quarters, he assented with enthusiasm. The guard seemed amazed at the idea of an officer sleeping there, so I explained that I had come to meet English prisoners and not to stay at German farms.

The conditions were certainly cramped. One room housed nine double-decker beds with very little space between them; the other room had a table, two benches, a few cupboards and a paraffin stove. The water was drawn from a pump outside the compound at such times as the guard chose to unlock the gate. There were no bathing arrangements, and the men washed in old metal basins. Their spare kit was kept in a loft above the *lager* entered by a ladder from outside. Most of the men were there continuously for three and a half years. When I visited them again in 1944, the Germans were even considering reducing the size of the ridiculously small compound.

Arrangements were made for the three of us, Lovelace, Oldorp and myself, to have lunch on a farm a mile away. The farm buildings lay in a hollow, and were a good deal more prosperous-looking than most; this was no doubt because the farmer was a German who had displaced a Pole. Inside, the house was typically German, very clean, but full of heavy, unattractive furniture.

As we sat in the sitting room waiting for lunch, Jock Borthwick, the Scottish lad who worked on the farm, came in to speak with us. Strongly built and in magnificent condition, he was a fine specimen from a farming family, his father having a large farm in Aberdeenshire. He joined us for the excellent lunch served by the elderly farmer's wife.

After lunch we took a walk around the district, calling in at several smaller farms where other prisoners from Neuhorst worked. Most of these farms were in the hands of Poles who had signed papers and were classed as 'Volks-Deutsch' or 'eingedeutscht'.

We returned to the camp, and at about seven the eighteen men began to drift back from work. They washed and

128

changed and set about cooking themselves something for supper. Cigarette parcels had not been coming through for some weeks, so that those we had brought with us were well received. Lovelace and I were much struck by the friendly, homelike atmosphere of the camp. In spite of the exceptionally crowded conditions, every man seemed to think and act in a true community spirit. As one man was in hospital in Torun, I was given his bed, and the camp leader gave up his to Lovelace while he made up a bed for himself on the living room table. My bed was on the top shelf alongside Jock Borthwick, and as we were both over six feet, we spent a good part of the night bumping and boring. But it had been a long day, and I slept well.

In visiting farm parties on a Sunday, I did not usually suggest a service in the morning; Sunday was the men's free day, and they spent the morning cleaning out the *lager* from end to end, washing and mending their clothes, gardening, and cleaning their best uniforms and boots. At midday, dressed as for parade, they set off, each man to his own farm for lunch.

Jock again took us to his farm, and on the way told us about the place. He said that the old farmer, who looked a decent elderly man, was, what he called, a typical Hun. He treated Jock with consideration and respect, partly because he realized that Jock knew what he was doing, and being strong could be expected to pull his weight, and partly because he could see that he was too dogged a Scot to allow himself to be exploited. The rather simple Polish girl who worked on the farm was deplorably treated, however: wretchedly housed and fed, she was grossly overworked and not infrequently beaten by the farmer with a stout stick.

We were given a large lunch at the farmer's own table – Jock Borthwick, the farmer's daughter and her soldier husband, home on leave, sitting with us in addition to the farmer and his wife. Language problems apart, it was one of the more sticky social occasions, and I was amused to study the open contempt registered on Jock's face for this family for whom he had worked and with whom he had virtually lived for the last eighteen months. After lunch Jock harnessed up two good horses in the best carriage, a high four-seater open affair, on which we bowled off into the forest. Well into the forest we came to the large and handsome mansion of Borowke. Here we found about twenty men housed in a single room camp in one of the large farm buildings. This was not one of my happier visits. We were only there for about one hour, and the ice was barely broken.

We continued our journey in an astonishing vehicle produced from the Borowke stables. It was a very well turned out four-wheeler, like a little box slung low between the two axles. Lovelace, Oldorp and I sat bolt upright on red plush upholstery surrounded by elegant plate-glass windows. It was a conveyance better suited to Berkeley Square in the 1880s than the sandy Polish countryside.

Less than a mile away at Zempelkowo, we came to a huge state farm with a disused schnapps factory, a common feature of all the old estates. Here we found the *lager* door wide open, but to avoid misunderstandings Oldorp agreed to report to the local guard before going in. We ran him to ground in his room in the basement of the big house. He was obviously an easy-going fellow, and we found that not only was the *lager* door wide open but at least half the sixteen prisoners were out for a nice Sunday afternoon walk. (Later on, such liberties, where they had existed, were drastically curtailed, and except for short periods the men in many camps were locked in the camp buildings on a Sunday afternoon, without permission to use even the tiny compounds.)

The *lager* at Zempelkowo was a large roomy loft and two smaller rooms over one of the enormous barns. The men enjoyed three times the amount of space allotted to most farm parties, and electric light was an unusual amenity. They were a quiet crowd, but I was able to give them news of many of their old friends, most of them having been formerly at Torun, and this broke the ice rapidly. A cup of tea was soon produced, and they gathered round for a service, which, perhaps because it was a Sunday with old associations seemed to affect us all; they listened attentively to my short talk, which at the small parties I kept as informal as possible. I was touched on our departure when the very quiet, middle-aged Lance-Corporal in charge called the men together, spoke a few words of thanks to me on their behalf and called for three cheers. We were driven home direct to Neuhorst through a forest of magnificent oak trees, the largest hardwood forest I saw in

Poland.

Back at Neuhorst I tried in a simple service to convey to this small group of men my appreciation of the kind of life they had worked out for themselves, after three years of captivity, 'tilling an alien soil'. That kind of comradeship in adversity does not just happen; it meant that every member of the party had been putting the community and family life first, in the word of St Paul, 'edifying' one another. This even impressed the Germans and Poles among whom they were living.

After the service we continued to talk by the light of small carbide jets, and our talk soon turned into a sing-song which was accompanied and supported by Don Cotton on his trumpet. He was a talented player and no mean musician, and the support he gave to our singing was as good as a whole band. He and Jock Borthwick struck me as outstanding characters, but there was another member of the party who helped to make it a memorable evening. The camp had run out of tobacco and cigarettes, but this man produced a four-ounce tin of tobacco – his iron ration stored up for an evil day. To mark my visit and to cheer everyone up, he divided it into eighteen portions and we all had a smoke that night.

The next morning the men were up early, and I did not see them again after they had gone off to work on their farms. About ten o'clock a farm cart arrived driven by a young Pole who took us to Zempelfeld station. There we found the dejected-looking son-in-law of our farmer host, who told Oldorp that all soldiers on leave from Norway had been recalled urgently. Naturally Lovelace and I imagined all sorts of exciting possibilities from this scrap of news, which of course was a false alarm. But maybe the 'nervenkreig' was beginning to show itself. It was always interesting to note any dents appearing in the confidence of the Master Race.

We had a short journey by train, only two stations, past Zempelburg to Kamin on the line to Könitz. The station there was at one end of a very beautiful lake about the size of Grasmere, stretching away northwards to the German frontier. Along the north shore were woods of hardwood trees, but on the southern and western shores it was open country, with wide fields of varied colours stretching for miles and miles over gently rolling hills. Close to the lake on the further side, the red roofs and the 'onion' church steeple of

Kamin village were clustered on a small conical hill reflected in the still waters of the lake. I came more and more to love this part of Poland, largely because it is real watercolour country. The slightest ascent opens up views of vast extent; there are no exaggerated features, but the country is never really flat. Forests of pine added their rich contrasting colours, and in many of the hollows there were lakes, some of considerable size, which mirrored the clear blue of the sky. Most of the farms and hamlets were scattered in the valleys, but where a village was set on a hill the houses huddled together to meet the freezing winds that blow across this open countryside from Russia and the Baltic in the long winters.

It seemed to be country where nothing more exciting than the constant toil of farm-work could ever take place, but in a little cemetery by the roadside a mile from Kamin I saw one of the ugly wooden crosses the Germans designed to mark a soldier's grave. This man had met his death eight or ten miles inside the Polish frontier on the first day of September 1939, the opening day of the War. Perhaps he was the very first victim of Hitler's folly. It was over this peaceful countryside that the German tanks had swept forward to 'free a minority', many of whom by 1943 had come to speak of their twenty years of freedom as *'in polnischer Zeit'*. Through this same countryside eighteen months later, we were to see the battered remnant of Hitler's army desperately retreating from the Eastern front, in search of a last standing point beyond the Oder, while the disillusioned 'minority' gathered up a few possessions and stumbled back along the road to Germany, leaving behind their homes where they had known happiness and prosperity, and to which they could never return.

From Kamin we had a walk of some four miles, quite far enough with our packs in the midday sun. We passed through the village of Gros Zirkwitz, composed mostly of tiny farms grouped round the crest of a hill, and followed a selection of sandy tracks leading us into a fertile, well-farmed valley. Among these scattered farms we found Splonskowski's, which was to be our halting place for the next four nights. Sergeant Godfrey worked on the home farm and was there to welcome us to his camp. This was an L-shaped converted cow-byre. In the long section on either side were three double-decker beds, with a narrow table running up the middle. In the corner was an upright heating stove, and in the short part of the L were two single beds. There were no bathing arrangements, and water was drawn from the farm pump. The only light came from two small windows above one rank of beds and from a larger one by the stove. At the time of my visit there was no compound, and when the door was unlocked the men had the freedom of the farmyard and the immediate surroundings. Only twelve of the fourteen men were resident. They were an older, tougher and more assured party than most I had encountered, with an average age of around thirty. They had shaken down well together as a community. On their various farms they seemed to do well for food, and consequently tended to acquire a surplus of Red Cross food which they were able to share with other parties in the neighbourhood who were less well-off. They told me that when one of their number was not doing too well for food on his farm, they persuaded their guard to visit the offending farm and remonstrate with the boss. I came to see that there was much to admire in a party such as this, where they knew the value of prisoners standing together.

Next morning Lovelace and I rose at our leisure some time after the men had gone to work. We lit the stove and fried two eggs each, given us by Sergeant Godfrey. As arranged, Lovelace went across the yard to draw bread from Frau Splonskowski, when to his surprise she produced four fried eggs and bacon as well. So our breakfast was something out of the ordinary, even for prisoners of war. We spent the morning lazily sunning ourselves in the farmyard until Oldorp arrived to take us to lunch on another farm a short distance away. Here we found a German family consisting of an old man of ninety-two, his wife – a sister or niece of a Polish Roman Catholic bishop – and two spinster daughters. The daughters received us hospitably and gave us an excellent lunch in the best parlour. They tried to keep their old father out of the way, but he was determined to have an innings, and after they had chased him out of the room three times they gave up the struggle, and he came and sat by me. He apologised profusely at my having to sit opposite a large photograph of Field-Marshal Goering; he said that he did not dare take it down as it was a present to him on his ninetieth birthday from the Ortsbauführer, and if he visited the farm and found it missing there would be trouble. I was shown the family album in which there was a photograph of the old man as an army cadet in the 1870 war. After lunch he took us round the garden, showing us, among other things, a fine apple tree he had planted as a young man. At ninety-two he was still active enough to work around the farm, and later we saw him chopping wood. The English lad who worked on the farm said that he was always well-treated, but the spinster ladies did not entirely trust him: every time a hen cackled they rushed out to secure the new egg. During my remaining three days at Splonskowski's they sent me a present each evening by him; one night it was cake and another strawberries.

In the late afternoon we walked a mile up to the head of the valley to another camp of twelve men who worked for one Frau Bratz. Here we found a deplorable state of affairs. The men lived in one minute room; the ceiling was so low that in the upper bunk of each pair the men could not even sit up. Frau Bratz, a really mean woman, rarely gave them the rations to which they were entitled, although she had a large and prosperous farm. She had considerable influence with higher ranking German officers at Stalag HQ, several of whom regularly received from her liberal presents of butter and bacon. The guard in charge of the camp had often tried to effect improvements, but on each occasion she had countered by cutting his rations, or, if that failed, by ringing up Stalag and demanding his removal. Prisoners acting as camp cooks had sometimes been removed at her request because they had weighed the rations she supplied and complained about deficiencies. Other men had been replaced for alleged go-slow working and other forms of protest. Frau Bratz regularly stood over the men while they were at work.

At the time of my visit her star had begun to decline. Her first mishap had taken place in the course of a routine visit by Oberzahlmeister Mixa from Stalag. (He was the chief quartermaster who dealt with pay, rations and clothing.) Normally when a German officer visited the camp, she would waylay him and give him a super-fine meal before he carried out his inspection. Unfortunately for her, Mixa, who was probably suffering from a hangover, arrived one morning behind schedule, having had a puncture. He went straight to the *lager* without calling on Frau Bratz. She saw his car and dashed over to ask him to lunch. Ignoring her, he asked the guard who 'this woman' was, and ordered her out of the *lager*. He then wrote a strongly critical report on the state of the camp to Stalag.

Not long after this, the Swiss Representative of our Protecting Power, Herr Achentaler, on his half-yearly tour of our area, visited the camp with the British Man of Confidence for the Stalag, CQMS Granger. Frau Bratz gave them a sumptuous meal, but Herr Achentaler expressed grave dissatisfaction with the camp and instructed the German Commandant to issue an ultimatum to Frau Bratz that unless the work on the enlargement of the camp was in progress by 1 August, the camp was to be closed and the men withdrawn. I visited the place on 30 July. On that day, for the first time two of our men had been taken off farm work and told to start building an extension – neither of them knowing anything about building. As far as the letter of the law was concerned, she had accepted the ultimatum and reckoned that she had covered herself.

While I was inside talking to some of the men, Lovelace, who was a master bricklayer, was giving some instruction to the two young 'builders'. He was overheard by the Frau, and she immediately asked Oldorp to let him stay and supervise the job, explaining that she could get no civilian labour – or more likely did not want to pay for it. Here, then, was a problem. Left to themselves, the men would get no improvements done for a long time. Much would depend on the supply of materials and how frequently men were spared from farm work, and so on. Stalag was unlikely to close the camp, the influence of Frau Bratz being what it was. On the other hand, was it our business to get her out of trouble by doing the work?

That evening I asked Oldorp to telephone Stalag and explain the position – if possible to Major Loeffler, the officer most likely to understand the situation. I asked him to say that the work had only just started and showed no probability of being finished for a long time, if at all: that I was prepared to leave Lovelace there – a full rank NCO who had no obligation to work – not in order to help Frau Bratz or the Germans, but voluntarily to provide better quarters for our men. Further, so as not to prejudice any action Granger might be thinking of taking towards getting the *lager* closed, I said I would only sanction Lovelace staying if Granger approved. Unfortunately Oldorp found that Loeffler was away, and the objectionable Hauptmann Duvet of Arbeitseinsatz told him in no uncertain terms to mind his own business. Duvet had regular bounty from Frau Bratz.

Morale was high in this party, in spite of their tribulations. They were a young crowd and full of humour, including seeing the funny side of Frau Bratz. The only blight was the British sergeant in charge – a mean, complaining sort of creature as I thought, and an ineffective leader of the party. He had recently weakened his position by an incredible piece of folly. He had asked to be relieved of his job and returned to Stalag, which was his right as a full rank NCO. He then changed his mind and asked permission to stay. To this the Germans replied that he could do so only if he would sign his willingness to work for six months. By signing, he had forfeited all rights he had as a sergeant and all the position of independence he had as camp leader.

From Bratz farm we walked back past Splonskowski's and two miles in the opposite direction to Obkas (Oberwalden), a small village on the railway. Here we found a particularly lively party of sixteen men, housed in a good billet which looked like a village school. The camp leader, Cpl MacIlroy, who had asked me to visit the camp, was away at Stalag with two other men, so I promised to return another evening. One of the men went to his farm and returned with a carriage and pair, in which he drove us back in style to Splonskowski's.

Next morning, while Lovelace and I were at breakfast, the guard from a party in the village of Gros Zirkwitz arrived on a bicycle and asked if I would pay his party a visit that evening. Soon afterwards Oldorp came in and asked me our plans for the day. He then produced a piece of paper which he handed to me, saying, 'You can take this and go on your own today.' On the paper was written in pencil, 'The British Chaplain, the Rev. R D F Wild, and his batman Sgt Lovelace have permission to visit camps in the vicinity of Gros Zirkwitz *ohne Begleitung* (without escort). signed – Oldorp, Unteroffizier. Abwehr, Stalag XXA.' It transpired that Oldorp fancied the progress he was making in his efforts to charm the daughter of the farm where he was staying. Unfortunately for him, she was only interested in the English lad who worked there, as he subsequently discovered.

Armed with this curious and highly improper pass, Lovelace and I set out to yet another farm, a poor grubby place and a poor meal. The Cheshire Regiment lad who worked there then sent us on our way to Resmin, a few miles away. It was a lovely walk, taking us a long way along one side and round the head of a considerable lake. None of the civilians we passed challenged us, not even the manager of a small sawmill of whom we asked the way and with whom we chatted for a while. He had been a prisoner in England in the last war.

It was teatime when we reached Resmin, a large state farm where twenty of our men were employed. All but six of the men were at work a mile from the camp, and there was no prospect of getting them back for a talk or a service. However, we had a cup of tea with the six, who had a half-hour break. From conversation with them and from stories I had heard, I formed the impression that Resmin was one of the ill-starred camps. Half the men had settled down well, but the rest were week-enders, replacements from the Stalag 'clink', who after a few days or at most weeks, during which they made no attempt to fit in, pushed off, expecting to be rounded up, spend a few days in the bunker and then be sent elsewhere. At first sight it was hard to understand the reason for this; the billet was as good as any farm billet that I saw, with several rooms and plenty of space for everyone. It was well-kept, clean and supplied with all kinds of gadgets to add to the amenities. Apparently the farm inspector was at the root of the trouble and worked the men unreasonably. The British NCO in charge seemed a nice but weak fellow, and I felt that good leadership and a united front as found in some other camps would soon have fixed the inspector. One or two barrack-room lawyers may also have been creating divisions. I was sorry I did not have a chance to spend the night there and see all the men together.

The camp had been open when we arrived, and no guard had put in an appearance while we were there. As we were about to leave, an elderly Obergefreiter walked in, slightly perplexed to find strangers. I introduced myself as the British chaplain from Stalag XXA, and he immediately saluted. Then, and only then, I produced Oldorp's scrap of paper. He read it through and saluted again. He then asked me what I would like to do, and whether I would like the other men brought in from work at once. When I explained that I could not stay longer, he appeared quite distressed that they would not have a service. However, he said that he would see us on our way, and accompanied us for half a mile along the lake. Then, saying that we must return another day, he shook hands, saluted and left us to go on alone. It all seemed faintly ridiculous and Lovelace and I sat down by the lake and had a good laugh. I would like to think that any self-respecting British camp guard finding strangers on his camp premises would have arrested them on sight and left them to explain themselves to an officer. As a serious document, my pass from Oldorp was patently worthless, and the guard had started saluting me before he had even seen it.

At the far end of the lake we crossed some marshy meadows and climbed a short hill into the outskirts of the village of Gros Zirkwitz. As we walked along the village street, several British lads who had finished work for the day joined us and escorted us to their camp. This was an ample loft overlooking the main street in the middle of the village. One large room provided plenty of space for fourteen men. It was well distempered and very clean. They also had single beds, not even the normal two-deckers. The fourteen men were the liveliest lot that I ever met in prison, all of them young and bursting with high spirits. All had learnt to speak fluent colloquial German and, I think, Polish too. Their guard clearly did what he was told.

They told me hilarious stories of their escapades. They tyrannised over the village, playing football in the main street, breaking odd windows in the process. On Hitler's birthday and on other regulation festivals when a Nazi flag appeared at every window, they hung a sack outside the *lager*. When the guard protested, they claimed that it was Churchill's birthday and if the Germans hung out flags for the Führer they had to fly a sack for Churchill. A tougher guard was sent from Stalag to bring them to heel. On his first morning he rampaged about the camp trying to get them up, firing shots through the ceiling with his revolver. Pointing it at one lad as he lay in bed, he said that he would count three and then fire. He duly counted while all the rest of the men lay in bed and jeered.

138

The threatened lad never moved while he counted; the guard retired defeated and never again recovered face.

After supper and a short service I had some talk with the Lance-Corporal in charge, who was worried because his wife in Liverpool had been bombed out and was writing from what he said was a bad quarter of the city. I wrote to the Red Cross for him, and in due course had a very reassuring letter from a woman visitor, giving helpful news and advice. I forwarded it to the man, and I know that he was grateful to the Red Cross for their sympathetic help and advice.

One of the men produced a carriage from his farm and drove us back to Splonskowski's at a spanking pace. He told me that he had been a bank clerk in the City, and had never been near a horse in his life. No guard escorted us, and Oldorp looked somewhat relieved when we rolled into the farmyard at about ten o'clock.

Next day, having the Bratz party on my mind, I went up there again after lunch and told them that Lovelace would not be allowed to stay and help them with the building. They said that they thought that they could manage with the help he had given them. Subsequently I heard that they had managed to finish the job, but six months later, after further trouble, Frau Bratz decided that she could bully Russians with greater impunity, and the British were withdrawn.

From Bratz we walked to Obkas, Oldorp again remaining to pursue his *amours* on the farm. MacIlroy and his party again gave us a great welcome and an excellent supper, after which we had a service. Like the Gros Zirkwitz party, they seemed to have their whole village under control and all the best jobs on the farms in their hands. One man told me he had done nothing but cow-herding for the last eight months, just driving a few cows down to the meadows and sitting watching them all day. I know that this party regularly sent one of their numbers into Stalag once a week on some excuse, taking with him at least one sack full of ducks and chickens, rabbits and eggs for their friends.

A young Australian borrowed a carriage from his farm, and we travelled back to Splonskowski's in state; and there we concluded a memorable visit with a very warm-hearted service.

Our journey home was a chapter of accidents. We thought

139

that there was a train to Torun via Könitz and Graudenz; but at Könitz we found that there was no connection. So we turned back again through Kamin to Nakel and Bromberg. At Bromberg we found that there was a fast train to Torun in one hour, but that POWs were not allowed to travel on it. There would be no slow train for six hours. Oldorp confidently said that he would sort out the Bahnhofsoffizier RTO, to whose office we duly retired. We were shown into the room of a genial-looking elderly major who looked as if he might have been a schoolmaster by profession. Oldorp spun a long story about my not really being a POW, and that I had an important service to take back in Torun. The old major listened politely, but as one accustomed to hearing 'sad' stories from his pupils. When Oldorp finished, he raised his hand with an air of finality and said quietly: *'Dass kommt nicht in Frage.'* ('That is out of the question.')

We adjourned to the large refreshment room in a hut erected for travelling servicemen and, ignoring the notice over the door – *'Nicht für Kriegsgefangene'* – went in and sat down in a corner. A Red Cross girl hospitably brought us soup and bread, and made us a pot of good English tea from a packet supplied by us. A blaring wireless and a few old magazines helped us to while away four hours. I particularly remember a rousing radio performance of a stirring marching song which Oldorp said came from the time of Frederick the Great, *'Ich sah ein Schifflein fahren'*, a far finer piece than their modern marches.

But a rude shock was in store for us. Our friendly waitress was replaced by the chief Red Cross superintendent, a vast figure of a woman. She took one look at us and shouted *'Heraus!'* Oldorp tried to remonstrate, but she continued to shout and in a few seconds had bundled all three of us out on to the platform. It was a fine performance, and I reckon that she came from a long line of Prussian Feldwebels.

Our belated return to Fort XV was uneventful, but as we approached the *Wache,* Scarface came out to greet us like long-lost friends. As this was the first trip on which I had been accompanied by a member of the *Abwehr* staff, I was anxious to know what he might be on the lookout for. Throughout our trip he had been innocuous, even cooperative, but I thought that there might be a sting in the tail, that he might want to search our kit to see if we had brought back any contraband or messages from the working parties. I was therefore acutely embarrassed when Scarface started patting our packs in jest and asking whether they were full of ducks and geese. For an anxious five minutes I tried to get free and hustle Lovelace into the Fort, knowing that his pack was full to the brim with screws, nails, higher watt light bulbs than we were allowed, hammers, chisels and all kinds of tools supplied to us by the men at Zempelburg Sawmill.

A week later Oldorp disappeared from Stalag HQ, returning, as I heard, to a mental home.

10

Autumn 1943

5.7.43

. . . a fortnight since I last wrote, as I was on tour again . . . stayed two nights with a party of ninety men, two with one of eighteen, and four with one of sixteen, all except the large one being farming ones . . . fun to see ducks, geese, chickens, deer, wild pigs and any number of storks. I even saw Big Business do his stuff on one farm [Big Business was the bull in Stella Gibbons's *Cold Comfort Farm*] . . .

also 5.7.43

. . . interested about *'Against Oblivion',* and hope it will come through all right. [This refers to the biography of my great-grandfather, Joseph Severn, just published by Sheila Birkenhead] I find the 'Severn' in me stands me in good stead; I am often disgusted with myself for feeling so contented with my life here. I think life anywhere is interesting, even if one is not actively forwarding a world war, and all the little calamities and quarrels and disappointments we get here are so trivial com-pared with the rest of creation groaning and travailing. I feel I ought to be making myself an expert in English Literature, and yet I pass a morning away quite happily playing piano duets or letting a very self-pitying man tell me how he hears

Funeral at Garrison Friedhof, Torun

Fort XIII, Torun from the main gate

143

Doctors, Dentists and Chaplains at Stalag XXA, 1943

144

CQMS Reg Granger, BEM, Man of Confidence at
Stalag XXA, with his clerk, Rifleman Maurice Atkins,
'backed' by the Geneva Convention.

Cookhouse at Fort XIII

145

Fort XV, Torun

Midwinter crossing of the Vistula at Torun

146

Boxing at Fort XIII

Library at Fort XIII

Railway bridge at Torun destroyed
by retreating Germans

British and French medical staff at Fort XIV

The author, David Wild, at Oflag VIIC, 1941

150

his brother has been killed. I am afraid my easy-
goingness will make you bash me with a chopper
one of these days . . .

11.7.43

. . . another lovely clothing parcel, most of it as usual
designed to clothe the inner man . . . When the
colonel saw the razor blades he said that either you
were in the rackets or all the Oxford Diocesan clergy
were growing beards . . .

In the late summer I conducted a number of funerals of
British POWs in the Garrison *Friedhof* [cemetery] in Torun. At
that time the Germans permitted a party of about twenty men
to attend these services. The men selected for the funeral party
were always faultlessly turned out and took special pride in
carrying out the simple ceremony. After the service, taken in
the small cemetery chapel, the bareness of which was relieved
by some fine wreaths, six men carried the coffin, draped in a
Union Jack, to the graveside. After the committal a bugler
sounded the Last Post. With rare exceptions, the German
guards present behaved with reverence and kept well in the
background.

The graves of our men were in small groups, scattered in
various parts of the already congested extension of the
Garrison *Friedhof.* A small party of volunteer British NCOs
worked on the graves daily for several years, and kept them
beautifully. In addition to the grass and flowers that they had
planted, each grave was marked with a simple standard white-
painted wooden cross, with the names and regiments painted
in black. Such a cross marked the grave of every British or
Commonwealth soldier who died in the Stalag area, both in
the cemetery at Torun and in many village graveyards, far and
wide over the countryside. Probably eighty per cent of the
graves, more than a hundred, in the cemetery at Torun bore
the date of the winter of 1940/41, a very severe winter when
little or no clothing, food or medical supplies had been
received from home.

The care of graves at Torun and throughout the area reflected credit on all concerned. In particular, CQMS Granger took great trouble in identifying and marking graves of men who had died before he became Man of Confidence, in seeing that they were properly maintained and in ensuring that arrangements for funerals, often at short notice, were made with all the fitness that was permitted by the German authorities.

18.7.43

No letters again, fourteen days . . . One funeral, a Liverpool militia lad . . . a good book, *Wife to Mr Milton* by Robert Graves, though I hope M was not quite such a shocking cad. I am afraid that the diplomat [Italy] must be shockingly worried, but I hear that Mary H [Russia] is blooming. [Sicily had been invaded, an event which exposed a weakness in our private code. Mary had written that Mrs Macindoe had gone to prison. Her name was Cecily. I thought that she was referring to the exceedingly respectable wife of the Bursar of Eton College, and even thought of writing to him to condole]. . . . Had a misery-making complaint, a boil under the eyelid, but it burst with a vengeance on Thursday. Today I had to read the lesson about motes and beams; glad it was not last Sunday's lesson . . . two Scotsmen doing orderly for us now in place of postman Fry, one young and nice, the other not so young . . .

25.7.43

. . . I seem to be extraordinarily busy these days. By that I mean I have at least one thing to do each day. You would not believe how long one can spend as a POW preparing to do a simple thing, doing it and then talking about it afterwards. It's the way we live, and it is going to be a painful process accelerating the tempo of life again. I should not worry about the way Cressy [RAF mass bombing] is going on. I am not sympathetic, but no doubt we shall have arguments about it when I get home. I think he is right . . .

2.8.43

. . . another funeral, and Padre Lathaen had another, a young Welsh guardsman I knew well, accidentally drowned . . . pianos do not like this excessively hot weather, in spite of the attention of our expert, CSM Brinsmead, of the piano firm. Two good books, Belloc's *Path to Rome* and Lindsay's *Two Moralities* . . .

8.8.43

I kept the day [our wedding day] as suitably as possible, five years and I don't feel at all hen-pecked yet . . . One day we shall wake up and find it was real after all, and then what shall we do to redeem all this misspent time, (are there enough ss in that, and how do you spell 'ss' when you want to?) Like the man in my English class who wanted me to write on the board, 'There are three ways of spelling the word "awe" in English,' the dirty cad, in front of my English class too. . . One hundred of our NCOs are going soon, the usual saying farewell to many friends, which I always hate. But these are sad times in many ways, and I wish it would end quick . . .

In late summer and early autumn the Germans imposed a clampdown, and it was no longer possible to obtain a guard to make journeys outside the Fort. No reason was given; they had just become nervous about something, and the ban lasted until October.

24.8.43

. . . most of my visits to the hospital and elsewhere

153

have been curtailed, at least temporarily, so like anyone else I just do my daily round in the Fort . . . I have unearthed a really good baritone among the new arrivals, who not only likes singing but can read and learn quickly. I hope to spring him on an audience in a week or two. Pianos a great anxiety; we had the guts out of one today and part of the action, and then had great difficulty getting it all back again. At our last concert the E in both octaves above middle C went silent out of cussedness, and finally the loud pedal fell off. Perhaps you can send a piano in your next parcel . . . Much enjoyed Edith Olivier's *Country Moods and Tenses* . . . so many good things I long to share; it seems wasted having them to myself. . .

29.8.43

. . . much interested in your latest news about repatriation, but please do not expect to see me. I know you feel like me about it, thank God, the old 'putting the hand to the plough' business. Sept '39 and Jan '40 were bad enough, and I do not want a repetition of all that. Anyway Celia is probably right; I suppose I am being more useful here than I shall ever be again, or ever have been . . . But one question is enough for the moment, and I know you will be with me when I give my answer tomorrow . . . Two interesting books this week, both of social interest, *No Mean City,* MacArthur, not very pleasant about razor gangs in Glasgow, and *The Child and the Magistrate,* Watson, as good as his earlier one, *Meet the Prisoner,* which I read before the war . . . Soon we may see the amazing sight of a hundred storks circling over the camp . . .

5.9.43

. . . a beautiful (pocket) Communion Set from Lady

Hester Bourne, it belonged to an uncle and as executor she thought this a good place to send it. She has done magnificent work for POWs . . . Every case I send her she looks into and reports most admirably . . . Well, the old question repatriation raised its head after all. The Colonel wanted to decide between me and Lathaen, but I knew what he would say and refused . . . I refused to toss a coin, which seemed to me a poor way of choosing a vicar for Stalag XXA, smacks of simony or something. Those are the facts, my love, so you can open proceedings on grounds of desertion if you like . . .

12.9.43

. . . dull week for weather, only redeemed by reading Borrow's *Lavengro,* splendid . . . Two grim cases this week, one of a man who died here; he had done four years prison in the first war and in this one his wife ran away, leaving two children; the other's wife bolted, leaving five children scattered all over the country, the address of only two of them known; the man is only thirty-three. All the talk of this camp is of repatriation, as we have over two hundred medical personnel here and they are all on tenterhooks. I had hoped to pay another series of visits . . . but am much battened down these days and can no longer get to the hospitals. In fact we can no longer take concerts there from this camp, a pity as our bands and entertainment here are good . . .

26.9.43

I disgraced myself last Sunday and never wrote, but owing to a bit of friction and musical temperament I got landed at the last minute with accompanying the band for intermissions of a four night show. It was good fun and the show excellent, 'The Fourth Wall' by A A Milne, the best piece of acting I have seen in prison. Now I have turned playwright myself and have hashed up a show called 'Talking of Music' . . . The difficulty is to get new ideas for shows after three and a half years . . . I am doing a good deal of work with men taking exams, so not much reading on my own . . . On the other hand all my work practically at hospitals and visits to working parties is stopped now for nearly two months . . . No letter at all for one month.

2.10.43

. . . yesterday came your first for four weeks. . . Still in throes of practising for this musical do next week; going well . . . What excellent things the powder or flake eggs we get in parcels now; two tins make a fine dish of scrambled eggs for us three. We have been feeding like lords all this year with parcels coming every week; you have no idea how we appreciate the excellent service . . . We have lost our piano-tuner; Eric Williams and I, mostly he, do our pianos now. It is a ghastly job. Bach did not know what he was doing when he wrote the *Well-Tempered Klavier*. He should have tried writing the '48' for ours . . .

16.10.43

. . . an eventful week here, continual comings and goings. We have lost nearly 200 RAMC men and nearly all our Aussies, and several hundred other medical orderlies and invalids came for a night or two, all ostensibly to be repatriated. All very exciting while it lasted, but after Sept 1941 many like myself take a very cautious view and will not believe anything until news comes that they are out of the country. We are left now with very few, about a hundred NCOs and about a hundred medical orderlies from another Stalag, who came this far and are now wondering if they are going to get any

156

further, the main body having left two days ago without them, poor lads. Apart from invalids I know of no doctors or chaplains having left from anywhere; poor Lathaen is very disappointed as a month ago we were asked, as you know, for the name of one padre and assumed that he would go. We have lost our complete dance and military bands in one go; but on the night before they left we had a marvellous military band concert, twenty-eight first class players, all our own band, plus the best of those from other Stalags, who were here for the night. It was really well worth hearing. All we have left is the pianist, Eric Williams, and the double-bass and a drummer. I have had a stack of books from home, including *Against Oblivion,* a good lot for winter reading. I am hoping that I may go out on tour this week. I told at least two men who were going home to give you my love . . .

On this occasion the repatriation scheme was completed successfully, but contrary to expectation it was confined to chronic sick and did not include doctors or chaplains.

11

Autumn Trip

The unexplained security ban imposed on Fort XV in July put a temporary end to expeditions, and I was confined strictly within the Fort like everyone else. However, following representations made to Stalag HQ I resumed my fortnightly visits to the Reserve Lazarett and my twice-weekly visits to Fort XIV. Occasional walks were also again permitted for doctors, chaplains and medical orderlies.

It was late October when I was at last granted permission to go on another tour of farm working parties. I took as my bag-carrier the young pianist from the Fort, Eric Williams. We were accompanied by an unprepossessing representative of the Wehrmacht, Obergefreiter Münch, one of the censor staff. He was short, with a slight hunch-back, and had had a strange rolling stone career. At one stage of his life he had hitch-hiked around the United States in search of a fortune, as he said; but, unsuccessful in his quest, he had returned to eke out a precarious existence as a guide to foreigners in his home town of Mannheim. He was intelligent and quite well-read, but he was sly, mean and cynical, and was much disliked, not least by his own comrades. Probably owing to his failure in the States, he bitterly disliked the British. His approach was outwardly friendly and light-hearted, but he was dangerous. His command of colloquial English and troops' slang was extensive, and we had learnt that when he was joining in conversation with a group he was listening intently to the remarks of others. When he conducted searches he was more thorough and more vindictive than any other censor. He had a weakness, however, which we were to discover.

Williams, a blunt Yorkshireman, took the offensive from

the start; smartly turned out, on the two mile walk to the station, he lectured Münch on the filthiness of his uniform and boots, which was indeed remarkable, even for a German garrison soldier.

We took the train to Bromberg, and from there on the Danzig line fifteen miles to Prust. At Prust, a dreary little village in flat country, we called briefly on a small party of twelve men who worked in a flour mill. One of the men came off work and showed us the camp, where we ate a picnic lunch before moving on.

Carrying our packs, we set forth along a country road. After two miles Münch, who disliked walking, hailed a passing farmer who gave us a lift another two miles to the scattered hamlet of Brachlin. Here the British camp for about ten men consisted of two large ground-floor rooms in what had once been a pretentious small Junker farmhouse. The rest of the house was a tenement for various Polish families, all very sordid in appearance. All was dark and gloomy; a few broken cupboards and a bare table were all the furniture in the first room, which had been the front hall of the original house, and in the old dining room with its flaking, discoloured walls were five rough double-decker beds, all looking very untidy.

From one of these beds a sleepy figure scrambled to his feet; he told us that he had stayed off sick for the day. He asked the unpleasant-looking guard who had admitted us to the camp why no food had been brought to him all day. Normally where a man took his meals on a farm, if he stayed in the camp sick, someone, the guard, the farmer or another prisoner, was supposed to bring his rations from the farm to the camp. This was the guard's responsibility, but the responsibility for seeing that this was done was naturally assumed by the British camp leader. At 4 pm this man had had nothing to eat all day. Mentally registering a black mark against the camp leader, I helped the sick man to complain to the guard, who hurried off and returned soon after with food and apologies.

My first impression of the camp was confirmed by the manner of the Scottish Corporal when he came in from work. He immediately, without any prompting, started grousing about the camp, the work and everything else. Although he had known that we were coming, no arrangement had been made to fit up beds for us, nor was this done until it was dark.

159

No one made any move to help feed us, until the youngest man on the party realized the position and, taking some food that we had brought with us, heated it up and brewed us some tea. The average age of the party was higher than most, and they seemed an ill-assorted crew. The two rooms that formed the camp were larger than most parties enjoyed, but the men had done little to make themselves comfortable. They had not scrounged a decent stove to cook on, their washing arrangements were quite inadequate, and there were none of the gadgets that most camps had fitted up to make the place homely and convenient. I was cold in the night, and this upset my stomach. We were bolted into the camp without access to the latrine, and better arrangements could easily have been made to cope with such an emergency.

In the morning the surly guard took us for breakfast to the Polish farm where Münch was staying. He and the guard had breakfast in the best room while Williams and I were given ours in the kitchen. The farmer's wife was much distressed about this, and was more than usually attentive and apologetic. After breakfast we strolled over to a State farm at Lushkau, about two miles away, lying in a hollow off the main road. The estate had at one time been owned by a German baron, but in Polish times it had been some kind of settlement for young offenders. With the return of the Germans in 1939, the young baron had resumed possession; but he was away in Russia as a war artist or correspondent, we were told. We did, however, see his old mother, a distinguished-looking Junker lady, walking with two lovely dogs. The mansion stood in the middle of a large wood of magnificent hardwood trees. On the outskirts lay the farm, the usual large quadrangle of buildings with a schnapps factory in the middle. We looked around the outbuildings and eventually found a wiry, small Englishman in the pig sties. When he saw me he grinned broadly and, standing in a pig sty he held a muck-rake in one hand and saluted smartly with the other. We talked briefly and he directed us to the camp – one large room for about eighteen men, although half underground, it was nevertheless an attractive *lager*. The guard, a decent, elderly, fatherly Saxon, showed it all off with obvious pride, the clean whitewashed walls, the tidy beds, the well-arranged cupboards and shelves, and the well-scrubbed tables and forms. I discussed with him some possible improvements, and he showed by his interest that he was really keen that the men should be comfortable.

We returned to the farm where we had breakfasted, and found that the Polish dame had boldly promoted us to eat in the second best room. After lunch I told Münch that I would like to take a walk, and led him by a route that I had been told would take us to a clearing in a wood where a number of Poles had been buried after being massacred by the baron when he returned to his inheritance in 1939. Walking with Münch was always a trying business; whenever he met a woman or found women working in a field he would try to engage them in conversation, in spite of the fact that most of them, being Polish, obviously resented his approaches. On the way back to Brachlin he said that the women of that area had no *Kultur;* in Germany, he said, a girl would always reply to his greeting, 'Good morning', but here they did not. When I said they probably only said it when they meant it, he asked why Poles should not want to greet him.

'While you were pestering those girls working in the fields,' I said, 'Williams and I were talking to another slave labourer, a pretty thirteen-year-old girl. She grubs weeds on her hands and knees seven days a week for the Germans. Only when work is slack can she go to school, and then she is only allowed one hour a week. Perhaps that is one reason why they don't say Good Morning.'

'We won't talk politics,' replied Münch.

I had a long talk that afternoon with the farmer at Lushkau. He was a Bessarabian, one of the many thousands of German origin brought back during the war to live once more within the frontiers of the Great Reich. They were given farms of varied sizes from which Poles had been displaced. Our men, many of whom were made to work for them, found them worse than any other employers, German or Polish. They observed all the Nazi regulations with exaggerated care, while their own standards of living were deplorably low. The Lushkau farmer was an exception; the son of a schoolmaster, he was obviously well-educated and cultured, and talked to me on a wide range of subjects, such as the Latin origin of the Romanian language. He had a good reputation as a considerate employer among our men who worked for

161

him.

Back at Brachlin we had an early supper on Münch's farm – this time in the best room – before returning to Lushkau. The men were all back from work when we arrived, and we found them a lively, cheerful crowd, just what our morning view of their camp had led me to expect. To my horror, after a pleasant service, two plates, loaded with fried eggs, bacon, Spam and a vast pile of potatoes were produced for Williams and myself. We had already had three farm meals that day, and at 9 pm this was a bit daunting. But the men of Lushkau stood around us and urged us to get to it; so to it we got. It was hard going, and even Williams, a good trencherman, had to admit defeat from the potatoes. At least we managed not to insult such grand hospitality.

Shortly before ten o'clock Münch arrived with the old guard, to bring a cheerful evening to an end and take us back to Brachlin. As I turned in the doorway to say goodbye, the senior soldier – there was no NCO – called the whole party smartly to attention. It was a moving gesture from these men in the little cellar where they had lived as prisoners for two and a half years. Even Münch was impressed.

The next day, Sunday, we took the morning easy, but later walked two miles to the next village, Gem Waldau, where we found eighteen men occupying the whole of a three-roomed cottage. It seemed a tight fit, but they had everything well under control. Quite a few of the men were out on part-time Sunday work, which always caused dissatisfaction, and they were not in a very good mood. But we had a pleasant visit and a good service, after which quite a few men shared Holy Communion. Two of the younger lads took us to lunch at the Ortsbauführer's farm where they worked. His wife was clearly far from pleased, and while Münch fed in the dining room, Williams and I were sent to the kitchen. I preferred this arrangement, and we had a cheerful meal with the two young men and a bashful Polish *'dienstmädchen'*. One of the men was from Stornoway and spoke with a delightful Hebridean accent, reputed to be the best diction in the British Isles.

A five or six mile walk faced us in the afternoon across a dreary agricultural plateau to the village of ~~Hasenau; it was a~~ longer walk than I had anticipated, and left us with less than two hours there. The *lager* was a reasonable enough building

162

for the sixteen or so men employed there. They gave us tea and we had a short service, but we never really broke the ice there, or at Gem Waldau. I was struck that day how tedious was the life of these small farm parties on a Sunday. They cleaned the camp and repaired their clothing and camp gadgets, and then they just sat around or slept in the camp or the tiny compound. The number of books supplied to these camps by the Stalag central library was small and the quality poor (I always thought that more of the better books could have been spared from the large libraries at Forts XIII and XV), and even when a man had some decent books sent to him from home, he could not carry many in his kit when he was transferred from one camp to another. Some of the men were as much as four years in one small camp, two hundred Sundays. In the eight winter months, with no illumination except two carbide jets or inefficient paraffin lamps, it must have been unbearably depressing.

Our long walk back to Brachlin was tiring, mostly in the dark, and we lost our way more than once. When we entered the camp, as appeared to be usual there, there was a first-class argument in progress. We had a short service, and I tried afterwards to say some pretty direct things about their way of life. I doubt if it did much good; I was too tired to be coherent, and I think that most of the trouble was due to a few incurable idlers and grousers, like the corporal. There were a few good men there: the young man who did most to make us comfortable, another fellow, Herd by name, son, I think, of the great Sandy Herd, the golfer, and a real straight honest Oxfordshire countryman, whose accent carried me right home.

It was exciting in this district to hear stories of the activities of Polish partisans. Barefaced robbery of livestock had occurred on a number of farms where our men worked, and evidently the partisans were in force in the neighbouring forests. German soldiers and civilians had been attacked on roads at night, and some had been stripped of their uniforms.

On Monday morning Münch came for us, and he was relieved when we acquired a ride to Prust on a load of potatoes being driven by one of our Lushkau lads. The small camp in a mill at Lushkau was one of the best. On the first floor above outhouses in the mill yard, it consisted of a landing and four rooms, kitchen, eating room and two bedrooms for twelve men. It was clean, well fitted-up with racks, shelves and cupboards, and very comfortable. The ablution place on the landing was better than most. The men, a young and pretty tough crew, had settled down well together and seemed to have things well under control under their camp leader, a Lancashire man, Gunner Birch. The boss of the timber and flour mill was an immense German, Herr Schmidt, who used his monopoly of flour and wood to wield considerable power in the neighbourhood. At first he had tried bullying the British prisoners; but one man had ended a contretemps by seizing him by the collar and dragging him, in front of Poles and other prisoners, the whole length of his own timber yard to the German guard. Since then he had come to treat the prisoners with respect and, what was more surprising, with a kind of rough affection and admiration. More like a huge beast than a man, he would appear in the yard roaring like a bull at some poor Polish worker; our men would roar back from the *lager* window, imitating him to perfection. He would either ignore them or just utter a coarse hearty laugh. Some months after my visit, when Birch, who had fought and mocked him for two years or more, came into our hospital for a long stay, he received several letters from Herr Schmidt, contrary to all regulations, asking him how he was and when he would be able to come back to work.

At Prust we had a spot of bother with Münch. Our next destination could be reached by one short train journey. Münch insisted that we must go via Torun, which was like going round three sides of a square. At one point in the argument I thought that the Prust lads were about to throw Münch out of the window, but he prudently withdrew. In the afternoon there was a visit from the Kontrol Feldwebel, to whom I explained the situation. Herr Schmidt and the local guard, a decent fellow and a barrister by profession, backed me up and the Feldwebel said, 'Where is he staying? I'll soon fix him.' He did, and next morning a much-chastened Münch arrived and took us meekly to the train we wanted.

Our destination was Dragas, a small village lying on a flat plain below the west escarpment of the river Vistula opposite the city of Graudenz. At Dragas we left the train and took a road that ran beside the immense dyke. True to form, Münch soon tired of walking and hailed a passing farm cart. He sat with the driver in front while Williams and I stood behind, swaying perilously, or sat on the low sides in extreme discomfort. Travelling in an unsprung hard-wheeled vehicle on a cobbled road is an agonising experience. Five kilometres on, we very willingly dismounted, in the small village of Gros Lubin, where we found the British camp across one field from the main road. It occupied the whole of an attractive, well-built thatched cottage, surrounded by a small barbed wire compound. It contained three light, cheerful and not over-crowded rooms. Finding no one at home, Williams and I ferreted around and found the wherewithal to make a fire and brew a cup of tea. To this and some food we had brought with us, we summoned Münch who had not spoken all day and had sat gloomily in another room since our arrival. He thawed a bit at the sight of food, and later, when he had gone out to find the guard, Williams told me what had been happening.

Apparently Münch had cornered Williams and asked him why I had reported him to the Kontrol Feldwebel. The Feldwebel had given him a terrific dressing-down, and among other things had reprimanded him for his disgusting appearance and filthy boots. He had also told him that if he gave me any more trouble he would put in a report about him to Stalag. Münch asked Williams if I would forget the incident, but Williams had replied, 'Certainly not. The last guard who gave trouble to a British chaplain was given fourteen days bunker arrest.'

We had no more trouble from Münch. In fact he went out of his way to ensure that I saw as much as possible of the men at the parties we visited subsequently. He also borrowed Williams's boot polish and cleaned his boots at least once during the next four days.

Corporal K, in charge of the camp, arrived and said that he would arrange for us to have supper and breakfast on a neighbouring farm. He was a young Irish corporal, lively, energetic and talkative, who obviously had his camp well in hand and efficiently run.

In the afternoon, as all the men were at work, we walked two kilometres along the Nowe road to Gros Sanskau to tell the party there that we would like to visit them the next day and stay a night. There was something about the exterior view of the camp that suggested that it would be better not to go in and have a look round. On the way back to Gros Lubin we stopped to look at the farm where Cpl K worked for the Ortsbauführer. While I was talking to the corporal, the Ortsbauführer, a dapper, middle-aged German, came up to speak with Münch. He was obviously embarrassed and uncertain how to behave with an English officer, and kept fidgeting with his hand backwards and forwards. Eventually I shook it, just to see what would happen. He looked much relieved and altogether more comfortable.

Our supper was a mean affair, a poor milk soup, eaten at a table in a back passage of the farm to which we were sent. The farm family were particularly mean Germans who treated the Englishman who worked there very poorly. Back in the camp, however, we discovered that conditions at Gros Lubin were pretty good on the whole, and certainly the camp was lively enough and the men a well-assorted crew. I am sure that the personality of Cpl K was the chief factor in the success of the camp. Even the two rather inexperienced guards seemed to depend entirely on his judgment. During the evening, one or other of them came in at least six times to ask him about some order that they had received, how it should be carried out, or what answer they should give to the Kontrol Feldwebel when he came round. We had a good night at this camp and managed to deal with several useful pieces of family business with the men.

Next morning we carried on early to Sanskau. Immediately on our arrival, the younger of the two guards in charge insisted on taking me inside and showing me round the three large rooms where some thirty men were billeted. He rushed about, lifting up mattresses and exhibiting dirty clothes underneath, opening lockers and producing mouldy food and unwashed utensils. The word 'Schweinerei' was freely used. I was glad to get an idea how things were, but I would have preferred to look around on my own without a German demonstrating it in all its shame.

When he had gone, I looked closer into the mess. On a verandah exposed to the elements I found a gramophone, a gift from the YMCA, in working order – few parties were lucky enough to have one – and a quantity of Red Cross dressings, which should have been kept in a proper medicine chest.

When I had seen enough I went upstairs to see the German Unteroffizier, a middle-aged lazy sort of bloke. I asked him to bring the British sergeant in from work immediately after lunch. When he asked why, I said the camp was far below the standard of other British camps, and I wished to tell him so before the rest of the men came in from work. He asked, 'Why the sergeant? The corporal is in charge.' I replied that I did not know what the arrangement was in that camp, but that it was not usual for a sergeant to be working under a corporal, and that I would only do business through the sergeant. He agreed that the situation was unusual, and said that he would fetch the sergeant in after lunch.

The younger guard came to take me and Williams out to lunch. He said that he had arranged to take us to two different farms and that he had told both that they would be entertaining a British chaplain and he hoped that Williams would play his part. As Williams looked rather less than his twenty-one years, I did not think that he would find it easy. I was left at a very small, neat, thatched farmhouse right under the towering bank of the dyke. My hostess, the eldest of three Frauleins Schmidt, a delightful old lady, farmed thirty acres with the assistance of one POW. She said that they were descended from a Dutch family, one of many that had come there a hundred years before to build the dyke. She was a Protestant, and said that many of these families had stayed on and that there were still a number of such Protestant families to be found between Sanskau and Nowe.

The farmhouse was spotlessly clean, and the parlour had walls and ceiling panelled with a light-coloured wood, all highly polished. It was a lovely experience to sit in this charming parlour conversing with this friendly, cultured old lady. She talked largely about religious matters, and asked many questions about the various denominations of churches in England. She also spoke with great sympathy about the various English prisoners who had worked for her. I heard later that she was a model employer.

When Williams returned, I asked anxiously how he had fared; Fraulein Schmidt's conversation would have floored him badly. Apparently, however, his hosts had been less ecclesiastically-minded and, apart from remarking on his youth and showing him the family Bible, they had caused him no embarrassment.

Returning to the camp, I found Sgt D waiting for me, an unimpressive, middle-aged man. I showed him some of the worst features of the camp and asked him to account for it. He said that originally he had been in charge of the camp, but had found the men too difficult to manage. I pointed out to him that he was wearing three stripes and was being paid as a sergeant; he had two courses open to him, to take charge of the camp and run it properly, or ask the Germans to send him to Fort XV as a *non-arbeiter*. In no circumstances should he remain there working for the Germans as a common labourer. He said that he was prepared to stay and assume responsibility for the camp again.

Though there was little chance of seeing the men at Montau, four kilometres further on the road to Nowe, I thought at least I would visit their camp as my time was running short. So we walked there after this interview and luckily found that four of the eighteen men were in the camp, 'light sick'. The camp, four small rooms, was the whole of a single-storey cottage and made a favourable impression. Camps always seemed better, cleaner, healthier and more contented when the men were not all together in one room. Montau was a good example, and I felt that morale there was high.

It was dark when we walked back to Sanskau, and we arrived just as twelve men from a second camp at Sanskau were coming into the camp to spend the evening with us. The difference between the men of these two camps was plain to see; the men of the large camp were under the weather, ill-disciplined and quarrelsome, while the men from the smaller camp were cheerful and well turned-out, even though they had been at work an hour earlier. I was particularly impressed with the young Lance-Corporal in charge of them, a bandsman in the Duke of Wellington's.

Before getting the men together, I explained to the corporal of the first camp, a Manchester policeman and a tougher, smarter man than Sergeant D, that so long as D was there he must be in charge, and he appeared to agree. Then, asking the men from the smaller camp to excuse any remarks of mine that might seem unfair to them, I pitched into the others really hard. I told them that when I arrived that morning they had had twenty-four hours warning of my visit. In spite of that, I had found the place filthy, more like a Russian or French camp. They were a hard-bitten crew, and it took time to make an impression. But in the end I hit the mark when I spoke of the Red Cross supplies and comforts that I had found rotting away on the verandah, and the filth of their latrine, the cleanliness of which I had found to be as good a test of camps that I had visited as any other. When I asked for comments, there were truculent sallies from a few men, but on the whole they seemed to accept the justice of my comments, and most of them clearly did not resent them. At least the atmosphere of the service with which we closed this unpleasant business made me feel that they might have appreciated some of the more constructive advice which I had given them. An occasional 'strafe' of this kind did no harm, and word of it got around. Nearly a year later in a camp many miles away, a man said to me, 'Was it you who chewed up Sanskau?' A few months later Sgt D chucked up his job and came into Fort XV; he told me that they had cleaned up and whitewashed the camp; but I do not think that the morale of the camp improved much. There were too many poor types there, who, as I saw a year later, made the efforts of the better ones ineffective and discouraged any raising of standards.

Next morning Williams and I were given an excellent breakfast by the farmer's wife, who lived in the other half of the building that contained the camp. Although a Bessarabian family, she and her husband, and the children struck me as pleasant, well-educated people, and unusually natural and kind. Before leaving the camp I went upstairs again to have another talk with the lazy old Unteroffizier in his room, which he never seemed to leave, allowing the officious young Gefreiter to run the camp. As usual, attack seemed to be the best means of defence, so I told him that, while I thought the British in the camp had fallen short of acceptable standards, I was sure that he could do a lot more than he was doing to encourage cleanliness. I also said that all the men complained that the Gefreiter was always contradicting his orders and that there could be no good discipline as long as there was dual control. I myself had seen evidence to confirm what the men had told me, that the Gefreiter was unbalanced, probably as

169

the result of a head wound, and that he had threatened men with his rifle. The Unteroffizier admitted that the Gefreiter had a metal plate in his scalp, and was possibly not fit to carry arms. I told him that, if he thought that, it was his duty to report it to his superior officer, and I warned him that he could be held responsible if any serious incident occurred as a consequence of the Gefreiter's condition. He took the whole of my tirade like a lamb, but I think he was an incurable sluggard, all for the quiet life.

A Northumbrian lad from Morpeth produced a four-seater carriage and an aged horse to take us on our way to Nowe. A mile from the camp we turned off to have a glance at the subsidiary Sanskau camp just under the dyke. As I expected, from what I had seen of the men the night before, it was a clean, tidy, well-appointed camp in a thatched cottage. Only one man was in, and I asked him to congratulate the others on their high standards.

We drove along the main road past Montau and stopped to look at the camp at Treul, where about sixteen men lived in one large room of what had once been the village school. The camp was well-kept, and the men evidently were musical. A variety of instruments in the room included a very old instrument, something between a piano and a harpsichord, which was in surprisingly good condition and had been bought by the men from the local pub. Was it a forte piano? In a field near the camp I stopped the carriage and had a word with a fine-looking corporal of the East Surreys. He turned out to be a nephew of my old Eton tutor, A B Ramsay, the Master of Magdalene College.

The road to Nowe ran through flat farming country; this was fortunate, as our horse showed increasing signs of collapse and a strong reluctance to continue. Towards Nowe the escarpment came closer and closer to the river, and the road rose sharply from the plain up a long steep hill into the town. This was clearly too much for our ancient horse, so we dismounted and, saying goodbye to our Morpeth friend, climbed the steep slope to a camp at Gut Konschütz, a camp that I had visited previously for a funeral.

When we arrived the men were just coming in from work for their dinner, and we had our meal, as on my previous visit, alone with the elderly Highlander, Sgt Mac, in the inner room.

Somehow I became aware that there was a feeling of tension in this camp which had previously seemed so harmonious. After the men had returned to work, one man who was sick stayed in with us, and after a short while asked if he could speak with me alone. He told me that a difficult situation had arisen. Mac had become very irritable, and resented any request from the men to make complaints to the Germans on their behalf about food, work conditions and so on. He said that they 'ought to be thankful and content with what the Lord provided.' When pressed, he had lost his temper and twice struck my informant.

Later in the afternoon I walked with Münch and Williams to a newly formed working party at a sawmill in Nowe itself. The men were all old members of the former 'P' (pioneer) hut-building party of skilled tradesmen who had been stationed at Fort XIII in Torun. Their very small camp of three rooms was in the yard of the sawmill, and showed every sign of being inhabited by skilled craftsmen; it was beautifully fitted up, with all kinds of new shelves and cupboards. I had a look round the yard where the men worked; though employed only on unskilled work, all of them knew far more about the work going on than their German and Polish bosses. One man, who at home was the highly skilled Clerk of the Works at Winchester Cathedral, had nothing to do but carry planks about the yard. When they had finished work we had a splendid tea and a very cheerful service. These men had little to learn about making themselves comfortable and handling their employers.

It was dark when we returned to Konschütz, and in the tiny camp I had no chance to talk with Mac on his own. Consequently the feeling of strain persisted throughout the evening, particularly since the rest of the men clearly knew that I had been told of the position, and no doubt expected me to say something. All that was possible was a hurried word with Mac before I left next morning. I told him that the men did not think he was fighting their corner with the Germans, that he was said to resent legitimate grievances being aired, and that he was said to have struck one of the men. He hotly denied this. I told him that I admired what he had done in the past for these young men and could probably do again; but he had not their confidence as camp leader. He ought to talk the

171

whole thing over that night, without recriminations, and find out if they wanted him to stay or not. If not, he ought to apply to the Germans to let him come to Fort XV as a *'non-arbeiter'*. Anyway, I said, he must report to me through CQMS Granger, the Stalag Man of Confidence, on the result of his conversation with the men when he paid his next routine visit to Stalag the next week. I also said that I would have to mention the alleged striking offence to Colonel Mackay, the Senior British Officer in the Stalag.

We left early in the morning, and had an uneventful train journey back to Torun via Hardenburg, Lassewitz and Graudenz. On parting I told Münch that I would withhold my complaints in view of his improved conduct! This paid off; on subsequent journeys, Padre Lathaen and I both found him useful, and slack in his supervision of our activities.

Colonel Mackay interviewed Mac the following week at Stalag HQ and was satisfied that Mac realized the serious view taken of his conduct. Evidently the men had settled their differences with him and asked him to stay. Some months later I again encountered my informant, who told me that Gut Konschütz was once more a happy camp. I was glad, because Mac, though he could be terrifyingly austere, was a thoroughly good type of Highlander, who really concerned himself for the men in his care.

After this tour Padre Lathaen and I agreed that such journeys in the winter months, largely on foot, were too severe. Instead we asked the Germans to allow us each to spend a weekend at one of the larger camps once a month until the spring. This was granted.

12

Winter 1943

31.10.43

. . . Life is very quiet here now, not to say deadly,
with only about 100 men left. I have been away for a
week, visiting farm parties . . . most of the men work
all day separately on farms, and, in consequence, in
the evening they discuss their work, using German
words for everything. It is funny to hear them. Some
have quite genuinely forgotten, if they ever knew,
the English names for implements, crops, animals,
farm buildings, vehicles etc. . . . I had the pleasure of
playing, for a week only, for the first time with a
really good violin player . . .

7.11.43

. . . we had our first hard frost. At this time of year I
feel like someone navigating gingerly up an estuary
full of shoals, hoping to get well up before one feels
the keel grate on something seriously. So here we
nose our way through the early weeks of winter,
hoping not to bump into the really cold spells until
we have got some way through. Last year we came
through without touching bottom once. But with
good clothing and plenty of Red Cross it is not like
the first winter when I wore my boots right through
to my socks and was still wearing my old Belgian
breeches . . . today the beginning of my third year in

this camp, a longer stretch than I have done in any one house since 1918. But I doubt if I shall decide to buy it; I don't feel entirely suited . . . I wonder if, when I get home, I shall keep looking out of the window to see if the guard has been changed . . .

In November I had a pleasant three day visit to Schülitz, where I stayed at Camp 48. I again took Pte Williams with me, because both Camps 48 and 129 at Schülitz had pianos, and I knew that he would give them really good concerts. In fact, both kept him at the piano for hours, and at 48 they even danced one night . . .

15.11.43

. . . I went berserk last Monday and played my first game of rugby for, I think, seven years. Good fun, but was I stiff next day? I have lost another molar . . . I am practising with a new singer; he has not sung for three years and his voice at the moment is not quite what he thought and told me that it was; so he goes all temperamental, tears up his words, throws them on the ground and sits down with his head in his hands, moaning – all rather exciting; must be what they call barbed wire fever . . .

21.11.43

. . . have finished Vol 2 of *War and Peace,* one more to go. It rejoices my heart to see the glamour taken out of Napoleon . . . I like to see history written in terms of misery, perfidy, tragedy, cruelty and the fear that war brings. It is a crime to portray it otherwise. You are going to find me a funny mess when I get out. For twelve months, the year in which more than any before in my life I have needed a 'chopping block' on which to hammer out hundreds of new ideas and ideals, I have had no one, no one at all, and they are

174

all left teeming inside. I do not know what I want to do, or be, or anything, always excepting . . .

28.11.43

. . . I do not think there is a single subject on which we [I and my room mates] agree, but I have given up arguing; it does no good and only makes me angry, and anyway I am just a 'young pup' . . . I hope by now one of those repatriated see you . . . I can just imagine what they feel like being home . . .

5.12.43

. . . There is a new system of sending home savings; living in a camp in which hardly anyone except me is paid I have not saved much, but, as a token of esteem and what all, I have sent you £50 for your own self . . . the only present I have sent you in three and three-quarter years . . .

12.12.43

I have been in the doldrums spiritually for the last few months; I know why, perfectly. By no stretch of the imagination can I claim to be in love and charity with all men in these trying circumstances, and this tension seems to affect my whole outlook on life. Ultimately I fancy the cause is Pride, but the cure is hard to find. I am busy hunting for it in Burton's *Anatomy of Melancholy*. The most helpful lines, seeing that 'moderate Venus' is not available at the moment, are 'rectifying evacuations', 'purging upwards', 'purging downwards', and 'aid of the saints'. But there are others if these don't work . . . Where will you be for Christmas? It is a strange time in wartime. One thing only makes sense for me about it, that is that what we are doing and have been doing for four years is in the end going to be the foundation of better things for a greater number of people . . .

19.12.43

. . . Having failed at the first attempt we have raised a small choir for Christmas and are hard at work trying to learn carols. I am horrified at the small number of Englishmen who can either read music or hold a part. But the practices are fun and they are all very keen. The Christmas parcels have arrived . . . we can hardly speak of the rigours of POW life; I expect that those repatriated exploded that idea anyway. I hope so, though Fred Parslow can tell as good a hardship story as anyone I know . . .

The December visit of the Swiss Protecting Power confirmed rumours that Herr Achentaler had lost his job. We were aware that he had found it increasingly difficult to restrain himself in dealing with German obstructiveness and prevarication, and an undiplomatic comment made on his last visit had been reported to Berlin by our Stalag Commandant, Oberst Kokail. The Swiss were asked to withdraw him from the job, and substituted a Herr Braun, who was disappointingly irresolute in presenting our case to the German authorities. Unlike Achentaler, he was always aiming for a compromise, a game at which we were more adept than he.

27.12.43

. . . Another Christmas come and gone . . . services at three camps in the morning with a twenty minute walk between each . . . a real white Christmas . . . Only one sad note; news had just reached us of the death in a mental hospital of young Alan Dickinson, a civilian in the Friends' Ambulance Unit, which

went to Finland, Norway, Egypt via Russia and
Greece before ending up here . . . he ran our library,
until he had a mental breakdown in August. A very
sensitive, over-scrupulous, conscientious fellow,
very kind and gentle, and much respected and liked
here . . . I got your 12 Nov on Christmas Eve, which
put the crown on a good weekend . . . how much the
only thing that matters each day is what the postman
brings me from my love. He owes me a lot at the
moment, as yours does you . . .

It was a long journey to take Alan's funeral. I took with me
our new Camp Leader, BSM Rogers, and Sgt Dowling of the
Rifle Brigade. We left with Münch at 4.30 am and after two
changes of train and a three hour wait at Bromberg, we
reached Preussich Stargard well up the line towards Danzig at
2 pm. It was a mile walk from there to the enormous asylum at
Konradstein, and when we arrived I found that the burial
service had been taken already by a chaplain from Stalag XXB.
I was, however, in time to say a few words to the small Guard
of Honour of men from Stargard camp, telling them what
manner of man it was that they had just buried, a Quaker
conscientious objector, who by his devoted service in an
Ambulance Unit from Finland to Greece, and in Poland
among his fellow prisoners, had won honour, respect and
gratitude from hundreds of British and Commonwealth
soldiers. I also spoke with a pathetic small group of British
mental patients who had been brought to the service. I have
often wondered whether any of them survived their incarceration in that dismal place.
    I had to see the asylum authorities about Alan's effects, and
while we waited for various formalities to be completed, I had
some talk with a Polish male nurse, who told me something of
the appalling conditions in the hospital. Food, he said, was in
very short supply, and I noticed in the register that I had to
sign that there was a death rate of three to five inmates
daily.
    As there was no train to Torun until morning, Münch took
us to a British camp at Stargard. It was a large camp from
which 120 men went to work in jobs all over the town. A

177

strong, competent Cpl Macintyre of the RAOC was in charge. During the evening he took me to a recreation hut, where twenty of our lads who had done a strenuous day's work were engaged in an even more strenuous physical drill and sparring under a middle-aged corporal. They were the fittest POWs I ever saw, including three cheerful lads from my own battalion. Macintyre told me that the civil population were a particularly fine, intractable type of Pole, and that they had done a great deal for our men.

We left the camp for a train at 8 am, a very slow train which shunted three or four times at every station, and at Schmentau we found that we had a five hour wait. As we sat in the dreary station buffet, through the window I saw a British POW driving past in a farm cart. I had not realized that there was a party so far up the Danzig line. Münch enquired, and found that there was a party only two kilometres away.

We started to walk there, but close to the station Münch, who hated walking, waylaid a carriage and pair driven by a young girl, which was going in our direction. She stopped and we climbed on board. Münch, needless to say, sat in the back with the girl, while Rogers, Dowling and I sat in front, Rogers, a gunner of twenty-one years service, taking the reins. The horses were fresh and Rogers took us along at a spanking pace, which did not slacken at all when we left the main road and followed a gently rising track. We were approaching a deep valley and suddenly found the track at an end and a precipitous slope falling away under the horses' noses. I was half out of the vehicle when Rogers, thoroughly enjoying it all, pulled the horses up on the edge of the abyss.

We dismounted, thanked the girl and walked on down into the valley which ran between wooded hills. On the farther slope we came to a group of cottages clustered round what was obviously a large State Farm. In the middle of the group we found the *lager* and about twenty of our men coming in for their lunch. They were surprised to see us such a long way from Stalag, and the guard was reluctant to let us in without a pass. I found that he had the Kontrol Feldwebel in his quarters on a visit, and when I explained to him how we came to be there, he agreed to our meeting the men.

They turned out to be a good party under a L-Cpl of the KRRC. I had met most of them before when they were in Fort

XV one Christmas, after a large camp at Schlusselmühle had been closed. I was particularly pleased on this occasion to find the camp a model of cleanliness and tidiness. I had often sung the praises of the small farm parties to seasoned old soldiers like Rogers and Dowling at Fort XV, and had my eulogies received with polite scepticism. Here was confirmation in convincing form, no advance warning of our visit having been given. The hospitality of this camp was a worthy example of the type. They would not let us touch the soup they were having, but, breaking into their Red Cross reserves, served us with a special meal. After lunch their guard allowed them to stay in while we talked and had a short service; and when they went back to work, the lance corporal was allowed to remain with us until it was time for us to leave.

The trains to Bromberg and then on to Torun were very crowded, and after a twenty minute walk through the snow to Fort XV I was very tired. There was so much interest in such journeys that a thirty-six hour absence from the Fort seemed more like a week, and our small diet, ample for pottering around the camp, hardly provided us with sufficient energy to cope with the extra exertion and mental excitement of such journeys. It is also worth remembering that the temperature at that time of year was usually about minus ten degrees centigrade, and often much lower.

On New Year's Eve a successful fancy dress party was held in our recreation room at Fort XV. A diversion occurred when Scarface entering the room, was confronted by a man convincingly made up as Adolf Hitler in SA uniform. He went straight up to him and pulled his nose, saying that he had wanted to do that for a long time.

Seeing in the New Year on an excellent bottle of illicit champagne produced by a Scottish sergeant did not produce our release within the next twelve months, but the atmosphere within the camp was good; there was plenty of food and drink and plenty of hilarity, but there was no drunkenness and no unpleasant rowdiness. Everyone seemed to be soberly wishing everyone else better times in the coming twelve months.

[It was a strange fact that the quality of wine consumed at our Christmas celebrations improved from Christmas to Christmas. In 1944 we drank French wine of the highest quality. We

179

bought it off a guard who, when pressed, explained how he obtained it. Wine of this quality was being sent from France, where the Germans requisitioned it to bolster the morale of their army, languishing on the frozen Russian steppes. In the railway sidings at Torun, just down the road from our camp, Poles cut their way into trucks, extracted cases of wine and spirited it away to a village several kilometres from Torun. Our guard had to bicycle out to the village in his off time, bargain with the Poles and then bring back his loot to the Fort, where he flogged it to us.]

2.1.44

Once again a very, very Happy New Year and pray God I may be able to share some part of it with you . . . So glad you got some of my letters at last. Sorry about your 'daily'; there are going to be some ugly days of reckoning after this is over, though I often feel sorry for some of the girls who have tripped up. Some of the letters men write from here in a bad mood are enough to make anyone revolt . . .

9.1.44

. . . I am alone now with Col Mackay, the Polish officer having gone after a long stay of seventeen months. [He had escaped, and reached England with RSM Hawtin of the Oxf. and Bucks.] He was a wonderful room companion in spite of our language difficulty. By many accounts coming from letters of those who reached home they seem to have had an astounding reception and a great time; you have no idea how pleased everyone here was to hear of it, not that anyone here had grounds for thinking POWs had been forgotten, far from it, but it was lovely to hear what had been done for them. I find it hard to imagine what it must feel like to be free again, to sit and be able to talk without having to think twice . . . What a day! Where would we begin? . . .

Early in January I spent three nights at a hitherto unvisited camp of about ninety men at Strasburg (Brodnice). On the station platform at Torun we saw the all too common sight of a group of about fifty cowed-looking civilians under arrest, men and women, some well-dressed, others not, under a strong police guard, no doubt on their way to some prison. We supposed that they were Poles or Jews, but we did no know that their probable destination was a gas chamber.

Strasburg was not a very happy camp. Some of the men worked for the municipality in jobs that produced plenty of rackets, and were anyway well led by a splendidly enterprising and energetic Lance-Corporal Macnee, a cheeky card who feared no man and could get away with anything. The other half worked loading and unloading stores of all kinds at the railway yard, hard work and irregular hours, as the authorities, urged on by the new *'Räder müssen rollen für den Sieg'* (Wheels must keep rolling for victory) campaign, insisted that trucks must be dealt with at whatever hour of day or night they arrived. Things might have been improved under a better Camp Leader, but the sergeant in charge was weak and ineffective. He was not at all happy about my visit. The German in charge was no better; on my arrival he tried to persuade me that the Bible said it was our duty to persecute the Jews. I asked him to fetch his Bible and show me the relevant passages, but when he could not turn any up he assured me that they were there all right.

There were some good men there. I remember Jack Parris, a Cockney of unbounded good humour. The story he told of his enlistment was that he and a friend had gone to a recruiting office with the intention of joining a cavalry regiment. They ran a finger down the list of regiments on the wall and decided on the Seaforth H, which they interpreted as Seaforth Horse. 'The next I knowed,' he said, 'we was walking down the Old Kent Road in a kilt.'

A rather pathetic creature was a pleasant young Cypriot who showed me two letters from his home, one written in Greek, the other in Turkish, neither of which he could read. I could make some sense of the former, and by reading aloud the words as they were written in Greek I appeared to convey to him the sense of the rest. I also read out to him the Turkish letter, as it was written, and to my surprise, after each sentence

181

his face lit up in a huge smile and he told me the meaning of what I had been reading without any comprehension. On my return to Stalag, I arranged that all letters for this man should be intercepted and translated by a more literate Cypriot in Fort XIII.

By coincidence, at the next camp that I visited I was to find another problem Camp Leader, a CSM in a well-known regiment. A magnificent looking man, I imagine he was an impressive and thoroughly efficient Warrant Officer back in England, but interested primarily in one thing, impressing his officers with his appearance and efficiency. Unfortunately, in prison the German authorities took the place of his officers at home. The camps that he ran were by all accounts models of efficiency, but though the men in these camps benefited from his efficiency, they abhorred the way he had to cut a figure with the Germans.

In the camp where I had gone to take a funeral, he was in charge of thirty men doing odd jobs in some large barracks. The CSM was in his element. Looking very smart and impressive, he circulated around the campus, ostensibly supervising the men under his command, but giving ostentatious salutes to anything in field grey he could see or be seen by. Before the funeral he insisted on taking me to the office of the German colonel, 'My Commandant,' he said, 'an awfully good fellow.' Whether this was to show me off to the colonel or him to me was not clear, but I could have done without the encounter. It was all harmless vanity, but in spite of all the good things he had done for the men under him, they did not like it, and I could easily understand why. It was uncharacteristic among the British Camp Leaders elsewhere.

16.1.44

. . . your 25 Nov telling of seeing Sgt Perkins, [a repatriee], bless 'is 'eart, a very decent lad. So you did get some first-hand news . . . I expect you find such interviews worth dozens of these wretched letters. I wish you could send someone out here to recipro-cate, though I cannot recommend coming yourself; you would be miserable at the endless inactivity, though I could supply you with two months' sock darning to start with. Tony Egan [also repatriated] seems to have done his stuff by us most conscientiously, even to the extent of taking out Capt Macmillan's girl friend to the Café Royal. Poor Mac's suspicions were hardly allayed by Egan saying, 'Needless to say we talked of you most of the time.' . . .

30.1.44

. . . glad to hear about Cyril [News of him in prison in Singapore had reached Celia, his wife], a small mercy, but one for which she must be very glad, because I know from medical journals here how terribly bad conditions are for many of them. Our life must be paradise to theirs, poor fellows. I had a considerable sweat getting together a talk I gave at the chief camp on Education in England after the War. Fortunately I had the White Paper and books like Livingstone's *Education for a World Adrift* . . . Last night we started a new series of Sunday night concerts. Our vocalist failed at the last moment, so I had to perform. Apparently some thought that I was crooning, and it is rumoured that I am now known as 'Scats Wild' . . . I hope that your VADs will be satisfactory lodgers; at least they should know how to make their beds . . .

8.2.44

More good mail . . . Garbett says did I know he had been abroad? [The Archbishop had been to Russia] You can tell him that all his activities and sayings, mostly apparently highly nefarious, are reported at length in the local press; in fact he seems not a nice man to know . . . I sympathise with your erring 'daily'. I am surrounded with the correspondence of four unfaithful wives. The trouble is that whenever I persuade an angry man into a forgiving mood his wife turns out to have become a common whore, while the absolutely obdurate men all have very repentant, hopeful wives. Meanwhile on Sunday I had to tell perhaps the most happily married man in the camp that his wife had died . . . Your Pa tells me what least of all I have to be told, how much you continue to be to so many people . . .

29.2.44

. . . sorry to hear of the old accidie, but I don't blame you . . . we lost our pianist, Eric Williams, a blow to our entertainment in the camp. The Welshmen are having a supper and concert tomorrow night and I am turning out a small Welsh choir again; they certainly don't sing as well as they should . . . When you are accidious remember that I am too, but it won't last too long . . .

5.3.44

. . . the Welsh 'do' on St David's Day was a great success, a splendid supper, all saved up, followed by a most entertaining sing-song . . . I stayed last weekend at the hospital and one of the things I most enjoyed was discussing post-war and other prob- lems with the three young doctors, which I cannot do here without laying myself open to a lecture or three . . .

Early in March I paid a Friday to Monday visit to Graudenz, taking with me a Cpl Williams of the Corps of Military Police, in civilian life an AA Inspector. The weather was miserable; it was either raining or snowing, and the streets were in a filthy mess. I stayed two nights at the Internat with the Australian doctor, Lionel Sapsford, and one night at the notoriously hospitable Neue Heimat camp.

On the Sunday afternoon I paid my second visit to the *Strafe Gefängnis,* and on arrival there, before doing anything else, I asked for permission to see a British officer, Flight Lieutenant Thompson, who had been reported to us as being in serious trouble. Highly strung and hot-headed, he had reacted violently against all the authorities since he had arrived at Graudenz to serve his sentence for assaulting a guard. The sadistic guards at Graudenz took pleasure in humiliating any British officer who came there, and Thompson had attempted the impossible by fighting the whole regime of a German 'glass-house'. He had been sentenced to solitary confinement and while there he had assaulted and laid out a Feldwebel. For this he had been given a hiding that resulted in serious bodily injury. He asked to see the prison doctor, Paulsdorf, but refused to go to see him, demanding that P should come to him, justifiably no doubt, since if he went to see P, P would say that if he could walk he was fit enough.

When I was shown into T's cell, I found him lying in bed. He talked in a very excitable way, and I formed the impression that his mind was seriously disturbed. The censor who was with me seemed to think that P ought to come and examine him, but I knew that T and P had quarrelled so violently that an impasse had been reached. The Germans both hated and were scared of T, particularly Feldwebel Österreich, whom T had laid out. I was really worried about T's future. In April he was due to face another Court Martial for his recent escapades, and his sentence was certain to be increased.

Before going over to the chapel I had some useful talk with a Sgt Thompson, the most energetic and successful of the succession of admirable men who had held the job of Man of Confidence in the *Gefängnis.* A well-educated, intelligent fellow, he was keen to do all that was possible to improve the lot of his fellow *Strafe* prisoners. During the next few months, working in close cooperation with CQMS Granger at Stalag XXA, he managed to work up to a remarkable level the amount of Red Cross food and other supplies admitted into the prison. By the autumn of 1944, men in the *Strafe* prison were by various means getting as much, if not more, Red Cross food than the ordinary prisoner. Thompson and his predecessor had also managed to wangle some English men on to the kitchen staff; this stopped a deplorable, long-standing French racket by which the British prisoners received only the liquid part of the daily soup while the French got all the more solid stuff.

As I was taken across the parade ground to the chapel, I could see that the men drawn up on parade looked better nourished than on the occasion of my previous visit eight months before, when they were not receiving Red Cross food. They were also better clothed and shod. At the service they again sang lustily and listened attentively to what I had to say, and quite a number stayed on to receive Holy Communion.

After the service I was again allowed to visit the sick bay. Almost all the patients there were Italians, but there were a few French and two British lads. Both were extremely sick, one of them a half-Maori New Zealander, Thomas by name, very young. I asked the German medical orderly why they had not been sent to our hospital at Torun, to which all the seriously sick were usually sent. He said he did not know, but they were in fact sent next day, both with acute pneumonia. Four more pneumonia cases arrived during the following week from the *Gefängnis,* all pretty sick; but all made a good recovery.

We returned to Torun next day. On the following Tuesday Herr Braun arrived on his quarterly visit for the Protecting Power. He told me that he would be visiting the *Gefängnis,* and I urged him to look into the case of Flight-Lieutenant Thompson.

Braun went to Graudenz and returned later in the week. To my astonishment and disgust, he made the following statement, that he had seen T and told him he ought not to be so difficult. He should go to see P, and P had said that he would give him proper treatment.

In my opinion the only proper treatment was to get T into hospital. This was not done. Instead, news reached us in the early summer that T had broken out of the *Gefängnis* – an incredible feat – he had been recaptured outside the town, brought back to the prison and done to death in cold blood in a cellar by Feldwebel Österreich.

Following the escape of Felix in January and more recently that of a doctor and sergeant-major from the hospital at Fort XIV, the Germans had been keeping a close watch on Colonel Mackay, whom they erroneously suspected of having hatched the plot. It was therefore no surprise when, early in March, he was suddenly removed from Stalag XXA and sent elsewhere. We had shared a room for sixteen months, more than enough for both of us, I suspect. I was joined by the Australian doctor, 'Quag' Meyer, a delightful man, who during his previous stay in the Fort had been overshadowed by his boisterous compatriot, Brooke Moore.

14.3.44

Well, the colonel has gone . . . unfortunately taking with him three of my best friends in the camp, the three young militia medical orderlies . . . I am busy plugging away at the accompaniments for this riotously funny cowboy show, that has been written here, about a Cockney who wins £50,000 on the pools and goes out to buy a ranch. A genuine little Cockney plays the lead, and I am reduced to helpless laughter at every rehearsal . . .

21.3.44

. . . I doubt if I am pleased that you have met Scatty [RSM Hawtin who had escaped with Felix]. One can never be certain what people will say . . . People here are crazy about more 'repat' rumours and talk of nothing else. Dozens of insane letters from people at home who do not realize the difference, even in wartime, between 'negotiations' and 'agreements' between two countries at war. I have been 'negotiating', rather one-sidedly, for two and a half years for certain privileges, but 'agreement' has seldom been reached . . .

28.3.44 (from Fort XIII)

I seem to remember that you used to have an old proverb, 'He who laughs last, laughs last.' Anyway the break-up of the triumvirate is complete after two and a half years and you will see that my address has changed. there are hundreds of reasons why I am sorry, but it could not be helped. John will tell you what a Pyrrhic victory is, if you do not already know. . . I am superfluous here for church, education, entertainment or any other activity . . . I wish you had seen me trying to pack; I had not only my own two and a half year accumulation, but all the 'left-behinds' of twelve officers I have lived with at one time or another; a Wild box-room had nothing to it. . . Anyway I hope my next move will be more than one mile in the right direction.

The Germans had once more imposed a security ban on any movement of prisoners out of Fort XV. As usual I put in my routine complaint about not being able to visit the hospitals. This time, instead of giving me a dispensation, they decided to send me to Fort XIII. After two and a half years I was really sorry to leave Fort XV, where I had so many friends on the staff, who had remained almost unchanged since November 1941.

13

Spring 1944

Fort XIII was the Stalag central camp where everything went on. But it was already supplied with two doctors, a dentist and two chaplains, C of E and RC, and there seemed no point in my being there. I applied for an interview with Oberstleutnant von Tiedermann, the Stalag second in command, whose job included the control of all our work as chaplains. He was reserved and absolutely *'korrekt'*, but very easy to talk to, and he was always ready to look for commonsense solutions to the problems that arose between prisoners and the authorities.

I told him that I was redundant at Fort XIII and that, if Fort XV was barred, I would like to go to Fort XIV, the hospital, which had always been part of my 'parish'. I knew that there might be a problem, as the hospital was officially the domain of the unspeakable Oberstabsarzt Weidermann, who had once told a French chaplain who made a similar request, *'Hier ist kein Kathedrale.'* Von Tiedermann said he would try to make the transfer. He then added that there was something that he felt that the chaplains could help with in their visits to camps. 'There is,' he said, 'as you know, an increase in the number of cases where men are being shot while away from camps where they are meant to be. These men are not seriously attempting to escape, and being outside their camps they are taking grave risks. At this stage of the war, for men to get shot in this way is particularly regrettable. The guards that we now have to employ are older men, more nervous and quicker on the trigger. I hope that you will do what you can to discourage men from taking unnecessary risks with their lives.' I had not the slightest doubt that he was entirely sincere in what he was saying, and I was glad to have his authority to discuss with men in the camps matters that might not be considered our concern. He also discussed with me the increase in cases of mental disorders among prisoners, and showed interest in our experiences of such cases in the hospital.

Within hours of my arrival at Fort XIII, I received orders to proceed next day to Fort XIV. I was delighted to go there, as I should have work to do, and I would be living with the two best doctors in the Stalag, Macmillan on the surgical side and Irwin on the medical side. Irwin, a splendid man, I had shared a room with at Fort XIV. Macmillan had come to the Stalag way back in the bad days of 1940, and had painstakingly built up the surgical unit and trained his staff with efficiency, enterprise and total dedication. All the men in the Stalag, particularly his old patients, French and British, regarded him with affection and admiration for all that he had achieved.

3.4.44

... since I wrote my address has changed again and I am now where I have often thought that I ought to be, at the hospital. I arrived on Thursday, but was away from Friday to today at the two large working parties [Schülitz] that I visited before in March and November 1943. It has been a whirl, but the end is very satisfactory . . . am sharing a nice room with Mac and have John's room on one side and our mess on the other, where we mess with the French doctor, Liévain.

9.4.44

... a stupendous parcel, bursting with chocolate; in fact the mess are quite pleased that I came here. Yesterday was one of the great days of prison life; word arrived at ten for two patients and five medical orderlies to pack and leave for my old camp, to be repatriated some time later this week. Another birthday this week; how old will I be when I totter home to you?

190

17.4.44

'Awake, thou wintery earth, shake off, shake off thy sadness.' On the tree outside my window today I have seen a tree sparrow, a long-tailed tit, a chaffinch, a tree-creeper and a redstart . . . Last night I got two convalescent patients on the stage to give an hour's concert, a violinist and a singer. We worked out a programme and put it on at six hours notice, and the audience, French and British, took it well. The effect was what I had hoped; the instrumentalists on the hospital staff, many of them army bandsmen, who had never got going as a band, came along this morning to ask what we could do, and tonight we had our first rehearsal, two violins, and a double bass, tenor and alto sax, clarinet, and, for dance music, guitar and drums. On top of this I have bid and made my first Grand Slam . . . But in spite of all this I would still like to go home . . .

20.4.44

. . . an eventful week; in the course of two weeks all the doctors here were sent away to my great regret, and their successors arrived . . . Here I am now with a young surgeon, Darlow, and a forty year old, Allen from Co. Durham; both were in Italy. It is hard for them to take over all the reins at once; they do not know a soul in the Stalag, and the personal side counts for a great deal in prison doctoring. Irwin and Mac will be greatly missed. We have just heard that there is a stoppage of all mail leaving England since 1 April . . . [Was this an anticipation of the Normandy landings?]

No one knew for certain why all the doctors were removed. The whole operation was carried out as discourteously and as inconveniently as possible, with no regard whatever for the welfare of the patients.

17.5.44

I am writing this in the middle of an interesting tour
of distant working parties . . . None has had a visit
before, so you can understand they made me very
welcome . . . The journey so far has been done
almost entirely on foot and I am feeling very fit . . .

In May I started out on the longest and most interesting trip
I ever made in Poland, taking with me Pte Harry Machon, a
Jerseyman who had assisted me greatly over church matters in
the hospital. He had left a fiancée in Jersey, who had been
brought to Germany as an internee. As escort we had Unter-
Feldwebel Müller. Tall and blond, he had had a university
education but was steeped in Nazi ideas. He prided himself
that he was a regular soldier and frequently spoke of his
exploits in the Polish campaign, in which I suspect that his
regiment had been employed as 'moppers-up'. He had
subsequently been invalided with heart trouble into less
arduous service as a Stalag censor; but he retained the
unbounded arrogance of a young soldier in Hitler's
Wehrmacht at its prime, and he loved to throw his weight
about in the presence of simple and elderly camp guards.
Among POWs he had an evil reputation for being over-
zealous in his activities as censor or searcher. I had been
warned that he might be difficult.

On the way to the station he said very seriously, 'I have to
warn you that on the slightest attempt on your part to escape, I
shall shoot without warning.' I thought he was joking and
laughed, but he was clearly shocked. In the train he prattled
away pompously in atrocious English, learnt obviously at
school, mainly about his army service, about his wife and
beautiful 'baybee'. It was almost too much for us when he
said, 'My wife thinks I am the second best soldier in the
German army.'

We had the usual 6 am start from Torun, and after two
changes arrived at Zempelburg, which I had chosen as the

starting point for our trip. The new barrack built by our men for themselves seemed even more luxurious than on my previous visit.

After a snack lunch we set off along the Tuchel road in hot sunny weather. Three miles on we came to a tiny British *lager* close by the road at Zahn. On approaching the wire we were greeted by a single private soldier, the camp leader and cook. He told Müller that the guard was away in Zempelburg and the key a mile away at a blacksmith. While Müller went off to fetch it, he explained to us that in fact the guard was fishing nearby, and he had the key himself in the camp. While Müller was away on his fruitless search, he called up another lad on a farm nearby and told him to run and warn the guard. The exasperated Müller arrived in due course and a few minutes later the guard arrived having been informed what story had been concocted on his behalf.

Over a cup of tea we learnt some of the troubles of Zahn camp. There were only ten men, and they worked on one large farm belonging to a German woman. She was supposed to feed them, but she was so mean that the men had found it better to draw their bare POW rations from Zempelburg and cook and eat them in the *lager*. In three years the owner of this huge farm had never given them a single scrap of food, not even at Christmas. When we arrived, they were right out of Red Cross food and smokes, but two of them had gone that day to Stalag and were expected back that night with supplies. I felt that they were keen that we should stay, and decided not to go further as I had intended. Just as the men were coming in from work, all hopes of a cheerful evening were dashed by a message from the guard that the ration party would not be returning until the next morning. I felt acutely for the men; like every other camp, they would have wished to entertain us well, and they had nothing but dry bread. Though we had a pleasant service and a long talk after our frugal meal, I could hardly persuade them that I did not need a sumptuous meal to make my visit enjoyable. I liked the men well and was impressed with the cleanliness and harmonious atmosphere of their tiny camp, which they had achieved in spite of the meanness of the woman who employed them.

The next camp we reached was in a substantial building in the attractive village of Scharfenhof (Skarpi). Sixteen or so men lived all together in one large room with plenty of light and space. As we entered the camp, two ugly-looking Feldwebels were taking their departure. They were professional searchers who paid surprise visits to camps, ransacking the men's possessions. One of their interests was to find notes from Polish girls, and photographs and other evidence of illicit intercourse between prisoners and the civilian population. Our men only too often carelessly retained such things in their possession; the result was a heavy court martial sentence for the man in whose kit the incriminating material was found, and an even heavier sentence for the woman. There were many such charges.

There was only one man in the camp when we arrived. He was sick, and acting as cook. He showed us enormous varicose veins on his legs and said he could not get treatment. When Müller came in with the camp guard, the latter obviously realized what I had been told, and he was embarrassed. I asked the man to show his leg to Müller, and the guard admitted to us that he had refused to take the man to the Zempelburg doctor. On our return I asked Müller to report the case to the Stabsarzt at Torun, and within ten days the man was in hospital at Fort XIV.

When the men arrived back from work we had lunch, mainly of Red Cross food, and a delightful service followed by Holy Communion. Müller attended my service, and appeared to follow my talk intently. I found that in spite of his Nazi opinionativeness he was not without sense, and came to realize that the visits and particularly the services were appreciated by the men on these remote scattered farms. After this he rarely insisted on attending my services, and became increasingly helpful in arranging suitable conditions for my visits and ministration at each camp.

To reach the next camp at Salesch, a mile and a half away, we followed a footpath through meadows and woods rising to higher ground. At the summit, just short of the village, we were confronted with a marvellous view. We were looking northwards across miles and miles of rolling country of forest and farmland. I could trace out the whole course of my trips of the previous summer, in the middle distance the Gros Zirkwitz district, and further to the north Könitz, Osterwitz and Goetzendorf. I could even pick out individual villages and farms that I had visited.

At the camp we persuaded the guard to send word to the various farms to let their prisoners come back to the camp by four o'clock. While they were being collected we inspected the camp, which was one of the best I ever saw; the men had the whole of a five room cottage between twenty of them, and they had made themselves very comfortable, decorating and furnishing the rooms themselves. We talked to the men as they came in until, completely unexpectedly, the sergeant, a Grenadier Guardsman, announced that they had a meal for us in his room. There we found a table with a clean white cloth and a marvellous meal, cold meat, Spam, salad with hard boiled eggs and elegant bread and butter, the whole served on a service of patterned china. It transpired that when the men at work heard who was waiting to see them at the camp, many of them had immediately collected eggs, cakes and so on from their farms, and one man had borrowed his farmer's best china and tablecloth. It was hard to speak when faced with such a spontaneous demonstration of kindness and hospital-ity from men whom I had never seen before and would probably never see again, men who had been cut off for three years from all normal forms of comfort and home life.

After the meal the men gathered for a service and talk, and as I reluctantly left this friendly crowd, a young soldier of my own battalion handed me three hundred cigarettes and said: 'The lads thought you might find these useful. We have plenty here, and we know you may be visiting camps that are short of them.'

It was after six o'clock when we left Salesch, and more than four miles to be covered before our next halt at Dorf Waldau. The road dropped steeply into a hollow and then climbed up to a high plateau. We were all three tired, and Müller, who for three days had regaled us with tales of his prowess as an infantryman of the Führer, was at his last gasp and demanded a rest when we reached the summit. Thus it was nearly eight o'clock when we dragged our weary feet into the village of Dorf Waldau. Here we found a party of over thirty men housed in odd corners of what had once been a schnapps factory. It was a high building, with strange stairs and corridors leading up from a large living room on the ground floor. Nobody seemed to be in charge of the party, which appeared to be composed of small, ill-assorted cliques.

I refused food as I was beginning to suffer from a violent stomach ache, and it was after ten before the men finished their various suppers. I kept our service very short and talked with a number of men until midnight, when I crept miserably to bed in the lower bunk of a double-decker in a crowded room on the top floor. Within half an hour of my tumbling into bed, all the bed-boards between my shoulders and my knees had given way, but I had no energy to do anything about it and spent the night with my body sagging through the gap on to the floor. Dorf Waldau is one of my least happy memories.

We had a wretched walk next day through uninteresting, flat agricultural country. I was still feeling very sick, and seriously thinking of abandoning the trip. After a few miles, however, we came to a small camp in the attractive hamlet of Waldowke. There was no NCO at this camp of twelve men, all of whom worked on the same farm. The man in charge, B, a Londoner, greeted us and took us into the camp, which consisted of two rooms upstairs over some stables. I had not meant to stay here, but the whole place had been made so cosy and homely that I asked if I could have a hot drink and lie up quietly for the afternoon.

It was well into the evening when the men finished work, although it was Saturday, and by then I was feeling less groggy and was able to enjoy a cheerful evening. First impressions had been right, and we found this as nice a party as I ever encountered. Except for one tough regular soldier and a very hard-bitten Yorkshireman recently arrived after doing six months *strafe* (later he was given another four year sentence), they were very young, none of them more than twenty-one. Five young Scots and one Englishman lived in one room and six Englishmen in the other, with much back-chat between them. Two of the young Englishmen (one called Dove, from Leicester) were men of huge physique; for supper they had a large stew with a mountain of potatoes; they then ate my share of stew and finished off with a wash-hand basin full of porridge. With hard work on the farm by day, no wonder they looked fit.

The retired major who managed this large State Farm had lived here before 1914. By all accounts he was a decent man, and treated our men reasonably. I was surprised to see a tennis court, the only one I ever saw outside a large town in Poland.

Next day was a heavenly May day, and a quiet morning in the sun and a stroll around the farm buildings filled me with the kind of nostalgia for England in summer that at most times I kept severely repressed. I had my hair cut by a young Seaforth Highlander, the youngest of a family of eleven from a Lanarkshire home. He was so small he had to stand on a box to reach the top of my head when I was sitting down. We had a pleasant relaxed service, after which the young Scotsmen shyly invited me to have lunch with them for a change. During lunch we had a short visit from the district Kontrol Feldwebel, a tough-looking man. He obviously had a soft spot for this party of youngsters, and spoke with them in a friendly way. But I was to see him in a worse mood twenty-four hours later.

The cheerfulness and peace of Waldowke and twenty-four hours' rest had set me up again, and after lunch B drove us in a comfortable carriage lent to us by the major. It was a pleasant eight mile drive across country to one of my old camps of the previous summer, Neuhorst. The men were spending a dreary Sunday afternoon locked in their tiny *lager,* and welcomed us warmly. Time was short, but we had a good talk and short service, at which I spoke of my happy memory of their friendliness and good spirits. Another twelve months of captivity under such conditions had begun to tell on them, but a wonderful spirit of good comradeship was still apparent in their exceptionally cramped quarters. I seldom had a chance to revisit a camp, but revisiting Neuhorst was like revisiting the house of old friends.

With regret, I decided that time would not permit to revisit Borowke, a camp which I had found depressed the year before; so we cut across country, a delightful walk by field paths, to Zempelkovo, accompanied to the half way point by the lusty young Scots farmer, Jock Borthwick. At Zempelkovo we had a cup of tea and a short service with the men and set out on our last stretch to Maienthal, where we spent the night. I was feeling pretty tired, and Machon was showing signs of my stomach ailment. In spite of a twenty-four hour rest, we had been in eight camps in three days and covered over twenty miles on foot. In each camp I had conducted some kind of service and given a talk, and I found it quite a strain to spend every minute of each short visit trying to break the ice and establish as many real contacts as possible with men I had never met before.

We started early next morning, as we had a long hilly walk to our next destination at Sanskau. The weather had turned hot and thundery and we felt distinctly clammy after a mile or so. It was near noon when we reached the village and found the camp among the buildings of an enormous State Farm. We were met at the door by a guard who said that we might not go in. Two men had disappeared the night before, and the Kontrol Feldwebel from Zempelburg was addressing the remaining thirty-five men on the other side of the building. A few minutes later the Feldwebel appeared in a flaming temper and he refused us entry. Müller produced the passes authorising our visit, but he said that he would require further authorization from Stalag. There was nothing to be done but to despatch Müller to a telephone, while we sat about outside. Through an open window we were able to chat with the men inside, who told us that the Feldwebel had said, among other things, 'We are not allowed to treat the British as they should be treated; if I had my way you would all be beaten.'

It was nearly an hour before Müller returned. He reported that Hauptmann Goedecke at Abwehr had been furious to hear that his authorization had been rejected, and that there was no objection to our visiting the men. But by this time the men were on their way back to work, and we could do nothing. In the German office I found the Feldwebel and the camp Commandant, an elderly Unteroffizier, both looking rather sheepish over the fuss that had been made. I told them that I would wish to see the men the next day, and that I would want them off work for an hour and a half at lunchtime, not just for the hour that they had stipulated. I also questioned the Feldwebel about the remark that he had made on parade about beating, and a threat that he had made that the men would have to do Sunday afternoon fatigues for a month, thereby contravening two clauses of the Geneva Convention, points I intended to raise with Hauptmann Goedecke at Stalag.

While all this was going on, the Baron, who owned this

immense farm, and his son-in-law, who managed it, arrived on the scene. He asked what I was doing in the camp. This roused Müller, who shouted at him that, Baron or no Baron, he was just a damned civilian, and though he might employ forty prisoners, the camp was army ground and he had no business to enter it. Exit the Baron.

Inside the camp we had some lunch, and were just finishing when Müller arrived to say that he had had a message to say that the Baron wished him to bring the British officer to lunch forthwith. This seemed too good to miss, so I agreed to go. The house was a huge, pretentious Junker mansion. Müller took us to the back door. A nervous-looking serving woman admitted us, and escorting us along a long basement corridor, ushered us into a small, squalid room in which was a bare table and two chairs. She went away and returned with some dry bread and a tureen of some thin dirty-looking soup with a few potatoes in it. Such was the Baron's hospitality! I let out a hearty laugh, and Müller and the woman looked acutely embarrassed. She protested that I ought to be in the best dining room upstairs, but said that she had been told to give us soup down there. I had a feeling that it was not meant to be an insult; it was a kind of gauche hospitality. Poor Müller was miserable. He had seen in the last few days the kind of hospitality shown to me in POW camps, and this was the bounty of a German nobleman. While he gloomily ate his soup he told me that Adolf Hitler did not mean the useless, rich Junkers to run the country again.

After this banquet we found the Baron's daughter in the garden, a hard-faced middle-aged Frau. We had been told that she wore the trousers, but she graciously gave me permission to keep the men in camp next day from twelve to one-thirty. I had already decided to leave Machon at Sanskau for the night and go by myself to a small camp at Grünlinde. By the time Müller and I set off it was raining, and Grünlinde looked a pretty miserable place, a tiny two-roomed hovel standing all by itself in the fields by a rough track. Müller fetched me the key from a neighbouring cottage and locked me in the camp. I was wet and cold; I could find no fuel for the fire and no light; so I turned down a bed and tried to sleep for two and a half hours until the men arrived from work. There were only five men in this God-forsaken camp, and the size of their hovel can be imagined from the fact that it was uncomfortable with only six of us there. I was glad I had not given the camp a miss. The men were effusively grateful, and I could understand what any visit from an outsider must have meant to these isolated lads. We had a cheerful evening, and I chiefly remember the Cockney humour of one older man who had been many years sergeants' mess waiter in the QVRs. He was quite a father to the others, and to me too, giving me an excellent supper and leaving everything ready for me to cook my own breakfast next morning, when they had all gone out to work.

Back at Sassenau I had a long talk with the cook, an impressive young farmer from the Isle of Wight. From him, and from Machon, who had had the same story from others overnight, I learnt that the sergeant in charge, a regular soldier, who was away at Stalag for the night, was far from satisfactory. The German rule for a camp of this size was that they could keep one cook and one other man in the *lager* to clean up by day. By remaining voluntarily on the party, the sergeant in effect occupied the second of these positions. In fact he did nothing, and instead of having the camp clean and tidy when the men came in from work, he was completely useless, and on some occasions he had been found drunk. It was a pity that he was away, but on returning from my trip I made over the case to CQMS Granger at Stalag, who gave the man an ultimatum which he accepted, asking the Germans to send him to Fort XV as a non-worker.

When the men came in at midday, they told me that the foreman had told them that they would have to make up in the evening the half hour that I had obtained for them from one to one-thirty. It was obvious that they never intended the men to have the half hour off. I fetched Müller into the Commandant's room, and said that I did not intend the men to have to work late because of my visit, and unless they got off work at the normal time, I would withdraw my request for the half hour at midday and would hold no service, and I would report what had happened at Stalag on my return. Müller backed me up, and the Commandant, having gone off to see the foreman, returned to say that there would be no overtime or reprisals. I sometimes wondered how Hauptmann Goedecke, if he had known, would have appreciated my brandishing his name as a weapon in these contests, but it seemed to be effective.

The situation at Sassenau highlighted some of the problems of authority in these camps. I was told that on one occasion a prisoner had words with the Major, the Baron's son-in-law, while at work. The Major threatened him with his stick. The prisoner went in with his fists and put the Major on the floor. He turned round, expecting the guard to shoot him. Instead, as the Major picked himself up and shambled off, the guard said, 'Why didn't you jump on his face with your boots?'

After all the fuss we had a good service after lunch. It was a pleasant change to have a larger party for a service, though I always enjoyed the intimate atmosphere of services in the smaller camps, and so, I am sure, did the men.

In the afternoon we caught a train on the small branch line and travelled two stations southwards to a point where we could walk a mile along a country lane to the large State Farm of Karlsdorf. The *lager* was one fair-sized room, rather overcrowded, with double-decker bunks for sixteen men. As soon as Müller made known to the guard in charge the object of our visit, word was sent out to all the prisoners working on different parts of the estate that they could return to camp, and in less than half an hour they were all back. There was no NCO on the party, but most of the organisation was done by two young riflemen in the QVRs, civil servants at home, intelligent and competent. Captured together at Calais, they had stuck together; they had been registered in 1940 with consecutive POW numbers and had managed to remain together through several changes of job in the intervening years. Their wish that the contents of all food and cigarette parcels should be pooled had worked very much to the advantage of the other men, and made for a demonstrably happy atmosphere. The men fed on a completely communal system, all meals being cooked by one man, and each man in the party taking on the job for a month at a time. I never saw a better regulated party. It was men like these who had found the right recipe for survival under these conditions, and I often asked myself, where had they learnt it?

Müller said he would attend my service, but having returned at 8.30 and found us still at supper, he departed and we had our short service without him.

201

Next day we had a restful morning, and after lunch took a short journey on the train, partly along the shore of a beautiful lake, to the town of Vandsburg. We found the British camp in the yard of a farm which was run by the sisters of a Protestant nunnery and girls' school. In charge of the camp was a young lance-corporal who had played leading roles in stage productions at Fort XIII.

During the evening I paid a visit to the local cottage hospital. In a ward terribly overcrowded with Polish patients, I talked with a lad from Zempelburg who had broken an arm at football. Across the road I visited the infectious block, where I found a man suffering from scarlet fever. Müller, like many Germans I met, had a horror of any kind of infection, and refused to enter even the entrance hall of the building. The prisoners told me that they were attentively looked after, but the medical skills, as in many German hospitals at this time, left a lot to be desired. At a later date I saw a young man from the Oxford and Bucks whose hand, damaged in a farm machine, had been badly mistreated in Vandsburg hospital and was likely to be of little further use to him.

We had meant to leave early next morning after what had been an agreeable visit, but we failed to contact the milk van from Wilkenwalde, from which we were expecting a lift to the camp there, and at ten o'clock all traffic in the town was immobilised for an hour by a full-scale air raid practice. The nun who employed our men, Sister Edna, appeared in a new role. She had changed her nun's habit for a boiler suit. A fine looking woman, as strong as a horse, she looked most businesslike and hurried to and fro on her warden's job. In no uncertain tones she shouted commands to squads of girls armed with buckets and stirrup pumps. I sat under a large pear tree, ablaze with blossom, and watched the proceedings. When Sister Edna went off for a few minutes discipline in the ranks deteriorated, and the girls squirted their stirrup pumps in all directions. On her return she found their buckets half empty, and in fury called them up in two ranks and delivered a stirring harangue. I could hear a mention of 'Zehn Tage Bunker Arrest', (Ten days' bunker arrest.) and the closing words rang out, 'Luftschutz ist kein Kinderspiel!' (Air raid practice is not a child's game!). Our men on the party told me that Sister Edna, though she was kind and had a most attractive face, was not a woman to be trifled with. It was interesting to see such ARP activity carried out by a whole town in an area hitherto unaccustomed to air raids. The war was coming closer. It was also unusual in Germany to see a middle-aged woman in such an active role, but Sister Edna was no common type.

By midday we could set off on foot on our twelve mile trek to Wilkenwalde. It was hot, and the road was dusty and our packs were heavy. For about one mile in the middle we rode in a rough farm vehicle which almost rattled the teeth out of my head, and for the last mile we managed a lift for Machon and our packs.

I was glad, however, that we made this journey to an out-of-the-way camp that I could not have included in any other itinerary. Immediately after our arrival a violent thunderstorm broke, and when it was all over, the men, over thirty of them, started to trickle back into the camp from the fields. As they came in, they showed themselves to the guard, who certified them as too wet to resume work.

They were a mixed crowd, not too well-assorted, with a rather ineffective lance-corporal in charge, and a fair ration of professional grousers. A talk with some of them revealed that conditions were poor in various respects and could well account for poor morale. Weak guards were not protecting their rights against a dominating farm Inspektor on this large State Farm. Before their arrival he had been dealing with Russians, and his treatment of both had been much the same. Among other things, contrary to a clear and specific order from Stalag, he had made them handle a noxious form of *Kunstdung* (artificial manure) without protective clothing, gloves, masks or eyeshields. I was shown ample evidence of its harmful effects on men's hands and clothing. The *lager* too, quite a good building with several rooms and ample space, had a defective roof through which rainwater was penetrating. For me the last straw was when I heard that the Inspektor had said that, as the men were missing evening work to see a chaplain, they must make up time during the week.

I took Müller to the guardroom and lodged these complaints with the Feldwebel in charge. I pointed out that the guard in charge had certified the men as too wet to continue working, and that, by a Stalag order, time missed in this way did not have to be made up. The men had not been brought in at my request. My complaint about the roof was not helped by the fact that the three guards were dodging about their own room, shifting their beds and vainly trying to catch all the drips in buckets; their ceiling was worse than that of the *lager.*

At this point Müller decided to throw his weight about. He went off to see the Inspektor and told him, as I heard later, that he would have to watch his step. He was dealing with British prisoners, not Russians, and they, like Müller, were soldiers, which he was not. At my request, Müller also reminded the guards that it was part of their job to see that our men were treated in accordance with the terms of the Geneva Convention, and with orders from Stalag and Berlin about working conditions, and to protect them against any breaches of the rules by the Inspektor. The guards, who were simple folk, seemed quite pleased to be reminded that they had some authority over civilians. We had a pleasant evening in the camp, and some useful discussion about their problems. Things had not been too good at work. At one stage the whole party had nothing else to do for seven weeks except pick stones off the fields for eight to ten hours a day. Sick men had also been made to walk to hospital at Vandsburg and back, a round trip of twenty-four miles, instead of using the milk van, which went daily, or the train which called at the station a hundred yards from the camp. With the worsening war situation an element of petty vindictiveness was becoming more apparent among the camp guards.

Next day we returned to Stalag, an all-day journey including a four hour wait at Bromberg with nothing whatever to do. On all trains that day a rigorous checking of passes, military and civilian, was taking place, officers of as high a rank as major taking part. We were regarded with considerable interest and even some respect by the checkers, who were anxious to know what kind of work I was doing.

Two days after our return I went to Stalag to report on our trip to CQMS Granger and to Von Tiedermann. I found that Müller had already reported to the *Stabsarzt* on sick men we had seen, and to other departments other irregularities that we had encountered. He had done well, and some of the things he had seen on this trip had changed many of his ideas. To Von Tiedermann I confined my comments to a few outstanding points, chiefly concerning Wilkenwalde. I was convinced that he was concerned to see that our men were fairly treated, and that he was willing to listen to what we had found out as chaplains on our visits. He was also insistent that the guards who escorted us should give us a good run. At the end of my interview he found Wilkenwalde on a wall map, and said that, though it was a long way off, he would pay it a visit. I do not know if he ever went, but soon afterwards the British prisoners were withdrawn from Wilkenwalde, and the Inspektor got his Russians again.

24.5.44

. . . [on returning from the tour] . . . I visited and held services at fourteen working parties, and stayed in eight of them, a different bed every night. The men work late on the farms, so unless one stays the night one scarcely sees enough of them to make the visit worthwhile . . . Almost all the travelling we did on our feet, carrying our packs; weather perfect and countryside lovely, with pear and cherry blossom at best. After this life here the exercise, the continual change of scene, seeing new faces, trying to get past formality and quickly to the point, two or three services a day, is a big strain, but I love every moment of it, and I found my official escort most helpful . . .

14

Summer 1944

After my spring expedition to working parties I was out of action for a few weeks, and took life easily under doctor's orders. On a diet, I put on nearly a stone and felt a lot better. Fort XIV was a good spot to lead the quiet life. Some of the wards were more or less underground in the Fort itself, but most, including our staff quarters, were in good wooden barracks on top of the Fort. Trees covered the slopes that ran down to the moat, a real moat, about thirty yards wide, and a belt of trees beyond the moat cut us off completely from the dreary, sandy waste outside. There were masses of birds in this green oasis, and between the huts we cultivated gardens where we grew fresh vegetables.

But various strains and stresses had begun to appear in the hospital after the departure of Captain Macmillan. Relations between our new Senior British Medical Officer, Liévain, the French doctor and Oberstabsarzt Weidermann were deteriorating. Liévain was displacing British medical orderlies from the French wards, where they had done excellent work, and replacing them with totally unskilled French prisoners, mostly recruited from *Strafe* camps. Unlike the British, the French doctor and orderlies were allowed to wander round Torun and mix freely with Germans. Our internal security was being compromised, and a showdown with Liévain was inevitable. We explained to him that we could no longer share our mess with him so long as he fraternised with the Germans. For some time he appeared to watch his step and become more cooperative, having discovered that his *'vacheries'*, as his sergeant described them, were not unknown to us; but the improvement did not last, and it soon became clear that he was keeping the Germans well-informed about all that went on in the camp. One can understand the French attitude to a point: there were many who deeply resented the fact that the British, and later the Americans, by their resistance to the Germans, were responsible for the continuation of the war (a war in which they were no longer involved), and consequently for the continuation of their captivity.

At the end of my last interview with Von Tiedermann, he told me that I had had my last trip. As the German war situation worsened more and more restrictions were being imposed, and a new order from Berlin said that no British chaplain might spend a night away from his own camp. There were to be no exceptions. It was a sad blow; nearly one third of the hundred and ninety working camps in Stalag XXA had still never seen a chaplain, and Padre Lathaen and I had intended to cover most of these during the summer. We had had a surprising amount of freedom, more than was allowed to chaplains in most Stalags, and it must have been obvious to any German that our visits, the only visits of any kind to working camps by a British officer, were a source of considerable encouragement to the men, quite apart from any personal influence we might contribute or any spiritual work we might do. A humane man like Von Tiedermann might view our work favourably, but many others were highly suspicious of our activities. He did, however, promise that he would give us permission to visit such parties as could be reached in a day.

At the end of May I had to conduct a funeral at Könitz. Under new arrangements with the Germans, I was accompanied by a bugler, Pte Blaikie, and a British sergeant from Fort XIII, who was permitted to take photographs of the funeral to send to relatives of the dead man. We were escorted by Oberfeldwebel Kuba of the Abwehr department, an elderly man and a native of the former Austrian Tirol, who bitterly resented the Nazis having given his homeland back to the Italians. After a long hot train journey from 6.30 am to 1.30, we arrived at Könitz and went straight to the mortuary, which was a small building facing a wide open space in the very middle of the town. A British guard of honour of a dozen men arrived from the dead man's camp at Lichnau and a horse-drawn bier drew up. Before starting off, however, I asked to be shown the body. I found it still partially clothed, and caked with dirt and blood from a bullet wound. By this time quite a crowd, mostly of women, had gathered around, and I told the Germans that in no circumstances would I proceed with the burial until the corpse had been made ready properly for burial. Kuba agreed, and he and I set off for the hospital nearby, which was responsible for making the funeral arrangements. Having explained to the hospital authorities what had to be done, he then took me on to the Könitz Guard Company HQ, who also had responsibility for the arrangements.

On the way in the main street we met two senior German Warrant Officers of the company. They stopped and asked why we were not at the funeral. Kuba explained and I quite expected them to tell me to get on with it, but instead they fell to accusing each other in loud voices for neglect of duty, a strange scene in a crowded main street. Seeing how things were going, I joined in and said:

'It is no concern of mine what respect the German army pays at a funeral of one of our men; but in every other Guard Company area, at least two German soldiers from the company attend the funeral in tin hats. At the moment you appear to be represented only by my escort, Kuba, and the guard from Lichnau, who is the man who shot the deceased. Naturally we do not wish him to be present.'

This set them off again, while Kuba supported me. After the usual German protestations at this stage of the war, *'Gibst kein Mensch',* ('There aren't enough men') they agreed with Kuba that they would send men to the funeral, and that the Lichnau guard would be withdrawn.

When we returned to the mortuary we found that the hospital had sent two orderlies, and that the corpse was being properly prepared for burial. I had some talk with Private Vagg of Lichnau about the shooting. The unfortunate victim, a forty-year-old tough Scotsman, had been working on a rick with some Polish women. The guard from the camp, visiting the rick yard, started an argument with him and ordered him down from the rick. When he refused to obey, the guard hurried back to the camp, fetched a rifle and, without more ado, shot the man on the rick. He was not dead, but the guard told the women not to go up to him. The guard then returned to the camp and there told Vagg what he had done. Vagg hurried to the rick yard and found the man still alive on the rick, but soon afterwards he died. The Lichnau men asked to be allowed to prepare the man for burial, but permission had been refused, and he was removed as he was to Könitz by the hospital authorities.

When preparations had been completed we moved off to the cemetery, before a large crowd of civilians who were fully aware of what had been going on and were visibly showing their disgust with the negligence of the German authorities. After the service I thanked the Lichnau men, and we made our way to another British camp on a high hill the other side of Könitz. The thirty men there were employed on various jobs around the town and were in the charge of a good lance-corporal of the QVRs. We had supper and a short service, but I was tired and glad of a nice bed.

Next morning I had to look into the case of a man on the party who was obviously mentally unbalanced. The incompetent guards had done nothing about this, but they assured me that the man would be sent into hospital at Torun. He was hopelessly insane, and must have been for some weeks a great anxiety to the other men on the party, who had done well looking after him. His name was Salotti, strange for a man in a Scottish regiment.

As our train was not due to leave until midday, I persuaded Kuba to take us to the hospital. Of the six British patients we found there only one was seriously ill. He said he had had a high swinging temperature for ninety days, and no diagnosis had yet been made by the German doctors. On my return to Stalag I saw the Oberstabsarzt and said that if the doctors at Könitz could not make a diagnosis in three months, surely the man should be brought to the hospital where our doctors could examine him, and where he could have the atmosphere of an English hospital and English nursing, instead of the poor conditions of the POW ward at Könitz. Weidermann had heard nothing of the case and was disturbed by my report. Two days later he told me that the man could not be removed to Torun (no doubt they did not wish him to be seen by our doctors), but that a specialist from Danzig would see him. Later we heard that he had been moved to Danzig, where he died of an abscess on the liver before they could operate.

But for the incompetence and neglect at Könitz, this man would probably have lived.

On the morning of 6 June I was near the Fort gate when Padre Gallagher arrived on his weekly visit to say Mass. He told me that the Allied Armies had landed in France. This was the news that we had waited for so long, and I hesitated to believe him; he was a good leg-puller. Fort XIII ran an all-day news-listening service on their hidden radio, whereas our team only functioned on their set in the evening. The padre soon told us enough to convince us that this was the real thing. What could one say or think? Whole new prospects opened up as more and more encouraging news flooded in day after day from the Eastern front as well as from the Western. Less comforting was news of the flying bombs, the effect of which was proclaimed in all the German bulletins, and not entirely denied in the British news.

8.6.44

It looks like you'll have to think of shaking out all those moth balls, though I know that you will not start doing anything in a hurry . . . Like you I have so completely shut out all thoughts of going home for so long, that when the possibility rears its head I am quite afraid of how all the bliss of it will take me, the sense of being free, the sight of Oxford . . . I wonder if I can face it if God grants it to me . . .

Meanwhile I had a summons to yet another tragic funeral. This time I was accompanied by Cpl Steven Davis, RAMC, and Müller as escort, as we set off to Lowienek, a small working party near Prust, where another prisoner had been shot. After a very early start we reached Prust by 8.30 am. At the camp there, the only man not at work told us over a late breakfast about experiments being carried out in the nearby Tuchenwald by Germans firing a new kind of rocket. For some weeks we had occasionally seen amazing vapour trails ascending to incredible heights in the very clear sky from about forty miles away. He said that they were by no means reliable and nearly half of those fired had descended in the Prust area, causing damage in country villages. Of seven fired in one day, four had come down nearby and exploded. We know now that they were experimental V2s. The local form was that when you saw a rocket go up, you listened. If you then heard a noise like distant thunder, you breathed again; it meant that the rocket was on its way to a distant target. If you did not hear thunder, you took cover; it was a misfire and might land anywhere.

From Prust we walked several miles along a dull, flat, dusty road to Lowienek. There we found the camp in a poor, squalid room with a brick floor, housing eight men in cramped conditions. The shooting of one of their company had had a devastating effect on their morale. Their story was that two men had made an escape; one had not yet been recaptured; the other had been found by a Polish farmer lying up in a barn. He had summoned the camp guard, who had gone to the barn and shot the prisoner in cold blood, reporting that when arrested he had attempted to escape – the old familiar story.

The guard, a particularly unprepossessing type, made an angry, unnecessary scene soon after our arrival. After talking with the men I asked Müller to question him about some irregularities in his treatment of the men that they had reported to me. Why, for instance, had he locked them up in the camp from midday on Sunday until nine o'clock, without access to water or sanitation, not even allowing them in the tiny compound? Müller was good and pressed him strongly, but the man was evasive in his answers. I also said that all the men in the camp would witness that he had said that if he was sent to bring back the other man who had escaped, when he was recaptured, he would not bring him back alive. The man looked thoroughly embarrassed and denied that he had ever said this, but in case of accidents I said that we would report to this effect to the Oberstleutnant on our return to Torun. This was the worst type of guard, young and well-Nazified, and a bundle of nerves, probably from shell-shock sustained on the Russian front.

At this stage not knowing who had actually fired the fatal shot, I said to the guard that I assumed that the man who had been responsible would not attend the funeral. When he

211

made no reply, with mounting anger I asked, 'Was it you?' The man hesitated and then said, 'Yes.'

After some food the men produced a flat farm cart, and we set off to collect the body from the farm where it was lying. At the farm the Kontrol Feldwebel met me and took me into the cowshed where the man was lying. The men on the party had told me that they had not been allowed much time to lay out the corpse, but I hardly expected what we found. The man was still in his blood-soaked uniform, lying on a filthy floor in a grotesque, contorted position. In front of several civilian farm people, men and women, who had followed us into the shed, the Feldwebel exclaimed, *'Schweinerei',* and added more about the British *Schwein* who did not know how to pay respect to their dead. I asked Müller to come outside with the Feldwebel. I told him that I had no intention of burying the man in that condition, and that I understood that it was the responsibility of the Feldwebel to see that arrangements had been made for the funeral. He said that our men had been given time to prepare the corpse. This may have been partially true, but the men, in their ignorance and in their state of demoralization, had not done what they might have done. I asked him to withdraw his remark about *Schwein,* but he refused, and I could only say that I would report them to Stalag.

Meanwhile Steve Davis had produced water, soap and rags from the farm, and bandages and cotton wool from the camp. We cut off the man's clothes, only to find in the stifling atmosphere of the shed that the body was already decaying, which made the task of cleaning and laying out a grim ordeal for someone not used to it. Steve worked nobly, and in half an hour the coffin was ready. We placed it on the farm cart covered with a Union Jack and set forth for the cemetery, a mile and a half away.

Müller had told the guard not to attend, and we were escorted by two *'Hilfswachmann',* auxiliary guards, farmers with yellow armbands, carrying rifles.

The simple, deeply moving service took place in a small cemetery, on a plot of rising ground surrounded by thick woods. During the service a rocket went up, probably less than a mile away. I saw the civilians who were present listening intently, and then relaxing as we heard the sound of distant

212

thunder.

It was too late for us to return that evening to Torun, and arrangements were made for us to occupy the beds of the two missing men in this little camp. There was little we could do to cheer the party up. Apart from the effect that this tragic affair had had on the men, they had been too long together in this miserable place, three whole years. I told them that I would ask for them to be split up and sent elsewhere.

On our return to Stalag, I made a report to the Oberst-leutnant, and he seemed inclined to listen. On this, as on other occasions, he showed obvious interest in the question of taking steps to relieve the mental strain for men who had been so long in prison.

16.6.44

. . . I now employ as assistant in my garden one of our semi-mentals, whose profession at home is market gardening. These cases are a problem these days, increasing as they are after four years. In fact I don't doubt that we are all a bit loopy, and if anyone thinks that a month's leave is going to make POWs useful members of society again, they are wrong . . .

Our hospital staff of about forty men had a regular game of soccer, in which I took part with great enjoyment. The standard was quite high, and the players included at least one man who had played professionally in League football.

21.6.44

. . . Here we are 'facing facts' in the same way as you, but it is hard to be pessimistic these days . . . scored my first goal today, but I suspect that a couple of my staunch touchline supporters, both of Lancs, and one of whom played for Bolton Wanderers, had 'bought' the goal-keeper with cigarettes. They rushed on the field, shook my hand and, producing

213

a form, asked me to sign for Sheffield Tuesday next season . . .

30.6.44

. . . the humour of this life in prison and among troops generally is that most of it derives from the fact that to all intents and purposes no one can keep any part of their life secret; all their peculiarities are common property, all run gloriously true to form, and a joke does not become classic until it has been repeated at least fifty times, like music hall humour. The one unforgiveable crime is to be upstage, or pose as anything you are not . . . the golden oriole is sitting about ten feet from me as I write . . .

In June I had permission to take a party of medical orderlies to have a bathe in a large quarry pool about a mile and a half from the Fort. We were escorted by an elderly guard. As we passed some rough Polish shacks the guard staggered, and appeared to be in distress. We sat him down by the road, and after some discussion decided not to miss our bathe but take him on with us. Two men supported him down the road while another carried his rifle. The Poles looked on in amazement. Arriving at the pool, we laid him out in a shady place while we had our bathe. On the return journey we again more or less carried him back to the Fort, where he was immediately sent out for a spell of sentry duty. This was the second guard who had passed out while escorting me. The Germans were becoming stretched to find able-bodied men of any age for base duties in the summer of 1944.

24.7.44

. . . only one letter this week, a particularly illiterate one from a man's mother, asking me to tell him that his wife had had such a hiding from the family of another man she was going with that she had to seek

214

police protection . . .

By the end of July the weather had become too hot for anything more strenuous than our hospital routine, an occasional bathe, sunbathing and tomato growing. But we were increasingly stirred out of our composure by events in the world beyond the confines of Fort XIV. In the west the Allies had not yet broken out of the Normandy bridgehead, but in the east the Russian offensive was rolling remorselessly westwards. It was hard to realize that the war was coming close to us at last, but lying on top of the Fort in blazing sunshine we could feel, though we could not actually hear, the almost continuous roar of gunfire on a scale that no German could explain away as artillery practice. Round Torun itself military activity was increasing daily. The troops exercising near the camp were no longer raw recruits, but front-line soldiers, trained men. Outside the main gate was an autobahn, built largely by our men in 1940/41 to convey Hitler's forces up to the Russian frontier. For some months it had been little frequented, but now was filled with column after column of lorries, taking forward stores and ammunition. Planes were no longer a handful of training planes circling round Torun, but whole squadrons of busy fighters hurrying off to the front, and at night bombers on their way eastwards, well-loaded with bombs. We fully expected the Russians to bomb the rail bridges over the Vistula or the sidings between us and Torun, but we were only once out of our beds at night when the Russians raided a town twenty miles nearer to Warsaw.

On 25 July news filtered through of the attempt on Hitler's life. No one really knew what had happened. there was little faith in newspapers and radio among the Germans. One had the feeling during the following days that most Germans secretly hoped that he was dead. So long as he lived, they knew that Germany would fight on to a hopeless death; but, if he had gone, a final catastrophe might be avoided. One evening, at the moment of greatest tension, before the truth was known that Hitler had survived, I saw Oberstleutnant Von Tiedermann sitting pensively in the stern of a small boat on the moat, being rowed around by his two daughters. Evidently he had fetched them from Danzig to have them with him if the end came suddenly. He was exactly the kind of German one would have expected to be involved in or sympathetic with the plot. No one dared to say anything out loud, but there was no mistaking the general disappointment and despair on many faces when it was known that the Führer had survived, and that Himmler had now been made master of all security in Western Europe, armed with absolute power in defence of the Führer, who must now be protected against enemies inside, as well as outside the Reich.

In spite of all the excitement and increase of security measures, Von Tiedermann continued to issue permits for one day visits by chaplains to working parties. One that I paid to two parties in the area north-east of Torun was particularly interesting, because it gave an insight into the way in which small north-south branch lines were being used to transfer large bodies of troops and equipment to face the Russian advance north of Warsaw towards East Prussia, where the main penetration occurred five months later.

24.7.44

. . . had a long day travelling yesterday, 3 am to 1 am, fair amount of walking and a bathe included . . . I was pleased to find that I was feeling as fit when I went to bed as when I got up twenty-two hours earlier . . . lovely to walk in open country and feel the wind on one's face . . .

16.8.44

. . . give the incomparable Felix my love [having escaped from Fort XV, he had reached England and called on Mary in Oxford] . . . my tomatoes are coming up to eating stage . . .

26.8.44

. . . tonight we give another concert. How I long to

hear some good music again, though I sometimes give myself a treat and play Beethoven's 5th, *Eine Kleine N'musik,* or something else on the gramophone . . .

29.8.44

. . . it is too hot to stay in bed. Imagine the finest summer day that you can, rather hotter than anything in England; we have had about thirty of these on end . . . I have just finished reading Newman's *Apologia,* which makes me even more amazed at that church's capacity for swallowing camels. I am getting tired of this war; five years on Sunday next. What annoys us most of all is that we could have committed some pretty hefty crime to get a four and a half year sentence, if only we had known . . .

I was not surprised when we were required to vacate Fort XIV, which, like the other Forts, was to be prepared for the defence of Torun. Our destination was Kopernikus Lager, an immense camp of wooden huts three miles south of Torun, at a junction where the two main roads, Torun-Posen and Torun-Bromberg, divided. The camp at different times had housed Russians, Italians and British non-working NCOs. Nearly half of it was unoccupied by this time, while the rest of it held 3000 Russians and a small hospital, if it could be so called, for Russians and Italians. One compound next to the Posen road was allotted to us for our hospital.

The Germans were too short of manpower to give any assistance for the move, beyond supplying us with three large lorries with trailers, to be driven by our men. We were allowed to take anything we liked, and among the items we transported were over a hundred iron bedsteads, quantities of stores, much furniture, the whole operating theatre and dispensary, hundreds of books, two thousand medical comfort parcels, several tons of coal and potatoes, a hundred and twenty patients, forty staff and all their personal baggage.

The whole operation was completed in a day.

In normal circumstances, a move of this kind would have involved a thorough search by the Abwehr of all our possessions. Fortunately their searchers were all fully occupied that day, searching the twenty-five top French Generals who were leaving Fort XI, where they had lived since they were moved from the camp in Germany from which General Giraud had escaped. One particular concern of ours was the radio. It was being conveyed in a box under the front seat of an ambulance when the ambulance was stopped and boarded by the Oberstabsarzt. He travelled to Kopernikus sitting on the precious box, unaware of its contents!

Kopernikus was a dreary enough spot, acres and acres of wooden barracks with not a tree in sight. There was more space than I had known elsewhere, and a walk round the perimeter of the wire must have been little less than half a mile. The wards and staff rooms were smaller then at Fort XIV, and orderlies no longer had to sleep in the wards, but in small adjoining rooms, a great improvement. The kitchen, a huge brick building, designed to cater for a much larger area of the whole camp than the part we were occupying, was inconveniently far from the barracks, nearly four hundred yards from the furthest hut, which was ours. Water was available only from stand-pipes between the huts, and the latrines, which were appallingly primitive and far from rain-proof, were more than a hundred yards from the huts, not too bad in summer, but a daunting expedition in the depths of winter. The huts were likewise adequate in summer, but bleak in winter. We had indented for more than we really needed, and it was unlikely that the Germans would provide enough fuel to heat all the rooms that they gave us. After years of living in cramped quarters, it was easy to be carried away by the offer of so much space.

11.9.44

. . . such big things happening everywhere seem to make our petty life here even less worth recording than ever. However, we have had a rather more eventful week than usual, the whole hospital having moved a distance of three or four miles ... It was sad to leave our oasis of water and trees. Here we have sand and huts, and then more sand and more huts. No self-respecting blade of grass would deign to show itself in this waste. But accommodation is pretty good and space to move about enormous ...

At the end of August I had another day trip to three camps on the Vistula just north of Bromberg. I took Steve Davis with me, and we were escorted by a new Sonderführer, called Haberer. An unprepossessing man, he claimed to have been a traveller for a jewellery firm in French North Africa. He spoke perfect French and pretty good English. As Sonderführer he was in charge of propaganda, cinema shows, education facilities etc. in the Stalag. His real rank was only that of Obergefreiter, but as Sonderführer he wore an officer's uniform with a special badge of rank. I was told that he was not to be trusted, but I found that provided he had a square meal and a smoke he was in no way difficult to manage, and in fact he did many things for us of which his superiors could not possibly have approved.

After the usual early start we were at Prust station by 8.30. More than forty people came off the train, and most probably had long walks ahead of them. Koselitz had sent a smart little carriage for us, which was waiting with liveried coachman in the station yard. We drove off behind two elegant horses at a spanking rate followed by astonished eyes.

It was a fine autumn morning, with a slight nip in the air. The first part of our route was through country familiar to me, through Gem Waldau and past Lushkau and Brachlin. After Brachlin we crossed a short plateau and came out at a lofty viewpoint overlooking the magnificent valley of the Vistula. Our descent into the valley by a very steep, zig-zagged road lined with poplars was exhilarating, as our carriage appeared to have no brakes at all! In a village at the foot of the descent we turned southwards up the valley. The strip of land between the river and the escarpment was rich farmland, and the dusty road was lined on either side with apple trees loaded with ripe fruit.

While still a mile from Koselitz, following the usual Polish custom, the carriage shed a wheel. Fortunately we did not overturn and were able to reattach the wheel somewhat insecurely, so that the carriage could continue without us, while we walked on to the village, eating apples off the wayside trees as we went.

At a large farm in the village we met a British lad who directed us to the camp, which was reached by an outside stair and consisted of one ample-sized loft above some stables. We had hardly shaken hands when our original guide arrived from the cookhouse in the great farm with a superb breakfast of fried eggs, bacon and tomatoes. After breakfast Haberer said he would leave us to our own devices, and went off with the camp guard, leaving behind his belt, complete with revolver and ammunition.

It being Sunday, the men suggested that we should take a walk with them across the fields to the river, where they used a delightful sandy bay as a bathing-place. The river there was magnificent, something like half a mile wide. The far bank rose steeply, and away to the north we could see the towers of the cathedral and other churches of Kulm, high above the river. We had nearly an hour's walk, for once not accompanied by a guard, but by the friendly *lager* dog.

I was in an unusually optimistic mood, and for the only time in all my visits to working parties suggested to the men that there was a strong possibility of a sudden end to the war, perhaps in the immediate future. We discussed what we all thought they should do if they found themselves suddenly on their own, without guards, a situation that did occur to us at the hospital, but not until four months later.

When we arrived back at the camp we found a splendid lunch waiting, with Haberer slightly apprehensive as to whether I was going to reappear. He provided some amusement for the party when he produced, as was his duty as Sonderführer, a large bunch of propaganda leaflets and illustrated newspapers. He threw them on the table, saying, 'Here is something for you to read, or as paper you may find a better use for it.'

Before we had finished lunch we were joined by ten men from the neighbouring camp of Seehof, and when the meal had been cleared away we had our service. It was attended by Haberer and the pleasant-looking guard from Seehof. They sat, stood and sang hymns with the rest, but withdrew, I thought rather reluctantly, for the Communion, both being Roman Catholics. The Seehof guard was a cultured, middle-aged Austrian from Vienna and wore a string of Austrian medals from the First War. When the service was over we all adjourned to the large farmhouse where he sat down at the piano in the front room and, surrounded by prisoners, played Viennese waltzes magnificently for an hour. I seldom saw a more unwilling Nazi warrior. While he was playing, the owner of the farm came on the scene. He was a young, very smart tank officer in civilian clothes, who had been disabled in Russia. With him came his fashionable young wife, who handed round bunches and bunches of very small but very sweet grapes. It was all a lovely experience, entirely unreal, and I enjoyed every moment of it, sitting on the front steps of this beautiful house, looking out over the sun-lit gardens.

Another feature of this cheery party at Koselitz was their addiction to music. Among the twelve men they had started with perhaps two competent musicians, one of them something of a composer. In the course of time all the other men on the party had taken up and learnt to play some instrument, and so they had formed a band. When any of them heard of an instrument for sale in the neighbourhood, they pooled their available *lager geld* to buy it.

By three o'clock we most reluctantly had to leave this quiet, pleasant place, and one of the lads produced a carriage to take us on to our next destination, Weichselhorst. The road continued a mile up the valley below the escarpment and then rose up a steep hill, for which we dismounted. From the top the view down the valley was stupendous; two tugs with great strings of barges were winding a course between the sand banks down the magnificent river towards Danzig and the sea, a sea that we had not seen for four and a half years.

The Weichselhorst party consisted of about twenty older and tougher men than we usually found. They were thoroughly insolent towards their guards, and I had no doubt that they had things well under control to their satisfaction and convenience. They made us welcome and after a short service, gave us a good supper. It was practically dark when we set off at 8.30 in another coach to the station some miles away on the Prust-Bromberg line. There was a distinct chill in the autumn evening after our day in the sun. On the way we passed a large new landing ground and could just make out the shape of numerous fighter planes placed round the perimeter.

The carriage dropped us at a tiny country station where, as in the morning, at least forty people were waiting for the Bromberg train. At about 9.30 the station master announced that the train had been delayed and would be at least two hours late. As there was nowhere at all to sit Haberer walked coolly into the *Dienstabteilung* (Staff Room) which contained the telephone and signal equipment, and sat us down. A porter protested several times, but Haberer said I was an officer and must be accommodated in this way. The porter gave up the struggle, but after half an hour the station master himself walked in. *'Kriegsgefangene heraus'* ('Prisoners of war must get out'), he shouted, and there was no mistaking the tone of finality in his voice. Haberer did not go down without a struggle, and we were allowed to take two chairs into the crowded waiting room, where men, women and children were sitting or lying all over the floor.

It was after eleven when at last the crowded train arrived, and inevitably we had to stand for the ten mile run into Bromberg. We had by then missed our connection to Torun, and found that the next slow train did not leave until 7 am. A fast train was due at 1 am, but prisoners were not allowed to travel on it. Haberer was as keen as we were to get home, so off we went to the Bahnhofsoffizier, to whom Haberer explained at length that we were not prisoners, but Red Cross personnel travelling on duty. We received a flat refusal, so he took us off to the Red Cross hut and, marching us in under the notice saying *'Nichts für Kriegsgefangene'* ('No prisoners of war allowed'), sat us down and ordered soup. Over the soup he asked us if we had any identity papers. Steve had a Red Cross card, and I had my BEF identity card. Armed with these he went off to beard the Bahnhofsoffizier again. He was soon back without success, but he said firmly, 'We will travel on the fast train.'

Bromberg station had a subway, and passengers did not, as at most stations, simply walk across the line between platforms. Also between the pairs of lines running between the platforms there was a metal barrier with gaps at intervals, spanned by a pole that could be raised, as at level crossings. In the dark of the blacked-out station Haberer took us well up the platform opposite the platform for Torun and stationed us opposite one of the gaps. Suddenly he said, 'Over we go,' and led the way across, diving under the pole. I had followed him and had almost gained the opposite platform when all the station lights were turned on, ready for the arrival of the Torun train. Steve was in the middle of the rails, just diving under the pole. I waited for a shot, or at least for a policeman to accost us, but no one took any notice and we made ourselves scarce in the shadow of a building. Haberer was determined to get us on the train, but he was afraid that one of the minions from the office would spot us before we embarked. Once on the train, the next stop would be Torun; questions about our presence on the train could answer themselves.

In came the train, and with crowds of others we made for the nearest coach. There were no seats of course, and we stood in the crowded corridor. There was one bad moment before we moved off, when Haberer discovered that he was crushed up against a ticket-collector. Looking slightly rattled, he said something, and I heard the ticket-collector reply, 'Not on duty,' and we breathed again.

It was two thirty am when we reached Torun and half an hour after that when we reached the camp. It had been a great day, but for the second time in a month a strenuous day that lasted more than twenty-four hours made me wonder if we were really fit for that kind of exercise, a question that would soon seem irrelevant.

15

Autumn 1944

28.9.44

. . . Quite ten days since I wrote; am getting worse
and worse, but oh! there is little to say . . . Had a
good day out on Sunday, visiting three working
parties . . . a peaceful autumn morning, all lovely
orchard country . . .

6.10.44

. . . have just received letter a month later than any of
yours, which must be one of your first from
Uppingham; hope you will find the work a change
and the folk pleasant. At our new camp for the first
time I have a room set aside as a chapel, what an
asset! . . . I do not think we shall have long to wait
now, though I never let the thought grip me too
much . . .

The German regulations about access to and storage of Red
Cross food parcels was becoming increasingly tiresome. They
were worried that in the event of an uprising the parcels would
be useful to any insurgents. So it was forbidden not only, as for
a year past, to have unopened tins in our possession, but for
the common store to be within the *lager* at all. Whenever we
wished to draw from our supply, we had each morning to join
a party and, escorted by a guard, walk three hundred yards to

a store by the main German guardroom. There we drew such tins as we wanted and had them punctured by a German. They were always trying to keep pace with endless Berlin regulations, the latest of which was that every tin must not only be pierced but emptied out into containers provided by the prisoners. In the hospital we could plead that patients did not possess such containers. Early in October a new order demanded that all reserves of Red Cross parcels held by camps or Stalags must be opened up and the contents distributed forthwith. This order was carried out to the letter in some Stalags, but in Stalag XXA this disaster was averted for the time being by the skilful diplomacy of CQMS Granger. In October the Germans also cut our potato ration, the staple food, by more than half.

8.10.44

Mail goes well at the moment, both ways . . . Everybody who writes from home seems to have managed some kind of a holiday this year, which must be an agreeable change, and a restorative before what looks like being quite a long stretch more . . . Last week we had a visit from YMCA, a new, young chap, very nice, Swiss; all the previous ones were Swedes. [This was Hans Heinrich Zürrer; he paid us two visits before the end of the year. On the occasion of his second visit he agreed to take back to the Rolex firm a watch that I was wearing when captured, but which had subsequently ceased to function. I was hoping that it could be repaired and I could collect it after the war. His story and the story of my watch is best told in his words, in a letter to me of 1945, which is appended to this chapter.] They send a fine type of fellow, with a wonderful memory for faces and details of camps they have visited . . .

In September, October and November I managed to arrange three one-day visits to working parties. Roman

225

Catholic numbers being comparatively small, Padre Gallagher had not been granted the same facility as Lathaen and myself, but the resourceful Haberer managed to change this, and Padre Gallagher joined me on two autumn outings. The first was to the two large camps at Schülitz, where I always had a great welcome. The second was a less successful venture. Our destination was at Maxtal, north of Bromberg on the line to Danzig. There, forty men were employed by the Reichsbahn. We each travelled with a bag carrier and were escorted by Haberer.

We found the camp in a hut, situated between tracks, in the middle of an enormous marshalling yard. On our arrival half the men were out at work, although it was a Sunday. It became apparent that the men were completely out of Red Cross supplies and were also receiving much reduced German rations, and so entertaining five of us was obviously out of the question. Padre G and I quickly agreed to hold brief services for the men who were there, and then beat a hasty retreat without embarrassing the men by staying for a meal.

No passenger train was due to take us back to Bromberg, and at Haberer's suggestion we clambered up into the brakeman's boxes, perched high above the end of the open trucks of a goods train that was about to leave. Our two assistants climbed into one, and Haberer, Gallagher and I squeezed into another – not first-class accommodation, and I wondered whether a railway policeman might think we were escaping prisoners and take a pot shot.

On the way to Bromberg we noted a vast locomotive cemetery – hundreds of disabled engines, some elderly and worn out, but mostly modern locomotives bearing obvious battle scars, brought to this place for repair or as scrap. Close by were acres and acres of farmland turned into a vast ordnance dump for all kinds of stores and equipment brought back from the East Front. I doubt if it ever-went any further, and imagine that three months later it all fell into Russian hands.

At Bromberg we had the usual four hours' wait, and had nothing to eat but some bread and a tin of Spam that I had brought with me, between the five of us. It was a frustrating outing, though I had enjoyed much talk with Padre Gallagher, whom normally I rarely saw, a wise and good man.

My third trip was another of Haberer's bright ideas. He thought he could combine a chaplain's visit with a film show for several working parties lying close together. We set off on a Sunday early morning, a party of seven, four cinema carriers and operators, Haberer, myself and my assistant, Ernie Reoch, a young Scottish newspaper reporter. We were aiming for Sanskau and other camps near the bank of the Vistula opposite Graudenz. Transport was expected to meet us at Graudenz, but all that turned up was a small farm cart, large enough only to take the film equipment. So we set off across the river on foot, a good six mile walk to Sanskau, calling on the way to advise the camp at Gros Lubin that they could join us for the show in the afternoon. While the film crew prepared the hall, I went on two miles by carriage to Montau. After two hundred yards a wheel came off, and we nearly landed in the ditch. The driver took the horse back to the farm and reappeared twenty minutes later with an amazing vehicle. It was very old, very heavy and very shabby, a jet-black closed coach of enormous size. Inside it had shabby plush seats and very loose plate-glass windows. It must have been ancient, and caused something of a sensation along the road. It was a bit much for our poor horse, and we made slow progress. At Montau we lunched with the men, a good crowd, and invited them to the show. I had meant to go a stage further to Treul and call on the men there, but we had lost too much time.

At Sanskau the village hall easily contained the men from Gros Lubin, Montau and the two Sanskau camps. We had a short service and talk, and then the film show began. I had been told that the three elderly Frauleins Schmidt were agog to entertain the British chaplain again, so I persuaded Haberer to take me and Ernie down to their farm under the dyke during the show. I knew that he would not refuse a meal – he had already had breakfast and lunch on a farm, as well as sharing our lunch at Montau, and before we set out for home he was to persuade another farm to give him supper. The three old ladies were as courteous and charming as ever, and the visit was for us a delightful reminder of civilised home life.

It was dark when we set out for our return journey. A carriage was provided for the six mile journey to Graudenz, the only time that I ever travelled in a horse-drawn vehicle after dark, an eerie experience, as the two lamps do not cast any beam ahead. It was eleven o'clock by the time we returned to our camp at Torun. It had not been a satisfactory trip. It was no good combining a film show and a chaplain's visit, and Haberer saw the point.

It had been interesting, however, on this outing to note the widespread preparations for defence everywhere. Since the attempt on the Führer's life on 20 July Dr Goebbels had been working overtime on his propaganda, with truly remarkable results. He had employed two main themes: 'enemies within the Reich as well as without', and the Churchillian 'fighting in the fields and villages'. He had also mobilised for armed service an extensive Home Guard in civilian clothes, and, for digging, every man, woman and child who could lift a spade. No one was exempt; every Sunday, civilians of all ages were conveyed in their thousands to their allotted sites, and even the German Stalag officers, including doctors, had to turn out. As a seven day week had already been in force for some months, there was some grumbling, but less than one would have expected. Propaganda had had its effect and support for the Führer in his last suicidal stand was more general and in some cases more fanatic than at any time since the Golden Age of Nazism in 1940/41. As we watched all this frenzied activity, I could only think of the utter futility of the anti-tank ditches that we had laboriously dug all through the bitter winter of 1939/40, ditches that had been no obstacle to the Germans. On the Sunday morning at Graudenz we had seen hundreds of civilians digging and drilling on the banks of the Vistula, and all the villages around Sanskau were full of troops, resting, I was told, from the West Front.

23.10.44

. . . I am much enjoying Pepys' *Diaries,* which incidentally is part of a fine gift of books from the King and Queen for Christmas 1944; they have sent some lovely books each year . . .

23.10.44

Another placid week, ruffled only by a pleasant visit
from the Protecting Power, two Swiss gents . . .
Hospital very full, this week we get the Mixed
Medical Commission, so that if those who pass go
off we shall be much relieved. We have one or two
serious cases like a cerebral tumour, who has lost all
control of his functions, adding much to the work . . .

30.10.44

. . . Travelling no pleasure these days in icy winds.
We have temporarily in the camp possibly the best
pianist in prison, L/Cpl Thompson, an Aberdonian
solicitor; I plague him to play all the time . . .

6.11.44

I don't suppose you kept this day as an anniversary,
but it was on this day in 1941 that I first arrived here.
Looking back I am sure that I have been immensely
fortunate in my camps until recently, in my
companions and in my work, if I can so refer to the
ways in which I get through each day. Still I do not
want to see another anniversary here. We have lost
our first patient since I came to the hospital seven
months ago, a hopeless cerebral tumour. It says
something for the devotion of the medical orderlies
that he lay there helpless for a month, totally
incapable, and no trace of bed sores. One lovely
experience this week: a twenty-five-year-old RAMC
corporal, well educated with a good career before
him as an electrical engineer, has concluded nine
months of painstaking thought over his agnostic
position by telling me that he feels a compelling call
to be ordained; I had done no more than lend him
books and answer his questions as best I could. The
quality of his work here has been second to none . . .

Captain Allen says Saturday must have made me feel quite at home, with a funeral am and a whist drive pm. We would dearly like a present from Newcastle . . .

My recent visits had shown me that there was a marked decline in the morale of many of our men. The seven day working week, introduced in contravention of the Geneva Convention, for prisoners as well as civilians, was a severe trial for men who had been prisoners and working without any break for over four years. The Germans defended their policy by quoting a clause of the Convention, saying that prisoners must work the same hours as civilians; in fact it said that they must work not longer hours than civilians engaged in similar work, while another clause said that they must have a break of twenty-four hours in each week, preferably on Sundays. This clause they conveniently forgot. After the Normandy invasion, the supply of Red Cross parcels became very irregular at the same time as rations from the Germans were being reduced. Further, our men were finding it harder to evade regulations as they had been accustomed to do, or to manage things their own way with guards who were becoming more and more scared of supervision by the SS. This had increased since Himmler and the SS had assumed complete control of defence of the Reich at the expense of the Wehrmacht, which had hitherto jealously protected its right to be responsible for *bona fide* prisoners of war. There was also much understandable concern in our ranks that the allied offensive in the West had failed to force an issue and that we were consequently facing another winter, our fifth in prison, under steadily deteriorating conditions, as bad, if not worse than any we had known since the winter of 1940/41. Misunderstandings abounded, and tempers were shorter.

Nowhere was this more apparent than in the hospital, and towards the end of the year changes had to be made in the administration. The Senior Medical Officer was replaced by Captain Lake, who had recently been posted to the Stalag and had had considerable experience of administration in the Lamsdorf area. A general lack of tact and commonsense on the British side had not improved already difficult relations with the French doctor. By the end of the year it was increasingly apparent that he was telling stories to the Germans, and had not the Russians arrived in January, some drastic decision would have to have been made.

16.11.44

. . . three letters from you, all very cheerful . . . glad to hear some of mine have arrived. So pleased you too feel it hopeless to discuss post-war by post . . . Good of Michael Mounsey to write to you [a Quaker who had been repatriated]. We were close friends and worked together for two and a half years. He did splendid work for the camp . . . One cannot help feeling that many hard and tragic things may come before this business is through, but you and I have all to be thankful for . . . as no doubt you have been told by Mounsey life here has been clouded with domestic difficulties and loyalties to a more than reasonable degree . . . The problem has taken up all my time and patience to solve . . . actually there is no human solution . . .

7.12.44

I have just had a week's holiday, six days in bed, the only way one can take a holiday and I appreciated it much after the tension of playing an unwilling role in a domestic strife of some duration . . . I would like to have been a peacemaker, but it is not easy. It needs better judgment than I have got . . . I am pleased to find how much I like the new head of this hospital . . . it is a treat, believe me . . . Forgot to say 'Rabbits' this month . . .

A dramatic event early in the winter was the first demonstration of Allied air power over Torun. We were sitting at lunch one sunny day when a steady roar of engines drew

231

our attention to the fact that the sky was full of four-engined bombers, an awesome sight, several hundred Flying Fortresses cruising in a wide sweep over Torun and moving off in the direction of Warsaw. Our camp Feldwebel, never an ardent Nazi, came into the camp with a broad grin on his face and both hands held well above his head in mock surrender. We knew nothing of the tragic story behind this impressive raid. It was a forlorn attempt to deliver supplies to the beleaguered Poles in Warsaw in the last days of their desperate revolt against the Germans. Not only would the Russians give them no help, though they were within a few miles of the city, but they also refused to let the Allied raiders land and refuel behind their lines, and many of the planes were lost as they made their return journey or attempted to reach territory occupied by the Allies in Italy.

In November a Mixed Medical Commission for repatriation paid its six-monthly visit to review cases from the Stalag. Several cases submitted by our doctors were accepted when it was shown that the Germans had failed to carry out specialist examination or tests required by our doctors. The German medical machine, never very efficient, was showing signs of cracking altogether with the increased pressure of work, resulting from innumerable casualties from the East Front.

The British doctors from Einheit Drei attended this visit of the Commission, and I was able to provide a sumptuous supper. The French doctor, Liévain, had produced a goose, a present from a French prisoner who went out to work. He had hidden it in our Mess locker, and forgotten to tell me. I found it by chance and sent it to be cooked in the camp kitchen. When it came back it smelled distinctly high. I asked Liévain to vet it, and he agreed that it was 'un peu faisandé, mais il n'est pas dangereux.' ('a bit gamey, but not dangerous.') Private Barlow and I removed all the flesh and disguising the taste in a sauce made of strongly flavoured American soup powder, produced a most piquant dish. The taste was so unusual for palates accustomed to tinned food or German rations that we had little difficulty afterwards in persuading the Senior Medical Officer, much to his horror, that he had been eating cat.

Also in November, we had a visit from the Protecting Power, on this occasion an impressive Swiss diplomat. He expressed himself in more forcible terms to the Germans than his predecessor. He also gave us great pleasure by taking a meal with us, and in just sitting in our room wearing an immaculate pre-war Savile Row suit.

Nothing has been said yet about our neighbours, the permanent background to our life in Kopernikus Lager. Our compound was surrounded by the normal double line of barbed wire, ten feet high, with a tangle of more barbed wire between the lines. This was all that cut us off from the much larger section of the camp, occupied by about four thousand Russian prisoners. But we knew little about them, and our contact with them was minimal. They had a small 'hospital' compound close to the wire, which was always crowded, and for a time we were able to pass through to them small quantities of medical supplies and some of our German rations that we did not use. But there was little that we could do.

Apart from those in their hospital compound, most of the other thousands would in normal circumstances have been regarded as hospital cases. They were so damaged physically that they were beyond the state in which the Germans could get any work out of them, and they were consequently being virtually starved. Many of them lacked a limb, or more than one limb, and it was a common sight to see a man with no legs and his stumps bound up with dirty sacking walking about on them or dragging himself by his hands on a home-made sledge. Hundreds were so sick or mutilated, and so ill-clothed, that seen individually they would have caught one's eye and attracted one's sympathy anywhere. At Kopernikus Lager there were so many in such a condition, that after a time we ceased to notice them as anything unusual. The death rate was naturally high, and each morning a cart with about a dozen naked corpses left the camp for the cemetery nearby, where there were eight thousand Russian graves. (Naked, because the clothes of a dead man were too precious to be buried with him.) The men were desperately hungry, especially some boys, who cannot have been more than fifteen years old; each night some of these would at appalling risk squirm through the barbed wire into our compound in search of food from our men. We could not encourage this, but the practice continued, even after two of them had been shot dead in the middle of the entanglement.

On several occasions the Russians lined up a concert party, consisting of a band with strings, trumpets and guitars, and a very fine tenor, and gave us a concert across the intervening wire. In return we turned out our small band and gave them a concert. But this pleasant exchange was promptly banned by the Germans.

The trouble was our current Camp Commandant, Leutnant Führmann. He had had a long association with prisoners, having been Feldwebel in various camps since 1940. He was a smart soldier, and had been a reasonable taskmaster in the days when Germany was riding high, though his reputation with other nationalities, especially the Russians, was bad. Since the summer of 1944 he had been on an officers' training course, and in November he unexpectedly turned up as Leutnant in command of the whole of Kopernikus Lager, both British and Russian sections. We soon discovered that behind an ingratiating manner he was scared of blotting his copy-book as a newly promoted officer, and was tightening up the discipline of the guards. He was also becoming increasingly bitter about the course the war was taking. Soon after his arrival he turned out about forty guards and security men late one evening to do a snap search. Only by an amazing stroke of luck did they fail to discover our precious wireless set. It was in a large wooden box standing on a table in the middle of a room, with a flex going up to a ceiling light. When the searchers arrived, the listening team had not time to do more than pull down the flex, push it into the box and slam down the lid, leaving a small bit of flex still projecting. The intruders searched the room thoroughly, beds, cupboards, etc, but they never so much as glanced at the box sitting on the table.

I too had a strange brush with Führmann. There had been no deaths in our hospital since I arrived in the spring, but late in the year we lost three men from incurable diseases. To bury them in a plot attached to the Russian cemetery, I would leave the camp with the bier and a small guard of honour of our men. I was unhappy about the arrangements made by Führmann for the first two funerals, and asked him to give me a guard to go to Stalag to lodge a complaint with the Oberstleutnant. When he refused, I asked him to forward a letter, a request which he was not entitled to refuse, but he took the precaution of going himself to Stalag to counteract any effect my complaint might have; in vain, as Von Tiedermann came out the same afternoon to see me. He came into our room, and sitting down, asked me also to sit, leaving Führmann standing. I told him that our little cortège was on each occasion kept standing unnecessarily outside the German guardroom, and that the soldiers there and those who escorted us to the cemetery ostentatiously showed disrespect, unlike Poles in the road outside, who dismounted from their bicycles and raised their hats. One never needed to underline points like this with Von Tiedermann. To me he said, *'Dass geht natürlich nicht'* ('Obviously this cannot go on') and then, turning to Führmann he shouted a sharp reprimand and asked him what arrangements he proposed for the funeral due to be taken next day, saying finally, 'And don't let there be any mistake this time.' It was the last time that I saw Von Tiedermann, a man for whom I had great respect, and to whom I owed so much.

Appendix to **Autumn 1944**

Letter from Hans Heinrich Zürrer of the *Kriegsgefangenenhilfe* branch of the World Alliance of Young Men's Christian Association, Geneva.

21.8.45

Dear Sir,
  Mr Johannot transmitted me your letter. So I have the *plaisir* to answer you. First about your watch. I kept it hoping to bring it myself to Switzerland for repair. But as the Russian attack began, I decided to stay at Danzig with those of the French, Belgian and Dutch POW and deportees who I could see almost daily. I waited there until the Russians were in the town. It was a *wunder* that I could escape with my friends out of the total destruction of the old and beautiful town. But I lost

almost everything I had, my wartime log with all the addresses – yours too! – my Bible and other books, also my own watch and yours! I became a horseboy in the Red Army. I fell sick (dysentery), made acquaintance with lice, was hungry, had no clothes to change, no blanket for the night and was lost with a small group of Russians and Frenchmen in western Poland. I think I felt a little bit as a POW in the first days of his captivity. But after two weeks I escaped – as a POW – at midnight and after a long walk arrived at Bromberg, and the day after at Torun. This town has not suffered by the fightings, only the railway station and the part on the left side of the Vistula is destroyed. There I stayed a whole week with a Polish family. Then I returned to Danzig and departed on foot, by train and by motor cars through Germany to Switzerland. The trip during thirty two days was extremely interesting. I learnt to trust in God and to be free from cares. With one exception I received always food without asking for it. I think that you too made acquaintance with the Red Army and came home over Odessa, didn't you?

And now about your watch! You will have another in a few days. It will not be a Rolex, but another one which – as I hope – will please you. It is a new model of an automatic watch which you do not have to wind up. It is a gift of the YMCA as many others which have been sent to POW who did also excellent work for their comrades. Actually I am carrying the watch on my wrist to examine it until the papers are in order. So I hope that you will have it soon.

I regret that I had not more occasion to meet you at Stalag XXA because I know that I could learn many things from you. Sometimes yet I told about you to my Swiss friends. You have something which many clergymen in Switzerland are missing; a close relation between your conviction and your life. Here in Switzerland a clergyman has to learn dogmatics, while you in England teach the divine rules of social, political and personal life. For instance someone who declares God does not want from us religion but justice from man to man is in Switzerland considered an outsider, whilst in England as a wise man. Recently I listened to a sermon of the BBC. I held it for a typical English sermon. So I would like to have occasion to meet English padres, especially you. But for the moment it will be impossible, because I go soon into the territory occupied by French troops in Austria to continue the YMCA's work for the thousands of displaced persons who are awaiting there the day of their return to Russia, Poland, Yugoslavia, Romania and other countries. Mr Berg hopes to continue the work for ex-POWs in the American zone of Germany and my friend Soederberg has yet begun the work for German POWs in Belgium . . . In Sept. he will make a trip to USA to have a conference about the War Prisoners' Aid in Germany.

And you, dear Reverend, do you return to Eton College? I would like to hear something from you if you'll have time. And if you had the occasion to come to Switzerland, then you must come to me, please, I beg you instantly.

Yours truly,

Hans Heinrich Zürrer.

16

Christmas 1944

My Christmas began when an invitation arrived, authorised by the OKW Berlin, for a British chaplain to visit the *Strafe Gefängnis* at Graudenz on Christmas Day. I agreed to make the journey, and asked that the two large working parties in Graudenz should be included in the day's programme. The Germans agreed that I should be accompanied by CQMS Granger, the Stalag Man of Confidence. Taking him as my 'bag carrier' offered him the chance to see how his plans for diverting Red Cross supplies to the *Gefängnis* were working out.

As I was to be away on Christmas Day, I held a Carol Service and a Service of Holy Communion on Christmas Eve, and for my benefit the doctors advanced our Christmas dinner.

I made myself a cup of coffee at 3.30 am, and when my guard arrived we set off on an hour's walk to Torun station at 4 o'clock. It was a sparkling frosty night, with the temperature around minus fifteen degrees centigrade and with a brilliant display of stars. The beaten snow on the road was dangerously slippery. At the station we found Granger who had come from Einheit Drei, and Sonderführer Braun, who was to escort us. He was a welcome choice, having escorted me on a number of occasions. He was invariably sympathetic and cooperative, and when he spoke enthusiastically of Padre Gallagher's Midnight Mass which he had just attended, I knew he had appreciated it more as a devout Catholic than as an Abwehr observer.

The train at 5.39 was full but not overcrowded. Between stations the carriage got up a good fug, but whenever the door was opened a perishingly cold wind blew in. At Graudenz it was a short walk to the largest British camp, the Internat, where we were given a welcome breakfast by the Australian Resident Doctor, Lionel Sapsford. We discussed plans for an evening service there, and I set off with Granger and Braun for the *Gefängnis*.

On arrival, as on previous visits, we were closely scrutinised at the guardroom and were then escorted to the office of the Major Commandant. A dapper little man of about sixty, wearing his Sunday best uniform, he stood up to receive us. He would have been wiser to have remained seated as both Granger and I were well over six feet tall, and somehow seemed to achieve an initial advantage.

He began by explaining that our visit had been very specially and unusually authorised by the OKW Berlin, almost, he seemed to suggest, by the Führer himself. It was clear that he was in a state of jitters, lest something should occur in the course of our visit to displease his superiors.

'I have to welcome you,' he said in German, 'to this prison on Christmas Day. You are permitted by Berlin to preach for forty-five minutes, but not to have speech with any officer or other rank in the camp.'

I thanked him and said that I was not accustomed to preach for so long, but I assumed that the time allotted applied to the whole service.

'On a previous visit,' I said, 'I was allowed by your predecessor to talk to the men under supervision.'

'Nein,' he replied, *'dass ist verboten.'*

'But,' I said, 'would it be possible to make arrangements with the Senior British Officer or Warrant Officer to allow those who wish to join in Holy Communion after the service?'

'Abendmahl ist von Berlin streng verboten,' ('Communion is strictly forbidden by Berlin') he replied, and of this strange interdiction clearly no more could be said.

'May I visit the men in hospital?' I asked.

'Nein, dass ist auch verboten.'

He then directed us to sit at a table in the corner of his office while he gave meticulous orders to Braun and his own interpreter about what I could or could not do. Both were to attend the service. While he was doing this I opened my case and took out a sheaf of hymn sheets and carol papers. He rushed across the room and asked what they were. Braun picked one up and handed it to him.

'But they have no censor stamp on them,' he exclaimed.

Braun and I tried to explain to him that they were Christian hymns and carols, sent to us from Geneva by the International YMCA with OKW permission and were used in all POW camps. After some argument he asked for a translation, and I watched as a curious look of perplexity spread over his face. Braun had mischievously chosen to translate 'Now thank we all our God' *'Nun danket . . .'*.

'Dass ist deutsches Hymnus,' he exclaimed.

The point was made, and we set off for the chapel escorted by his interviewer.

As we entered the large Gothic chapel by the door into the chancel, I noticed that the interpreter and Braun walked away to the west end, where they remained throughout the service. Meanwhile all the 200 British and Commonwealth prisoners came in through the sanctuary door, passing right by me on their way to their seats. All of them nodded to me, some wished me a Merry Christmas, and some whom I had known in Stalag XXA left the column, shook me by the hand and asked for any news I might have of their friends. Not one of them uttered a word of complaint about the conditions under which they were living. While Granger walked round with the hymn sheets I had a useful chat with the Senior British Officer, a New Zealand colonel, and some of the other officers. The interpreter made no move to stop me.

Christmas is the family festival, and for most of those present at that service it was the fifth Christmas spent in captivity, separated from their families. They sang lustily and listened attentively to my inadequate contribution; the lot of all prisoners was bad enough, but these men were serving court-martial sentences under particularly rigorous conditions. It was a privilege to be able to visit them on Christmas Day and speak of the Christian message of faith and hope in a caring Saviour. I was sorry not to be allowed to administer the Sacrament of Holy Communion as had previously been permitted.

As the men filed out I had further talk with some of them, again without any interference from the censors, and at that moment a message arrived to say that the Major had changed his mind, and I had permission to visit the sick bay after all. (Perhaps he had rung the Führer.) I was glad of this, as I knew that among the patients there, who were mostly French or Italian, was a British merchant seaman who had been under sentence of death for the past three years. Granger was fully informed about the current state of his case, having been corresponding about it with the Red Cross and the Protecting Power. So I left them to talk it over while I spent most of the time with the others, all of whom were touchingly grateful for our visit.

Word then arrived that we were to return to the Commandant's office. So we ended with prayers for the patients and their families. Back in the office we found the New Zealand colonel and the Senior British Warrant Officer. The Major said that we could talk for ten minutes, but he refused me permission to offer them a cigarette. (He had probably run out himself.) We went to work quickly, and Granger discussed all kinds of questions about mail and Red Cross supplies of food and medicine. At intervals the Major anxiously asked Braun what we were saying and after ten minutes he closed the discussion. He called a guard who took the Colonel and Sergeant-Major out through one door, and when I had thanked the Major for his arrangements we were shown out with Braun through another door. We all met outside again in the corridor and continued our discussion.

From the *Gefängnis* we had a two mile walk to Neue Heimat camp, where the ebullient Corporal Williams had laid on for us a typical Neue Heimat feast, a real Christmas dinner with two large black-market chickens with all the trimmings. Braun was not the man to resist or query such temptation, and enjoyed it as much as we did. He was the last to realize what was happening when the tell-tale remains on our plates were hurriedly swept from under our noses and shovelled into the stove. News had reached Williams that a strange German officer had been spotted heading for our room. Williams was already awaiting a court-martial for illegal trading with the civilian population.

After lunch we had a service in the recreation room and watched a game of football played on a snowy ground before walking back another mile to the Internat. The service at six o'clock was the best I ever held there, a good turn-out, hymns and carols well sung and well accompanied by a competent small band, and afterwards quite a number shared in a service of Holy Communion.

A quick walk to the station, another mile, and a two hour rail journey brought us to Torun by ten o'clock. Then another long walk on ice-covered roads to Einheit Drei, where I spent the night. So ended the most arduous but certainly one of the happiest Christmases of my life. All day in such varied surroundings there had been a sense of togetherness and mutual support.

Less than a month later the Russians had begun to overrun western Poland. No letter of mine has survived with a date later than 7.12.44 except for my final one of 1.1.45. There must have been several, but understandably by this stage of the war, with Germany rapidly collapsing, mail had become unreliable. We were certainly no longer receiving mail from home.

1.1.45

I feel a cad for not writing lately, but my right hand and my forearm have been immobilised in plaster – tino-sinovitis. I have been wondering where you spent your Christmas. We have had a month of extreme cold, though not much snow until Christmas . . . [after a short account of my Graudenz expedition] . . . I slept twenty-four of the next thirty-six hours. You need not worry about food; we have not done too badly and today we received the magnificent Christmas parcels. I have been sleeping very well and enjoying the severe but fine cold weather. I dearly hope that you are also flourishing, and that this year is the last – the ONE . . .

It was.

17

Release

In the early days of our captivity in 1940 we passed the time weaving fantasies about the time and mode of our ultimate release. Dick Troughton imagined he was looking down from the upper windows of Oflag VIIC into the main street of the village of Laufen. A sports MG would approach the prison gate, conveying two gorgeous young ladies. One would get out and, having knocked on the main gate, say to the duty guard, 'I think you have a Mr Troughton here. We are taking him out to luncheon.'

My fantasy was rather different. I saw a British scout car drive up to the gate. From this slowly would emerge the long, lanky figure of an Old Etonian subaltern in immaculately creased battledress, with a coloured and braided forage cap and brown suede shoes. Approaching the guard on the gate, he would enquire in a well-bred drawl, 'I say, you fellow, have you got some British types in there?'

In fact, it was two Russian private soldiers who ultimately effected my release, well into the fifth year of our captivity. They even had snow on their boots.

On 16 January our wireless bulletin showed that a Russian advance of great magnitude was in progress. Next day we heard that Warsaw had fallen, and that one spearhead of the Russian advance was heading towards Torun. It became obvious that some kind of evacuation of the Stalag would be attempted by the Germans. Our doctors decided that preparation must be made to carry the lying sick, sixteen in number. Our camp carpenter was instructed to make stretchers with wood and blanket material.

The situation remained obscure for the next few days, but

on Friday 19th the censor Braun from Stalag told us that the Stalag was expected to be evacuated on foot next day, and that all files at HQ were being burnt. In the afternoon Captain Lake visited Einheit Drei, and there received orders from Oberstabsarzt Weidermann. All men in the hospital and elsewhere who could walk were to leave with the main Stalag party on foot, and all sick men who could not walk were to join those in Kopernikus. We decided that Lake, Feltham, the second doctor, and I should stay at Kopernikus with fifteen French and British orderlies, and that the rest of the staff should leave on foot under Captain Allen and Liévain, the French doctor.

When we went to bed on Friday night no precise orders had been received, but our wireless bulletin suggested that the Russians had advanced about halfway across western Poland. German transport of all kinds was streaming past the camp along the Torun-Bromberg road. The rout had begun.

At 4 am Führmann arrived in our room with instructions that the walking party was to leave at 8 am. Neither then nor at any subsequent stage did he question our decision as to who should stay. The Germans of all ranks were far too busy making their own arrangements for getting themselves and their baggage away. Lake told Führmann that he wished the Red Cross store opened so that those who were leaving could have one each of the 2000 invalid comfort parcels then in store. When Führmann said that he could not allow that without a *Befehl* (instruction) from Stalag, Lake told him in no uncertain terms that this was not a time for talking about *Befehls* from Stalag. The store was opened.

By eight o'clock the walking party was ready to leave, equipped with sledges of all shapes and sizes for dragging their kit along the snow-bound roads. It was more than an hour later when they set off, and, simultaneously with their departure, sick men arrived from Einheit Drei accompanied by Major F the New Zealand dentist, two padres and a number of medical orderlies. They were supposed to leave the sick men and continue on the march. While they were still in the camp, however, confusion was caused by an air-raid alarm and the din of an ack-ack battery just outside the camp. When this was over the guards were completely demoralised, and eventually decided that it was too late to catch up with the

Stalag, and that the Einheit Drei officers and orderlies would have to remain with us at Kopernikus. None of these showed much enthusiasm to join the walkers, but it was unfortunate that no doctors except Allen, and no chaplains accompanied the Stalag column on the long march into Germany, where their services during the next two months were sorely missed, and many of the marchers died.

Meanwhile, during the morning preparations were being made to fit the cellars under the cookhouse for occupation in an emergency. It was the only solid, brick-built structure in the whole compound. We also brought as many parcels as we could manage from the stores, wheeling them laboriously in hand-drawn carts across soft sand and snow for over a quarter of a mile. At this stage it was not the intention that we should evacuate our wooden huts, and some of the staff painted large red crosses on a white ground on the roofs and sides of the huts facing the Posen road, along which the Russians might be expected to arrive.

The Germans then withdrew all guards except those in the lofty machine-gun boxes outside the wire, whereupon our compound was immediately invaded by several hundred Russian prisoners from next door. They were a pitiful crew, many with missing limbs, and they crowded round our huts, hoping for loot. At first it was possible to keep them at bay, but after an hour or two their manner became more threatening; they were breaking into rooms and wards through the windows, and whenever a room was left empty for a moment they swarmed in and looted it from top to bottom. One party during the morning, not surprisingly, stormed the cookhouse and cleaned up our lunch which was cooking. It soon became clear that we could do nothing about this invasion, and Lake gave orders that everyone was to assemble in the cookhouse. We took with us what kit we could and cleared out. I was the last to leave our hut, and was nearly overwhelmed as a horde of Russian down-and-outs forced their way in and stripped the place of everything we possessed. It was a frightening encounter.

Throughout the evening things looked fairly desperate. Pickets posted round the cookhouse, unarmed of course, managed with difficulty to keep the Russians at a distance. Then the situation eased considerably when Lake arranged with some Germans to issue to the Russians all the remaining Red Cross parcels – amounting to as many as a thousand –that we had not managed to bring to the cookhouse.

The cookhouse was a considerable building with brick walls and a high roof of corrugated iron. The floors were of concrete, and below were four cellars, rectangular rooms of identical size. They were not connected, and each room had a doorway opening out to a narrow stair leading up to ground level. Brick walls and brick vaulting supported the concrete floor of the cookhouse above. We joined up the four rooms by knocking apertures through the brick dividing walls.

Our total strength was about one hundred and eighty French and British, and included three doctors, three padres and a useless French doctor who had appeared from a *Strafe* prison in Torun. Dick Feltham collected most of the seriously sick in one of the four rooms. For the rest of us it was a tight fit indeed; we just about found lying space for all. Electric light of a kind had been fitted up, but there was no sanitation except buckets, which at night could only be reached with difficulty by climbing over recumbent figures. The temperature at night was somewhere around minus twenty-five degrees centigrade, and by day not much better. It would have been total misery had it not been for the cooks upstairs, who managed at intervals to produce some food and hot drinks. Those who had set off on the march spent that first night, as we heard later, in an open field.

On Sunday there were still guards around the camp, but by midday no trains were running by on the Posen-Torun line. From the radio we learnt that the Russians might reach Torun within forty-eight hours. During the morning we had a visit from the chief Russian doctor, whom we knew quite well, and one of his patients, a Russian full-colonel parachutist, who had recently been captured. After lunch with some of our officers in the cookhouse, he agreed at their request to give orders to the Russian prisoners to keep away from the cookhouse. His order was only partially obeyed, and some hungry Russians continued to haunt us. They had thoroughly looted all the huts. Towards evening we could see some very large fires burning in the direction of Einheit Drei. I led prayers that night in each of the four rooms.

Late in the evening, when the radio bulletin was coming

through on Corporal Forster's set in the corner of a cellar, there was a disturbance by the door, and a very agitated Führmann appeared carrying a Tommy gun at the ready. He was a bundle of nerves, and at first it was hard to make out what he was trying to say. The situation looked distinctly ugly for a few minutes, especially as Führmann had not realized what was happening, and the radio continued with the bulletin. First he wanted to know if there were any Russians in the cellar. Then he said he wanted us all to go down to the German quarters a quarter of a mile away by the main gate of the camp, in the dark and through the snow. With difficulty we persuaded him to drop this idea, and then he calmed down a bit and stopped shouting. He told us that he had accompanied the marching column to Bromberg, but he did not explain why he had left the column and returned to Torun, where he obviously had no future. Finally he said that he would be staying until the Russians arrived; but we never saw him again after this strange interview.

Next morning there were no guards visible inside or outside the camp, but all day we could see small groups of Germans digging in at various points on the Posen road alongside the camp. By midday audible sounds of battle and aerial activity increased, and early in the afternoon we could see what appeared to be tank action outside the tank ditch that had been dug two miles away, near Fort XV on the east side of Torun. At about four o'clock someone reported that a Russian patrol in white overalls had been seen fifty yards outside the wire on the Posen road. Lake took Ivan, a young Russian who had been batman to Führmann and had attached himself to us, and went over the wire. He contacted the patrol, but they seemed hazy as to who we were and went on their way. Many of the Russian prisoners broke out through the wire at this point and raced off across country after the patrol, probably to their embarrassment, and soon after we heard shots and some of them came slinking back into the camp.

As it grew dark, machine-gun fire opened up all over the place, and a stream of tracer bullets came from the woods over by the railway. Most of them passed over the cookhouse in the direction of the Posen road, but some hit the building. Artillery fire also opened up nearby, and further off it was a continuous roar. I did not know what others were feeling; I only know that I was in a state of acute anxiety, a blue funk, to put it mildly. Most people seemed to think that the cookhouse was a good solid building, but it had been built by POW labour, for what that was worth, and the brick vaulting of the cellars was less solid-looking than that of the building in which I had been blown up by a shell in Cassel in 1940. Standing on a rise, the most conspicuous feature in a singularly featureless landscape and the only brick building in the area, visible from miles away, it seemed a thoroughly undesirable residence, and I felt certain that a direct hit would penetrate into the cellars, with devastating effect.

At about ten o'clock, without any warning two flash shells exploded with a terrific din directly above the building, extinguishing all the lights that we had improvised since the electricity supply had ceased the night before. I had an uncomfortable feeling that the Germans, expecting the Russians to occupy the cookhouse, were getting their range, ready for an early morning barrage. Everyone was nervous, but the men were full of lively backchat as ever. The Yalta Conference was in progress, and in the dark I heard one man remark in a loud voice, 'It only needs Churchill to call Joe Stalin a bugger, and we're all in the cart.'

Lake had been handling the situation with reassuring calm, and it was he who had taken the critical decision to abandon the huts and concentrate in the cellars. By this time he was desperately tired, and came to squeeze into the space next to me for some sleep. Partly to give him more room, and partly, perhaps mainly, because I was too cold and too frightened to sleep, I left him and went into the next cellar to sit with Dick Feltham, who was on duty with the sick. I talked with him while the men snored away, and I counted off the minutes, one by one, all night, waiting for the barrage that I felt sure would come in the morning after the two ranging shots of the night before. Lake had ordered everyone to come below ground, but overhead I could hear men walking about on the concrete floor of the cookhouse. About 4 am a little Cockney private soldier came down and told us that Sergeant Morice and he had the fires going, and intended to produce porridge and tea for all before daylight. It seemed a sporting effort, and not the moment to speak of orders being orders. Over the most welcome cup of tea that he brought us he told us that some Russian prisoners had invaded the cookhouse; he had stripped them and made them wash, and now had them stoking the fires and stirring the porridge.

There was no barrage, and we had our porridge and tea before dawn in comparative quiet. Shots still passed over the camp at intervals, apparently from Germans and Russians, but around ten o'clock someone on the lookout said that two Russians had arrived. Dressed in rough, warm clothing, with Tommy guns slung over their shoulders, they came down into our cellar. Lake spoke to them through Ivan, and then gave the order that we were to evacuate at once, taking no kit whatsoever. All fit men were to assist in carrying the sixteen stretcher cases. Inside the cellars there was turmoil; passing the stretchers through the doors, round the corner and up the steps was extremely awkward. A few men, chiefly Frenchmen, were blocking the way, trying to extricate their personal belongings. I pushed and struck two of them, and bundled them out of the way. Lake told me with satisfaction that he found an able-bodied Frenchman loading himself with kit and a large guitar; he threw him out and chucked the guitar into a corner. Speed was vital.

I took one corner of a stretcher bearing a French patient, and with three other men made our way through a small gap in the wire into the Russian compound. Crossing that, we came to the top end of the camp within a few feet of the Posen road; but to our horror we found that the wire had not been cut. All the men from our compound were assembling at this exposed point, and we were being joined every moment by hundreds more Russians, all delirious with excitement. Some were trying to climb the wire entanglement, ten feet high and four feet wide, impeding our men who were trying to hack a way through with choppers and other instruments. I was afraid that this mauling mass was presenting a perfect target to the nearest German troops, and I decided to hold my stretcher party some thirty yards away, under the shelter of a hut.

At last a small passage was made in the wire, and we moved up to find a way through. To my amazement, the brawling mob of starving and mutilated Russians shouted to each other as each stretcher came up, and they made way for us. Once out on the road, I took a last look back. From where we stood, the road stretched away downhill across the bleak Truppenübungsplatz to the main German defences three miles away in front of Torun. It was a morning of pale colouring, the snow sparkling in the wintry sunshine, and we had cut our way through the barbed wire to freedom. In less than ten minutes we had emptied the cellars, and in half an hour we had cleared all through the wire.

But it was no time for lingering. We started the stretcher party off at as fast a pace as we could manage, but the road was terribly slippery and twice one of our party went down, nearly toppling the patient off the stretcher. At intervals we passed Russian posts with light anti-tank guns pointing down the road in the direction of Torun. The soldiers, mostly in white overalls, simple Mongolian-featured types, stared at us with looks of surprise and no comprehension. Released Russians, many of them on stumps or wooden legs, streamed along beside us and shouted greetings to their fellow-countrymen, who made no reply and just continued to stare.

Our road soon plunged into a forest, and on either side we passed groups of cavalrymen, horse transport and light artillery, gathered under the trees, always in small numbers. After about five kilometres we halted, and our straggled party formed into a group. To our surprise, we found our friendly Russian colonel waiting for us with some other Russian officers; apparently he had slipped out of the camp the night before and had given news of our position to the forward Russian troops. A speech was made, and we were told that we would soon receive transport, and that within a week we would be in Moscow. Meanwhile we were in a danger zone and must proceed as quickly as possible.

The afternoon march was a nightmare. It was found that most of the stretchers, which were cumbersome and very heavy, would run if dragged on the icy road, but some would not and had to be carried. The further we went back from the front, the more troops we met advancing. There were thousands of them, almost all on foot. We saw no transport except horse-drawn vehicles, most of it commandeered farm vehicles, and all piled high with baggage and loot. We saw less than twenty tanks, and very few guns of any size. Motorised transport was almost non-existent. Except that most of the infantry carried automatic rifles, it might have been a

Napoleonic army on the move, seemingly endless columns wending their way across country in the snow as far as the eye could see.

We were in total ignorance of the local situation. The Russians appeared to be pouring an inexhaustible number of troops along this so-called main road with no apparent air cover of any kind. Clearly the German main force had been completely withdrawn, but the Russians seemed anxious about the existence of scattered groups in the forests on both flanks, and there were continual outbursts of sporadic firing at no great distance. The main Russian advance appeared to be by-passing Torun on the northern side and pressing on towards Bromberg, which, as we heard later, had already fallen, with scarcely any resistance. Several times in the afternoon we were urged on by our Russian colonel to keep going, as the area was not yet safe.

The Russian soldiers looked perplexed when they saw us, but as word of our identity passed along the ranks, they broke into broad grins and hailed as with shouts of 'Anglicani' or 'Amerikanski'. Occasionally we saw fine-looking cavalrymen galloping through fields bordering the road, a few wearing traditional Cossack dress. Most of the infantrymen wore thick quilted uniforms, and all had Wellington-shape boots made of stiff grey felt material.

After covering about fifteen kilometres we were halted at last in mid-afternoon, just off the main road by a group of cottages. After some delay, we were told that transport was available for the stretcher cases and a few others, while the rest of us were to push on to a town called Alexandrovo, ten kilometres further on. It was bitterly cold and we were extremely tired, more particularly some of the medical orderlies, who had carried almost without relief the two stretchers that would not run on the road. But there was no time to rest, as night was fast approaching.

For another five kilometres we continued along the main road; traffic was increasing all the time, infantry, often two columns abreast, horse transport and artillery, some American-manufactured lorries and a few large tanks. Against the tide, we could only walk in single file along the verges, and the going was difficult. Hundreds of Russian prisoners were going the same way, and we followed them when their column

251

turned off the main road by a field track. In the dark the going became worse than ever and the snow deeper. Many of the Russians turned aside to find shelter for the night in deserted and derelict cottages and barns, but it seemed risky to drop out in such company, and we kept plodding on.

After what seemed like eternity, we crept at last into the small town of Alexandrovo. There we found a small cottage hospital staffed by elderly Polish nuns, who made no fuss but quietly welcomed us in. We had covered about twenty-five kilometres. We were probably given something to eat and drink, but no memory remains of this. I simply lay down on a bare table and went to sleep.

Next morning we took stock. There was no one to give us instructions or order us about. The hospital was overflowing with sick and wounded Germans and Russians. The angelic nuns, only about half a dozen, made no distinction. They were just doing what they could with what they had got. We made a plan eventually. Most of our party, with Russian agreement, were to proceed to the town of Ciechocinek, about five miles away, while one doctor, two British and two French orderlies, and myself found some sort of a billet next door to the hospital. Our stretcher cases would remain in the hospital.

There was an eerie atmosphere in the village. There were few Russians about. Civilians of the Polish Resistance emerged from their various lairs from which they had been operating for five years, only to be rudely rebuffed by the Russians; they were either shot, or arrested, or retreated back into hiding. The splendid-looking Polish priest who had been one of the first to welcome us was arrested and led away, to the dismay of the poor nuns.

Meanwhile a makeshift 'parish council' had set itself up in a cottage across the road from our billet. They were a villainous looking riff-raff whom the Russians had unearthed to supervise the town, in preference to the admirable Poles, who for five years had formed the only valid resistance to the Germans.

For a week we tried to find out how we could move our non-walking sick on to Ciechocinek. I sent our French sergeant orderly over the road to the sinister Kommandantur to ask for advice and assistance. He found them sitting around in a sleazy den, smoking heavily and drinking schnapps, and formidably slung round with an assortment of lethal weaponry.

On his return, his delightfully understated verdict was, *'Je ne suis pas rassuré.'* ('I am not reassured.')

For two more days we continued to visit this unpromising establishment in search of information. We were anxious not to prolong our stay in the hospital, where all the beds and most of the corridors were filled with hideously wounded men, both Russian and German. At one point a Russian officer, finding a bed occupied by a wounded German, ordered his removal. To the dismay of the nuns the man was carried out of the hospital, dumped in the snow outside and shot where he lay.

Quite unexpectedly, a Polish farm cart appeared outside the hospital, and we were told we could load up our stretcher cases, now reduced to three, and be on our way. Gratefully we trundled off through the snow, and without further problems arrived safely at Ciechocinek some five miles away.

18

Last Lap

Ciechocinek, which for the past four years had borne the name of Hermannsbad in honour of the notorious Marshal Goering, presented a surprising appearance. It had been a health spa. Grouped around a wide square of formal but neglected gardens were a number of imposing hotels, straight out of Harrogate or Baden-Baden. Apart from this impressive town centre, the rest of the surrounding town consisted of singularly unimpressive and sorely neglected and scruffy houses.

A small hotel had been allotted to the British contingent of released prisoners, and with them, to our considerable relief, we were reunited. Conditions in the building were primitive, and it was uncomfortably crowded. Our numbers had swollen to about three hundred, a considerable number of former inmates of our hospital and of other camps having, by various means, dropped out of the westward march of prisoners towards Germany and found their way to Ciechocinek. Apart from the clothes we stood up in, our possessions were virtually non-existent; in order to carry the stretcher cases, we had abandoned all else. We were provided with a few blankets and a little fuel, and the rations available for the next two months provided us with half a loaf of bread and one barley soup a day.

The Russians, who had a small garrison in the town, showed little interest in our existence. From time to time a Russian officer, accompanied by some kind of political commissar and an interpreter, paid us a visit, listened to our complaints, shrugged his shoulders and disappeared again. One day an inebriated Russian soldier wandered into the building and left, taking with him one of our soldier's greatcoats. We sent for a Russian officer, who heard our complaint and departed saying that he would investigate the alleged theft. Two days later he returned and delivered a short formal address through his interpreter as follows:

'I have investigated your complaint. No Russian soldier entered your camp as you allege. It was a German soldier. There are many German soldiers masquerading as Russians, endeavouring to sow discord between two great Allies. Good day.'

The party then turned about and departed.

Realizing that we were in for a long stay, we were particularly anxious that the authorities at home, and through them our families, should be informed that we were 'safe' in Russian hands. After some days' delay it was agreed that the Russians should compile a nominal roll and forward it to England. A Russian officer, an interpreter and a young scribe armed with huge sheets of paper ruled in columns took up their position, and all three hundred of us lined up to supply the required information. We were asked innumerable questions, such as our forbears' names and places of birth, all of which was laboriously written down phonetically in Russian script. This presented problems when the scribe was faced with names like Maclachlan. We tried to persuade them to include the only item likely to make an impression at home, our army number. 'There is no such thing,' the officer declared.

It all took a long time, and we were not optimistic about the success of the operation. Two days later, the officer re-appeared with a different scribe. He said that he would like to check the list. One by one we filed up to the table and were asked all the same questions. At least fifty per cent of our original answers were crossed out and a new phonetic version substituted. The lists, needless to say, never reached White-hall, and would have produced many problems of identifi-cation if they had.

Rather surprisingly, we were provided one day with a truck and driver, and returned to the hospital at Torun in the hope of finding some possessions, but the camp had been thoroughly looted, and all our books and other treasures accumulated and preserved over five years had been

255

shovelled into a trench and buried.

Two dreary months passed by with few diversions. We were not confined to barracks, but though I took a few short walks in the town and in the neighbouring countryside, there was an ominous feeling of tension. The front had passed well beyond us, but there was quite a lot of unexplained rifle and automatic fire still going on, especially after dark. The few Poles with whom I spoke were desperately worried about their prospects.

One night a few of us were invited by the Russian garrison to attend a dinner to mark one of their national anniversaries, the anniversary, if I remember right, of the founding of the Red Army. We were liberally feasted with loaded plates of roast pork and with fiercesome schnapps, while endless toasts were drunk. Accustomed to a diet of one barley soup a day, I was sorely to regret this indulgence.

After our arrival at Ciechocinek the next door hotel was taken over and occupied by a contingent of nearly five hundred American troops, all of whom had been captured six weeks earlier by the Germans in the Ardennes winter offensive and, more recently, overrun, as we had been, by the Russians. They had managed to arrive with a surprising amount of stores, some of which they shared with us. They were also more suitably clothed for a Polish winter. Several evenings I went in and played bridge with some of their officers. They were an interesting study. Six weeks of captivity was almost more than they could endure, and they were childishly puzzled at finding themselves in the unfamiliar situation, in which the power of the dollar counted for nothing.

For us it was difficult to formulate any kind of plan. Our objective clearly was to get on the move and return home. The Russians appeared to have no plan for us and no information that gave us any clue about a future move. This was understandable; their job was to conquer the Germans and win the war. We had nothing to contribute, and plans for our disposal were to them a very low priority. To us it seemed best to remain together as a coherent unit. The senior American officer evidently thought otherwise; to the consternation of his brother officers, he went missing suddenly, without leaving any explanation or instructions. I doubt if he received a very rapturous reception when he caught up with the party he had deserted some weeks later at Odessa.

The maddening inertia of the Russians responsible for our repatriation was causing us problems. On the approach of the Russian army some working camps, like our hospital, had never been evacuated by the Germans, and had been overrun. Many men from the marching parties also fell into Russian hands at various points between Torun and Stettin. Such men found it difficult to establish their identity with the Russians and many unpleasant, even fatal, incidents occurred. Russian local commanders had no instructions or only very hazy notions about what to do with British POWs. Usually the stragglers were told to make their way to some collecting centre, among those mentioned being Bromberg, Hohensalze, Ciechocinek and Lublin. It became clear, however, to us at Ciechocinek that many British ex-prisoners were scattered all over the countryside, having drifted back to their farms and girl friends; others were going aimlessly from place to place, at increasing risk to themselves as the Russians found more time to round them up. To complicate matters, out of our three hundred men at Ciechocinek, eighty left the camp without permission, some, like the US colonel, because they thought that they might get home more quickly by pushing on (some did just that), others because they knew that they would live and feed better in Polish homes than in the camps provided and rationed by the Russians.

We took up this point with a Russian colonel who arrived unexpectedly in our camp. He was, as it turned out, the senior officer responsible for the repatriation of prisoners of war in the sector covered by the advance of Marshal Zhukov's army. After some discussion, he agreed to take me to the Bromberg area where he was based, and where it was known that many of our men were on the loose. It was also agreed that I would take with me Esther Lurie as my interpreter. She was by origin a Lithuanian Jewess. She was highly intelligent, spoke English, German, French and Russian fluently, and was an accomplished professional artist. At some time before 1939, I think in Palestine, she had acquired British papers. In 1939 she had been captured by the Germans while on a visit to her family in Eastern Europe, and since then she had been in a concentration camp. When the surviving inmates of that camp were marched out in January 1945, they were overtaken by the Russians. Esther produced her English documents, and, amazingly, the Russians accepted them and dumped her on us. With her command of languages she was invaluable to us, even though she was understandably not in the best of health.

The Russian colonel had arrived with three trucks full of Russian soldiers. He travelled in the leading truck, and Esther and I were allowed to travel in the driving cabin of the second. The column set off at speed on the icy roads, but after a few miles our truck broke down and we had to transfer into the open uncovered back of the third truck. This also broke down and Esther and I and all the troops packed ourselves into the first truck, where we lay in a huge huddle on the floor. We appeared to be making up for lost time as the truck raced along the icy roads, skidding past oncoming traffic and on one occasion striking one of the roadside trees broadside on and bouncing back on to the road. Our Russian companions seemed to find it all highly exhilarating, shouting and laughing at every twist, turn and skid. I was less thrilled.

At Bromberg we dismounted, cold and battered, outside the largest and smartest hotel. The Colonel escorted us upstairs to his private suite, where an orderly promptly produced a welcome meal with schnapps and excellent wine. With Esther as interpreter, the Colonel and I discussed all kinds of subjects until I eventually reminded him that I had come to Bromberg with a mission to complete. He summoned a truck through his orderly, and this conveyed Esther and myself to extensive barracks which were being used as a collecting centre for released prisoners. At the main gate a Serbian soldier, armed and apparently acting as sentry, made no attempt to query our right of entry.

Inside we found a disorderly conglomeration of all nationalities: Americans (about a dozen), French and Belgian soldiers and civilian conscript workers. Ukranian men and women, Jewesses, Serbs and many others. Among all these were five British private soldiers. They had no papers and no instructions. Several times they had been told to stand by for transport, and each time nothing had materialised. There were no beds, and food was poor. I learnt from them that at least fifty British soldiers were living with civilian Polish families in the town, including one British sergeant by the name of Glover of the Royal Sussex regiment. Later Glover told me that the number was far larger.

I found the Russian Commandant, a captain, who was surprisingly courteous and cooperative. When I asked him what steps were being taken to repatriate British prisoners of war, he assured me that everything was in train. I asked about men living in civilian houses, and he told me that he would start rounding them up next day and all would be sent to Odessa. (Glover later told me that no such round-up took place for at least four days.) At first the Colonel welcomed my suggestion that I should stay and assist in gathering up the stray British soldiers and despatching them homewards, but later he changed his mind and said that I could be of no use, and that anyway I was registered in a different army area, a splendid red tape objection.

I had also by then decided that without the backing of some recognized repatriation mission, it was useless for me to try to make further progress. But at least I had stirred the pot. As I knew well from my own army experience, a wonderful inertia descends on officers posted to behind the lines jobs. I was unable to contact Sergeant Glover before I was due to leave, but I left a note for him with an American sergeant, urging him to get as many British men as possible heading towards Odessa. This he did successfully, and later we met many of them there. On our way back to the hotel we ran into three British stragglers, who also made this journey successfully. They told me that under Russian instructions they had hitch-hiked by truck and train several hundred kilometres to Lublin. There they had found dismal conditions and no further instructions; in despair, they had made the long journey back to Bromberg, where they knew that they had Polish friends.

Back at the hotel, we found that the Colonel had ordered another sumptuous meal with liberal supplies of wines and spirits, and was obviously keen to continue our conversation. We discussed at length, and at times with some heat, the current tricky state of affairs in Greece. Even today I have difficulty in understanding the complex situation in that country following liberation from the Nazis, but in Bromberg in March 1945, both protagonists in a spirited argument were equally ill-informed about the hard facts of the situation, though equally prepared to fight their corner. I asked him about his family, and he proudly informed me that his son was graduating at an officers' training establishment. Asked how the son qualified for entrance, he replied, 'I have a nomination.' I wondered when that was last the method of entry to Sandhurst or Woolwich.

By midnight I was desperately tired, and my inside was in a turmoil after so much unaccustomed food and drink. At my request, the Colonel summoned his batman, who escorted us along the hotel passages and ushered us into separate bedrooms, apparently at random. My room was already occupied by a Polish family of parents and two children, but there was one free bed, on to which I gratefully collapsed. I was feeling much too sick to go to sleep. The only remedy appeared to be offered by an immense brass container holding a large potted aspidistra. There was nothing for it. I removed the aspidistra and was copiously sick into the container. The Poles appeared unmoved by this disgusting proceeding and, much relieved, I returned to bed and slept as best I could.

In the morning, feeling considerably battered, I found my way back to the Colonel's room, where he was tucking into breakfast with Esther. He agreed that we had better return to Ciechocinek, and summoned a truck to take us. On our way back I was allowed to call in at Schülitz, where I remembered the two large working camps, and where I had heard on the grapevine that some of our men in the neighbourhood had returned.

I found the Kommandantur, and asked the Russian major who was in charge what he was doing to repatriate British prisoners. He proudly presented me with a poster in three languages (Russian, French and English) which he said was being posted in every town and village. This poster is my favourite war souvenir, and hangs framed by my door in the hope that parting guests will respond to the final exhortation on their way to their camps of recollection. This is the English version.

ANNOUNCEMENT

Officers and soldiers of the allied armies freed from the German captivity by the troops of the Soviet Army and citizens of the Allied States which were interned by the ennemy, have to call on the next military commandant of town, common or county, and direct themselves by his order to the camps of recollection.

Besides they can march to the camp of recollection in the town of Wrzesnia and beginning from the 25th February, 1945 also in the towns of Lodz, Praga and Lublin.

Recording to that the further itineraries are designed by the representatives of the Allied Governements and that the further travelling to this points will be arranged by these camps of recollection, it is DEFENDED to omit them and to continue desorderly the route.

THE COMMAND OF THE FRONT

It had been an enthralling expedition, travelling about a large area of very recently Russian-occupied country. Whether it had been of any value was questionable, but the Russians we encountered had been surprisingly responsive, and most of the British soldiers we had found were apparently pleased that some concern was being shown for their welfare.

A surprise was in store for us when we returned, very tired, to Ciechocinek that evening. The whole British contingent was under orders to move immediately. It was cheering to be on the move again after two frustrating months, but a night journey by truck at a temperature around minus twenty-five degrees centigrade had its disadvantages. The trucks when they arrived were an impressive convoy of American vehicles, and fortunately were covered. There were enough of them to cope with 150 British and 500 American troops. We set off before midnight, and drove right through the night. The cold was intense and seemed to come up from the metal floor through the studs of my boots. My feet were aching with cold all night.

Early next morning we drove into the huge parade ground of the extensive barracks at Wrzesnia, east of Poznan. The camp was already crowded with troops of various nationalities. There was the usual endless delay while arguments went on about billeting and feeding. Eventually we were told to take over the totally unfurnished ground floor of a house that had been previously occupied by Italians. It was a mass of every kind of filth and excrement, and any wooden furniture or fixtures had been ripped out, chopped up and used for firewood.

By this time I was feeling dreadfully ill, past caring, and simply lay down and stretched myself out on the filthy floor. There were no latrines, and when I was smitten with diarrhoea in the middle of the night I crawled out several times into the snow outside while an air raid was going on overhead. Twenty-four hours at Wrzesnia was the low-water mark of my five years captivity. Twenty-four hours only it was, for by midday the following day we were heading for the railway station, where trains of cattle trucks were standing in the sidings. We were allotted our trucks, about thirty to forty men to a truck, and were encouraged to scrounge any material or fuel we could find lying around the goods yard. The centre of each truck was left as an open space with a stove, while living accommodation was provided on two levels at either end of the truck. Warmth of a kind came by day from the stove; by night we packed ourselves in on the shelves.

Progress was slow. Wrzesnia lies on one of the main lines from Warsaw to Germany through Poznan, but the retreating Germans had ripped up the track, and only a single line had been relaid by the Russians. The army's requirements for the drive into Germany had priority, which meant that for twenty-three hours out of twenty-four, all traffic was west-bound. For the first six days, consequently, we travelled for only about one hour and remained in sidings for the rest of the time. Accompanying our slow progress were other trains of cattle trucks, crammed full of Germans heading for captivity, or worse, in Russia. Nobody had told us our destination, and we only hoped that at some stage we would be separated from the

Siberia-bound trains. Our rations were the standard one daily meal of barley soup and half a loaf. During our long halts we were allowed to wander about or perform our natural functions in the snow, but the cold was so intense that we sat or lay around in the trucks, keeping the central stove going when we had any fuel. At night, although forty bodies generated some heat, metal bolts on the wall of the truck next to my face were covered with ice.

On the sixth day someone switched the points and, parting company with the train-loads of Germans at Brest-Litovsk, we headed southwards. The temperature began to rise, and we spent more time in motion than standing still. The dark brown earth of the rolling plains of the Ukraine began to show through the covering of snow.

On the platform of one station I got into conversation of some kind with a Russian officer who had dismounted from a troop train heading frontwards. He was intrigued by a train load of British and US troops. He pointed at the shoulder flash of one of our men which read 'New Zealand' and asked me to explain. When I managed to make him understand that the man had actually come from the Southern Hemisphere to fight the Nazis, he threw up his hands and exclaimed in surprisingly colloquial English, 'What a war!' I suppose, like most of his fellow countrymen, he had been fed with the usual propaganda that only Soviet armies were seriously engaged in war against Nazism.

On the tenth day our journey ended at Odessa. We formed up and marched for half an hour as respectably as we could through the streets of the city, but I do not suppose that the citizens who saw us had the slightest idea that we were samples of their Allies rather than enemy prisoners. Certainly there was no enthusiastic welcome. We arrived eventually, to find sparse accommodation in some rather tatty barracks. We were not allowed out into the city, and an armed guard was mounted at the gate to keep us in, 'for our protection' we were told, but protection against what or whom was not explained.

Conditions were primitive, though there was adequate space in the large barrack rooms. Food was as sparse as ever. There were no facilities for exercise, and the only sanitary arrangements were lines of open trench latrines dug in rows across a courtyard and overshadowed by the high walls of neighbouring buildings. Not long after our arrival one of these walls collapsed and buried three US GIs who were on the latrines – a tragic end for men who had survived the battlefield and were heading for home.

After three days we somehow heard that two British liners had berthed in the harbour, bringing loads of Russians who had been liberated on the West Front. With them had also come a US and British repatriation mission. They soon arrived at our billet. The British mission consisted of a colonel, a naval captain, a wing-commander, an intelligence officer, and two very elegant middle-aged Red Cross ladies. When they arrived in our barrack room I was in bed at the far end of the room, not feeling my best. Suddenly one of our doctors rushed along the room to me and exclaimed, 'The Old Etonian has arrived.' When he came across to me he was not the elegant young subaltern I had always expected, but a kindly, rotund, elderly colonel, sporting 1914/18 ribbons.

'I hear you were a master at Eton,' he said. 'I was at Impey's.' Edward Impey, I knew well, had held his boys' house for over twenty years at the turn of the century. This delightful Colonel Jackson had left Eton in 1900, and must have been over sixty years old when he was taken on as OC troops in the Canadian Pacific liner, now troopship, SS *Duchess of Richmond*. He was to exercise his benign rule over our fortunes for the rest of our homeward journey.

The repatriation commission more or less took charge of us as soon as they arrived. Things had not entirely worked out right for them. While the American mission was doling out masses of stores to their contingent, new uniforms, blankets and food, the British mission had comparatively little to offer to us. It was hinted that the stores intended for released British prisoners had been sent to Archangel in mistaken anticipation of our arrival there. The mission was housed in Odessa's best hotel; the intelligence officer complained that when he turned on the bath taps, the last occupant's waste water welled up from the plug. Hardships! It was an emotional experience talking to two perfectly ordinary English housewives after an interval of five years, a strange prelude to meeting our own wives and families. I know my feelings were shared by many others as we enjoyed the café service they managed to rig up from their depleted stores.

An almighty row brewed up when a Russian officer burst into our room and removed a wireless set that had been introduced by the mission for our benefit. War was in danger of being declared between 'two great Allies', but some face-saving formula was worked out and we retained the set.

Meanwhile some effort was being made on the Russian side to suggest that we were not still prisoners, in spite of the guard on the gate and the wireless episode. Some of us were taken to a circus, a humble olde-worlde affair with a splendid Toytown band in braided uniforms perched above the performers' entrance. Another day we were taken to the Opera House, one of the finest in Europe, for a performance of *Carmen*. The house was packed, and from our box we looked down on the stalls filled with high-ranking officers in uniform, loaded with decorations and epaulettes, and their ladies in wonderful fur coats, which they wore throughout, as the Opera House was not heated. Apart from that defect, we might have been back in the days of the Czars.

The performance on stage hardly matched the audience, which showed its disapproval with whistles and catcalls, while the elderly Toreador was hideously barracked. He was a charming man who deserved better, as we discovered when he, with other members of the cast, paid us a surprise visit in the camp next day, sharing with us some bottles of schnapps that they brought with them.

We seemed very near to embarkation when word reached us from the harbour that a signal had been received from the Admiralty to the effect that the *Duchess of Bedford* was to take off the 500 Americans who had been captured as recently as December, and that the *Duchess of Richmond* was to return empty to the Mediterranean for trooping duties, while the 150 British – prisoners since May 1940 – were to await the arrival of another ship. One could only imagine that the cable had emanated from some very unimaginative type in the Admiralty. Even if the *Duchess of Richmond* was not to be made available, there was ample room for us and the Americans on the *Duchess of Bedford*.

There was, however, a change of heart. Rumour had it that the crew of the *Duchess of Richmond,* being aware of the conditions under which we were living, informed the Master that they were not sailing without us. We had one more night of 'captivity', and next morning we fell in and marched off to the harbour to be confronted on the quayside by two lovely Canadian Pacific liners and to find ourselves almost within touching distance of British 'territory'.

Surely this was the great moment? But no! On to the stage stepped a Russian officer, accompanied by an interpreter with a large scroll in his hands. 'You will answer your names as they are called out,' said the interpreter. It was the nominal roll composed phonetically in Russian script at Ciechocinek. An unrecognisable name was read out. In desperation I replied 'Yes' and urged my neighbours to continue the farce. Nobody on the Russian side seemed worried, and our only fear was that the list would run out with more men on the quayside than there were names on the list.

All was well, and within minutes we were on our way up the gangplank to the friendliest welcome I shall ever meet in this life from the Master, Captain E A Shergold, and the crew of the SS *Duchess of Richmond*.

19

Homeward Bound

Lunch was the first meal served to us on the *Duchess of Richmond,* and for the first time in five years we were confronted in the first class dining saloon with restaurant service and a printed menu, with four courses, but no choice. The stewards, expecting us to be ravenous, were confounded when all of us rejected the first course. It was barley soup.

Once on board, we settled down to enjoy civilized conditions of a kind that had hardly entered our dreams. Our first sight of land after leaving Odessa was the entrance to the Bosporous and what I took to be the site of the British forces' base in the Crimea. At Istambul there was a delay, and for two days we lay at anchor in mid-stream opposite the Golden Horn, and could study at a distance the domes and minarets of the great city, especially beautiful when seen silhouetted against the western sky at sunset. I had no idea how strongly the current flows through the straits from the Black Sea, and when we slipped anchor we made rapid progress through the Dardanelles to the Aegean Sea. Our departure had been timed to take us right through the Aegean, a danger area apparently, at night and round the southern tip of Greece, so that we saw nothing of the Greek islands, but we had a splendid view of the Strait of Messina before we reached Naples, our next port of call.

There we were tied up in the docks for five days, but there was no question of our being allowed ashore. The war was still in progress and security was as tight as ever, and we were simply a batch of 'unidentified ex-prisoners' without any identity papers. On the second day, however, we were 'treated' to an ENSA concert party. We could have done without it. They were a third-rate bunch of singers and comics, who appeared to think that they were doing us a favour, pouring forth a string of obscene jokes of a kind from which our POW concerts had been remarkably free. The troops received them in stony silence and with scant applause.

Next day we were treated to a rather different concert of operatic music, belted out by a jolly group of robust Italian singers. This second concert was unexpectedly interrupted. That morning I was reading an English language newspaper published in Naples for the Forces. It announced that on that date the Archbishop of York would be visiting Naval Installations. I found Colonel Jackson and asked if he could send a message ashore to the Archbishop. I had been his chaplain in 1936, and he had married me and Mary in 1938, and he had shown great kindness to us both during the five years of my absence. Colonel Jackson tackled the Master, Captain Shergold, and between them they sent a message to the Naval HQ. Within an hour a despatch rider came cruising along the quayside bringing a message to say that the Navy would rearrange the Archbishop's programme to enable him to come aboard at 2 pm. I was invited to join the Master and Colonel Jackson on the quayside to welcome the party, who arrived on the dot in a procession of staff cars impressively headed by a number of motorcyclists in line abreast. It was an emotional meeting for me and for the Archbishop, and he delighted everybody by making his way up to the main deck, where the Italian singers gave place to him, to address words of welcome to all my fellow prisoners on their release from captivity.

His visit had a pleasing sequel. He wrote a line to Mary, saying, 'I am not allowed to say where I am, but I have seen David today.' Newspapers in England were simultaneously announcing that the Archbishop was in·Italy visiting the Forces. This was the first news Mary had had of me for five months. She had had no idea where I was since the Russians had overrun Poland, or whether I was alive or dead.

Meanwhile we passed the time as best we could. Even if we could not go ashore, we were no longer captives. I was press-ganged into enlisting a team to produce an eight page souvenir, to be printed on board, with contributions in prose and verse and some very competent cartoons. It was entitled 'Homeward Bound'.

After four days the *Duchess,* which had so far carried no more than three hundred ex-prisoners, was filled to capacity with hundreds of homeward bound troops of various units which had been fighting their way northwards through Italy all through the winter. Confronted with this horde of battle-hardened professionals, we retreated into anonymous obscurity. They were mostly fairly exhausted, not to say suffering from delayed shock, and in no mind to be interested in our years of profitless inactivity.

From Naples we sailed in quite a small convoy as far as Gibraltar, but after Gibraltar the convoy grew to some thirty ships shepherded along by busy destroyers and corvettes. It was at this stage of the voyage, on 12 April to be precise, that news came through of the death of President Roosevelt, and flags were flown at half mast on all the ships. None of us were in any doubt what we, and the whole civilised world, had owed to him. Rather less notice was taken of my birthday, the sixth since I had sailed off to France with the BEF in January 1940.

The last twenty-four hours of the voyage were unutterably tense. We were so nearly home, but we were told that German submarines were having a last fling and were still active around the British Isles. As we proceeded northwards during the night through the Irish Sea, I was appalled by the noise of exploding depth-charges around the convoy, almost to the level of panic. The crew of the *Duchess* were Liverpool-based and had hoped that they would berth there, but to their great disappointment the convoy divided and our half continued northwards to Scotland.

As day dawned, my first sight of home was Ailsa Craig appearing out of the early morning mist, and then the sight I knew well of the Ayrshire coast on one side and the Cumraes and the Isle of Bute on the other, all bathed in early morning April sunshine.

It was midday when we berthed at Greenock. We were all longing to go home, but that was not the way the Armed Forces proceeded. Our party was formed up on the quayside and a party of Red Cross ladies advanced, anxious to offer us refreshments. But as they moved forwards, two 'redcaps'

269

shepherded them back, to the sound of hoots of derision and obloquy from the ranks of POWs, many of whom had for five years been rehearsing what they would say to the first 'redcap' they encountered on release. It appeared, however, that they were simply clearing a way for a general who had been despatched from Scottish Command to welcome us home, a pleasant gesture. His opening words were, 'This must be a great moment for you.' From the ranks behind me, I could hear a voice saying, 'I can think of a better one.' The general tactfully kept it short, and we were soon bundled into a waiting train, where the Red Cross ladies had their innings, loading us with food and drink for what was to be a long and tedious journey.

The sad fact was that we were still officially 'unidentified ex-prisoners' with no papers, and though some of our party had been more or less in sight of their homes as we sailed up the Clyde, our designated reception centre was at Beaconsfield, where we were to be 'kitted out' with identity papers, uniforms, money and instructions. Consequently, all through a long day our train slowly progressed from Glasgow to Edinburgh, and then southwards through Newcastle and York, and then by the old Great Central line through Sheffield, Nottingham, Leicester and Rugby, and so to Beaconsfield, the same line that I used to take in the early nineteen-twenties from Newcastle to my prep school at Oxford. It was like a dream, seeing England at its best in April sunshine. There was one particular treat; our train obligingly halted on the viaduct at Durham, and we could enjoy for a short spell one of the noblest views in Europe, of the castle and the cathedral.

At Beaconsfield we were bundled into trucks and transported to the Reception Camp, a hutted camp in a particularly beautiful beech wood, with the trees just coming into leaf. But it was not idyllic scenery that we needed, and when, next morning, we were told by the leisurely staff that we would be there for some days, a number of our troops set off to walk to Beaconsfield station and had to be rounded up and brought back. The camp authorities belatedly got the message and decided that the necessary formalities could be completed in twenty-four hours. Meanwhile I had managed to contact my 'in-laws', and learnt from them that Mary was at Uppingham.

I was able to reach her on the telephone, and told her to expect me next day.

That, however, was not to be. It was four o'clock before we escaped from Beaconsfield. We were taken to the station and travelled to Marylebone, where we piled into a truck which set off on a round of London main line stations. I was dumped on the pavement outside St Pancras, where for the first time in five years I found myself alone and a free man. I felt absurdly lonely and totally bewildered. At the booking office I was told that there was no train to Uppingham before four o'clock next morning. I could have contacted old friends in London, but I appeared to be devoid of all powers of initiative and simply wondered how to spend twelve hours in a London railway station. I sat on a seat and watched hundreds of people hurrying to and fro, all purposefully engaged, while I, a free man at last, could think of no sensible way of spending my time.

I discovered a Salvation Army hut just outside the station, which provided rest and refreshment for service personnel in transit. There for company I found a pleasant assortment of strangers. They were the Third Officer of one of the Queens, a New Zealand subaltern and a black Jamaican RAF Flight Lieutenant. All three had abundant recent experience of active service, and when I let on that I had just emerged from five years of useless incarceration, my disclosure was clearly an effective conversation-stopper. This was a reaction to be experienced many times in the coming months by me, and I suspect by many others. It was like letting on in public that one was suffering from an unmentionable terminal illness. Most people were quite sympathetic, but did not really want to know how we had filled up five years of enforced inactivity.

In the early morning I caught a train to Kettering, and after changing there and at Seaton I caught the little train that chugged its short way up the hill to Uppingham. I need not have wondered what it was going to be like, meeting my lovely Mary again after five and a quarter years. We carried on exactly where we had left off. The world was all before us, and we did not have to bother about what was past.

Martin Lloyd, her kind Headmaster, was already looking for her replacement, and when news of my impending return

271

had arrived from Naples, Mary had opened a file on which she had inadvertently typed 'Applications for the post of Headmaster's Secretart' (sic). We spent the weekend at Uppingham, and in the parish church on Sunday the appointed psalm said everything, 'When the Lord turned again the captivity of Zion then were we like unto them that dream. Then was our mouth filled with laughter and our tongue with joy . . . They that sow in tears shall reap in joy.'

At Mary's home at Streatley I was reunited with all my old clothes which she had carefully put away in 1940, and at Oxford we stayed with my eldest brother, who, since I had last heard of him six months earlier in Poland, had married and had been appointed Master of University College. At Univ. the Common Room was temporarily closed, and he took me to dine in the Common Room at Queen's. After an excellent dinner, when the port had gone round once, the Provost started the decanter on its way again. A startled voice said, 'It's Thursday, Provost,' and he hurriedly recovered the decanter and put the stopper in. I realized then how wartime austerity had affected Oxford, when there was only one round of port on Thursdays in the Common Room at Queen's.

The army soon made it plain that I was unemployable and would soon be 'demobbed'. I was summoned to a Medical in the Examination Schools at Oxford. There I was examined by two doctors, a man and a woman. The woman expressed great concern about my skinny appearance and started to write out chits for me to receive various extra items of diet, but they were all torn up when the man quite truthfully said, 'I knew him before the war. He was never any fatter than that.' I was, however, like all other ex-prisoners entitled to a double ration card for six months, and Mary consequently put on weight.

Many months before my release, Dr· Hobson, Mary's former employer at Oxford, had promised that when I came home he would lend us his cottage at Birdham on Chichester Harbour, and to that we made our way. It was the perfect place for us to find our bearings again. It also brought home to me the real problems of sustaining life in wartime Britain. There was no village shop, and the only way we could feed ourselves was to bicycle five miles into Chichester and purchase there whatever the rationing system provided. After enjoying the riches of Red Cross parcels, I was surprised and shocked. A long queue at the fishmonger's was for me an entirely novel experience, but as the only man in the queue I was given abundant advice on my purchases by all the friendly ladies.

One memory stands out among all others of those days. Mary and I had made a complicated journey – three buses – to Pulborough via Chichester and Midhurst, to take lunch with Charles Clutsom of my battalion, whom I had last seen at Laufen in 1941. On our return journey we had to change buses and kill time at Midhurst. As it was Saturday afternoon, we decided to cash our meat ration at a local butcher. When I handed over the ration cards the butcher noticed that mine signified a double ration. 'POW?' he enquired, and when I agreed he said, 'Come inside,' and took us into the cold store at the back. 'Have what you like,' he said. We took a leg of lamb, much more than we were entitled to. Kindness like that from a perfect stranger helped me to feel that once more we belonged. The people of this country had wrought a great work at great cost, and even those of us in captivity had played a small part.

INDEX

275